THE OLD FARMER'S ALMANAC
Book of Weather and Natural Disasters

THE OLD FARMER'S ALMANAC
Book of Weather and Natural Disasters

BENJAMIN A. WATSON
and the editors of
The Old Farmer's Almanac

RANDOM HOUSE • NEW YORK

This book was originally published in hardcover by Random House, Inc.,
New York, in 1993 as *Acts of God: The Old Farmer's Almanac
Unpredictable Guide to Weather and Natural Disasters.*

Owing to limitations of space, all acknowledgments of permissions to
use illustrations will be found on page 246.

LIBRARY OF CONGRESS CATALOGING-IN-PUBLICATION DATA

The old farmer's almanac book of weather and natural disasters/
    Benjamin A. Watson, ed.
        p.   cm.
    ISBN 0-679-75788-0
    1. Almanacs. 2. Weather—Folklore. 3. Natural disasters—Fore-
    casting. I. Watson, Benjamin A.
    QC999.A28 1993
    555.6'31—dc20   92-42605
                                                              CIP

Manufactured in the United States of America
98765432

First Paperback Edition

To my sisters — Judy, Debbie, and Cynthia.

Acknowledgments

THE AUTHOR WISHES to thank the many people who have assisted in the creation of this book.

Michelle Seaton provided invaluable research assistance during the entire course of this project, as well as lending personal and professional support above and beyond the call of duty. She also penned many of the short boxes and asides that appear in the work and had the unenviable task of fact checking the entire manuscript.

Deborah Watson contributed materially to the author at the beginning of the project and helped him obtain the tools he needed to write this book, for which he is eternally grateful. And in her role as head reference librarian at the University of New Hampshire's Dimond Library, she helped to fill some of the author's most pressing research needs.

Sharon Smith acted as project editor and enthusiastic cheerleader for the book. Without her guidance, development, and thoughtful line editing (and, above all, her patience), this book would never have seen the light of day.

Jill Shaffer thoughtfully designed this book and gave it much of its visual appeal.

Jamie Kageleiry selected and edited the photographs that appear in this book and assisted in writing captions. She also participated in the developmental stages of the project and contributed many helpful suggestions along the way.

Barbara Jatkola copy-edited the manuscript and healed the author's sometimes limping prose.

Bob Trebilcock contributed his notes and ideas during the formative stages of the book, which proved useful throughout the research and writing process.

The author and research editor consulted many experts and eyewitnesses during the course of this project, to collect more detailed information and to check the accuracy of the manuscript. Thanks to David M. Ludlum; Tom Grazulis; Dr. Martin A. Uman, University of Florida, Gainesville; Dr. Robert P. Davies-Jones, National Severe Storms Laboratory; Tobin Morrison and the rest of the *Alaska* magazine staff; Dr. David

M. Stewart, Southeast Missouri State University; Jack Hailey; Virginia Carlson, New Madrid (Missouri) Historical Museum; Tim Marshall, *Storm-track* magazine; Mel Waskin; Bill Masterson, Seaton Publishing Co.; the *Rapid City* (South Dakota) *Journal;* and Eugene Auciello, Scott Kroczynski, and the rest of the National Weather Service staff.

Thanks also to the following individuals and institutions: The National Archives; the Wallace E. Mason Library at Keene State College, especially Alison Cook; the Ezekiel Dimond Library at the University of New Hampshire, especially Val Harper and Peter Crosby; Susan Peery, Tim Clark, and John Pierce of *The Old Farmer's Almanac;* and David Rosenthal, Della Mancuso, Amy Edelman, and Rebecca Beuchler of Random House.

Contents

2 Introduction

4 Watching the Weather

20 Hurricanes

46 Tornadoes

66 Blizzards & Wintry Weather

88 Drought, Dust & Conflagration

120 Floods

144 Earthquakes

176 Volcanoes

202 Lightning

224 Rain, Hail & Ice Storms

We can't hope to change
*the weather, but those
who know how to read
its signs can sometimes
profit from it.*

THE OLD FARMER'S ALMANAC
Book of Weather and Natural Disasters

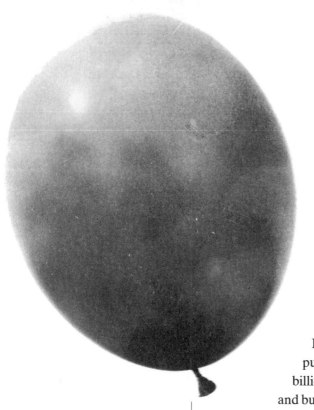

Introduction

IN HIS 1935 BOOK *Uncommon Law,* A.P. Herbert defines an "act of God" as "something which no reasonable man could have expected." Every year, throughout the world, we've learned to expect the unexpected in the form of earthquakes, volcanic eruptions, powerful storms, floods, and fires — natural disasters that claim the lives of millions and cause untold damage. In the United States alone, natural disasters cost the public and private sectors between $5 billion and $10 billion each year on average. And as our country grows and buildings dot our shorelines and our plains, we become ever more vulnerable to the destructive whims of nature. A single terrible storm — Hurricane Andrew, which struck southern Florida and Louisiana in 1992 — wreaked more than $20 billion in damage all by itself, forcing a million people to flee from its ravages and leaving 250,000 homeless in its wake.

Americans have always been intrigued by natural disasters, their impact and their aftermath. Perhaps, as some authors have suggested, this interest stems from the fact that the United States is bracketed by oceans and that, in our brief history as a nation, we have only infrequently had to fight foreign invaders on our own soil. (War, after all, is nothing but a manmade disaster.) More likely, though, Americans simply share the same normal responses — horror and fascination — that most humans feel when they witness, hear of, or read about a great tragedy. As author Beverley Raphael points out in her book *When Disaster Strikes* (Basic Books, 1986), people tend to "flock to the site of a disaster to see from a safe distance what they fear at close hand." For most of us, this "safe distance" is provided by the national media, and it comes as close to us as the headlines of our daily newspaper or the tragic images on the television screen inside our home.

Another reason why we Americans follow natural disasters with such interest is that our country, so large and so varied, plays host to many dramatic events each year. In the few months since the writing of this book began, there have been two major earthquake outbreaks in California (one centered in the south, near Joshua Tree National Monument; the other along the northern coast, in Humboldt County). Alaska's Mount Spurr volcano erupted, spewing ash over Anchorage and sending a gritty cloud sailing over the northern plains and Canada. During the 1992 hurricane season, Andrew, one of the strongest storms ever to hit the United States, flattened the city of Homestead, Florida; two week later, Hurricane Iniki did the same to the Hawaiian island of Kauai. In between these two disasters, Typhoon Omar struck a hard blow against the Pacific island of Guam. And aside from these dramatic, well-publicized weather events we have seen floods, forest fires, a record 1,290-plus tornadoes, and all manner of other weather-related events that have affected nearly every region of the country, creating havoc and sometimes causing death. The weather affects us more than we realize, and it stands still for no one — not even for a writer trying to capture its grandeur and excesses.

Great weather disasters have punctuated both the geography and the history of the United States — from the Johnstown Flood of 1889 to the Dust Bowl of the 1930s; from the great forest fires that followed the railroads, lumberjacks, and farmers westward to the Galveston Storm of 1900, in which at least 6,000 people died.

This book is a tribute to all the people who have weathered the storm: the heroes who saved others at the risk of their own lives; the survivors who lived to tell their tales; and all the legions of the dead, whose stories (and sometimes whose very names) may never be known. It also celebrates those innovative people — the scientists and researchers, as well as the quacks, cranks, and fakirs — who have tried to predict, control, or modify the weather over the years. Although we are still far from unlocking the secrets of nature and learning how to expect (and perhaps avoid) the unexpected, these men and women have worked to contribute to our traditional and scientific knowledge. Likewise, for more than 200 years, *The Old Farmer's Almanac* has published its famous forecasts and weather wisdom with the selfsame goal in mind: to make us all just a bit more weather-wise. ■

A meteorologist for the *U.S. Weather Bureau sends up a trial balloon.*

WATCHING THE WEATHER

SINCE IT FIRST APPEARED in 1792, Robert B. Thomas's *Old Farmer's Almanac* has become a part of our weather tradition, and millions of Americans still consult it for its long-range forecasts and its mixture of practical advice and entertainment. Forecasting the weather more than a year in advance can be, well, problematic, but the success of *The Old Farmer's Almanac* (the editors claim an 80 percent accuracy rate) proves that the formula — a combination of modern scientific methods and ancient weather wisdom — still works in this age of supercomputers and satellites.

If you think forecasting "normal" weather is tricky, though, try predicting a natural disaster. No one wants to look like a prophet of doom, so on the rare occasions when *The Old Farmer's Almanac* predicts a severe storm (as it did in forecasting Hurricane Andrew in 1992), it does so in the same spirit as the National Weather Service — simply to serve notice that a big storm may be coming. The difference, of course, is that the Almanac has to stick its neck out more than a year in advance.

The Almanac and the scientists have been watching the weather for years now and have become more and more skilled at predicting what lies ahead. Yet for all of our science and technology, the sheer power of nature still can take us by surprise and have a lasting impact on our lives. Disasters will always afflict us, but at least we can protect ourselves by staying alert and informed and keeping a weather eye on the sky. It's just like the old proverb says: Forewarned *is* forearmed. ∎

Any farmer can tell you that it pays to read nature's signs — and to make hay while the sun shines.

We've Come a Long Way, Baby

Time was, no one even knew the weather in the next town over.
Then along came a few far-sighted geniuses . . .

WHEN THE FIRST EUROPEAN SETTLERS arrived on the shores of North America, they found themselves ill prepared for the climate that awaited them. Far from being the paradise they had envisioned, the New World soon became known for weather that quite literally blew hot and cold, and the harsh conditions took their toll on many poorly equipped settlements. In 1604, a group of French explorers established a colony on an island in the middle of eastern Maine's St. Croix River. They found the winter there so cold and miserable that they decided to move to a balmier spot on Nova Scotia (otherwise, our country's founders might well have spoken French). Of the original 105 colonists who settled at Jamestown, Virginia, only 32 survived the famous Cold Winter of 1607–08. And even though the winter of 1620–21 was by all accounts a particularly mild one, it almost spelled disaster for the Pilgrims at Plymouth, Massachusetts; only 50 of the 102 settlers lived until spring.

The main priorities for the new colonists were food and shelter, but as life in the New World became less of a struggle, the first American arts and sciences began to flourish. America's first printing press arrived in Cambridge, Massachusetts, in 1638, and the second document it issued was Captain William Pierce's *Almanac Calculated for New England,* published in 1639. Indispensable for early mariners and planters, the almanac (from the Arabic *al manakh,* "the reckoning") contained tables giving the times of tides and astronomical events. The fact that an almanac was one of the first fruits of American publishing is by no means insignificant. As late as the nineteenth century, the only reading material found in many rural households consisted of the Holy Bible and the local almanac.

In the year 1644, the Reverend John Campanius made the first weather observations in North America, at Swedes' Fort near the present-day city of Wilmington, Delaware. While some early Americans were complaining about the weather and others were succumbing to it, a few enlightened souls had already begun to observe and study it.

During the eighteenth century, the science of meteorology was relatively crude. The basic instruments for measuring temperature, precipitation, and barometric pressure had been introduced and were in the process of being standardized and improved, but little was really known about the nature of storms and weather patterns. One of the first Americans to glimpse the true character of storms was Benjamin Franklin, a remarkable amateur scientist who contributed so much to our understanding of electricity. Almost everyone knows about Franklin's experi-

Left: The early Puritans *were ill prepared for the harsh winters of the New World.* Above, top to bottom: *Founding fathers Benjamin Franklin, George Washington, and Thomas Jefferson were early weather watchers.*

Members of the Lewis and *Clark Expedition charted the weather as well as the geography in their ground-breaking exploration of America's West.*

ment with the kite and key; less famous are his observations based on what historians now call the Franklin Storm.

On the night of October 21, 1743, Franklin was eagerly awaiting a scheduled eclipse of the moon, which he planned to observe at his home in Philadelphia. Unfortunately, a strong storm, a "nor'easter," raced through the city on the big night, obscuring the skies and making him miss the eclipse. Only later did Franklin learn that his brother in Boston had witnessed the event right on schedule, with a clear sky overhead, and that only four hours after the storm had hit Philadelphia, it had passed through Boston as well.

With only these facts and his common sense to guide him, Franklin theorized that the storm must have traveled at a speed of about 100 miles per hour up the coast, from southwest to northeast — despite the fact that the surface winds associated with the storm had blown from the northeast. To explain this apparent contradiction, Franklin decided that the winds must have rotated around the storm in a circular motion. These simple deductions, so obvious to us today with our satellite loop images, were nothing less than revolutionary for the time, for they suggested that if weather conditions were observed at different points (like Philadelphia and Boston) simultaneously, the movements of major weather systems might one day be tracked, understood, and predicted.

Eighteenth-century America had no National Weather Service, official or otherwise. What it did have were astute private observers — college professors and presidents, farmers and mariners — who watched the skies and kept local weather records, many of which are still studied today. George Washington, our first president, and Thomas Jefferson, our third, both kept weather journals. Jefferson bought his first thermometer while writing the Declaration of Independence and his first barometer soon thereafter.

Most of these citizen-observers in the new republic were isolated from one another; their instruments were often unreliable and not calibrated to a single standard. By the end of the century, though, groups of weather watchers had begun to share their observations and agreed to take simultaneous readings at various prearranged hours each day.

In 1778, Thomas Jefferson at his home, Monticello, and the Reverend James Madison of Williamsburg, Virginia (not to be confused with our fourth president of the same name), took the first simultaneous observations, noting temperature, barometric pressure, and wind over a six-week period, with readings taken daily at sunrise and again at 4 P.M. After comparing notes, Jefferson found the differences in the two sets of records

The Man Who Was Attached to Leeches

IN 1850, AN ENGLISH DOCTOR named George Merryweather invented a new kind of weather instrument that he called the Tempest Prognosticator and described as "an Atmospheric Electromagnetic Telegraph, conducted by Animal Instinct." The strange apparatus looked something like a carousel, with 12 pint bottles around the base and a bell at the top, surrounded by 12 hammers. Each of the bottles was connected to a hammer through a metal tube in its neck. The tube contained a piece of whalebone and a small wire attached to a little gold chain. The "animal instinct" was provided by live leeches — those traditional friends of doctors, who for centuries had applied them to suffering patients to draw and "purify" the blood.

The Tempest Prognosticator.

Merryweather relied on an old folk forecasting observation that leeches respond to atmospheric pressure and can predict when a change in the weather is about to take place. He poured an inch and a half of rainwater into each of the bottles on his prognosticator and then inserted one leech per bottle. When a storm was approaching, he reasoned, the leeches would rise into the metal tubes in the necks of the bottles, dislodging the whalebone and causing the hammers to strike the bell on top of the apparatus.

After thoroughly testing his device and satisfying himself that it worked, Merryweather exhibited the Tempest Prognosticator to an astounded audience in his hometown of Whitby, Yorkshire, and later at the Crystal Palace Exposition in London. He hoped that his invention would revolutionize weather forecasting and that eventually it would be distributed all over the world.

Alas, it was not to be. Unfortunately for Merryweather (though fortunately for leeches), a device that was not nearly so complex, not to mention disgusting, had been invented some years earlier. It was called the barometer.

most illuminating, showing clearly the cooler climate of his mountain home as compared to the warmer temperatures in the James River basin, where Williamsburg lies. During the course of his career, Jefferson also exchanged weather observations with fellow correspondents from as far away as Philadelphia, Natchez (in present day Mississippi), Quebec, and London.

A national leader in so many respects, Jefferson worked both as president and in his private life to create a national system of weather observers. As president, he supplied the Lewis and Clark Expedition with weather instruments and asked them to collect data on their travels through the previously unexplored West. And from 1797 to 1815, in his role as president of the American Philosophical Society, Jefferson lobbied for his observer network, which would have supplied one volunteer in every county of every state in the Union with accurate instruments with which to record local weather.

At the same time that private individuals began to collect their weather observations in a systematic way, various departments in the U.S. government were getting their feet wet in the weather business. In 1814, Dr. James Tilton, the U.S. Army's Surgeon General, issued an order for his surgeons to keep weather diaries at their posts. By 1838, doctors at 13 forts, mostly in the frontier states, were keeping general observations. At the end of the Civil War, some 143 posts were recording weather data.

Following suit, in April 1817, Josiah Meigs, the commissioner of the Treasury Department's General Land Office, requested that the registrars of the 20 regional land offices under his supervision begin keeping meteorological records and including them in their monthly reports to Washington. Meigs asked that the regional offices take observations three times daily: in the morning, at 2 P.M., and in the evening.

Finally, in 1845, the single most important breakthrough in the history of U.S. weather forecasting occurred when the first telegraph line was opened to the public. With telegraphy, the problems of communication between two observers at distant points became a thing of the past — or would become so, as soon as the telegraph network had spread to all corners of the nation. The possibility of almost instantaneous transmission of information made simultaneous observations that much more important, and made it possible to plot an up-to-the-minute weather map showing current conditions at all points. A weather system affecting one location could be tracked on the map, and its direction and behavior predicted. With the technology of the telegraph, the science of meteorology graduated from the exclusive study of weather past to the elusive prediction of weather future.

In 1849, the secretary of the new Smithsonian Institution, Joseph Henry, first began receiving daily telegraphic reports from a network of volunteer weather observers located all over the eastern United States. By the time the Civil War began, and southern reports abruptly ceased, Henry had built up a system of nearly

And Now for the Weather in Your Neck of the Woods . . .

ON MAY 1, 1857, THE *Washington* (D.C.) *Evening Star* published the United States' first national weather roundup, giving the current weather conditions at 19 telegraph stations, from New York to New Orleans, as collected by volunteer observers in the Smithsonian Institution's cooperative network.

As reported by James R. Fleming in *Meteorology in America,* six days later the *Evening Star* also published what was arguably the first weather *forecast* in America, probably prepared by the Smithsonian's secretary, Joseph Henry, and meteorologist James Pollard Espy. They didn't exactly stick their necks out: "Yesterday there was a severe storm south of Macon, Ga.; but from the fact that it is still clear this morning at that place and at Wheeling, it is probable that the storm was of a local character."

The cautious James Pollard Espy.

In January should sun appear, March and April will pay full dear.

"Old Probs"

IN JANUARY 1871, PROFESSOR Cleveland Abbe went to work as the chief forecaster for the U.S. Army Signal Service (the forerunner of the U.S. Weather Bureau) in Washington, D.C. His first official weather predictions, which were called "probabilities," were published on February 19, earning Abbe the affectionate nickname "Old Probabilities," or "Old Probs" for short.

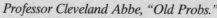

Professor Cleveland Abbe, "Old Probs."

600 observers, whose information was transmitted free of charge and as a top priority by nearly every telegraph company in the country. The weather information that the observers sent to Henry in Washington, D.C., arrived at his office around ten o'clock every morning and was plotted on a large map that hung in the lobby of the Smithsonian. By 1857, Smithsonian reports were running daily in the *Washington Evening Star* and in many of the observers' hometown papers.

The Smithsonian's observer network fulfilled the dream of Jefferson and others, becoming the first widespread weather service in the nation's history and proving that, given standardized instruments and a little training, volunteer observers still offered the most cost-effective option for reporting the weather. These lessons were not lost on the government weather service that developed over the next few decades. Even today, the National Weather Service uses some 12,000 cooperative observers in locations throughout the 50 states and in other U.S. territories.

But the federal government, despite its modern-day preeminence, was a Johnny-come-lately to the field of weather forecasting. Not until 1870 did Congress authorize a government meteorological bureau, under the auspices of the U.S. Army Signal Service. The move made good sense, since the Signal Service, under the direction of General Albert J. Myer, also was charged with the task of stringing telegraph lines across the western territories.

FOR THE RECORD

ON APRIL 12, 1934, WEAther observers Salvatore Pagliuca, Wendell Stephenson, and Alex McKenzie logged the highest wind velocity ever recorded on earth — 231 miles per hour — at New Hampshire's Mount Washington Observatory, 6,288 feet above sea level. On the same day and in the same spot, the trio also recorded the highest sustained (five-minute) wind speed ever for the United States — 188 miles per hour.

On November 1, 1870, the Signal Service started sending out weather reports to some metropolitan newspapers. These reports on current weather conditions came into Myer's office in Washington from observer-sergeants posted in 25 cities and shore points, as far west as Cheyenne, Wyoming, and as far south as Key West, Florida. Within eight years of its founding, the Signal Service network had expanded to 284 stations from coast to coast and had established cooperative stations in Canada and the Caribbean. In addition, Myer's men built meteorological observatories atop two key mountains — Pikes Peak in Colorado and Mount Washington in New Hampshire.

In 1890, Congress decided that the government's growing responsi-

An early weather observer's *son poses at his station on Oahu* (inset). *At the other extreme, the observatory on New Hampshire's Mount Washington has seen all kinds of cold-weather phenomena, including the freakish rime ice.*

In this century, a new era *began for the science of meteorology when airplane pilots started helping to collect weather data.*

bilities for weather forecasting would be better left in civilian, rather than military, hands. So on July 1, 1891, the stations, equipment, and most of the personnel belonging to the Signal Service passed to the newly created U.S. Weather Bureau, which was housed within the Department of Agriculture. Since that time, the understanding of weather and the atmosphere, as well as the improved technology and accuracy of forecasting, have moved light-years beyond where they once were.

Along with the telegraph, the airplane ranks as one of the most important technological advances for the study of meteorology in the past 150 years. In 1917, meteorological instruments were installed on some military aircraft in France, and in 1925 the U.S. Navy and the Weather Bureau began taking daily soundings from airplanes over Washington, D.C. Finally, researchers could reach up into the clouds (even into the eye of a hurricane) to obtain data straight from the realm of the storm.

The improving quality and quantity of Weather Bureau data were soon reflected in the increased confidence of its forecasts. By 1910, the bureau had begun issuing regular weekly forecasts, which in 1940 were replaced with the familiar five-day forecasts we still have today. But in 1950, for the first time, the Weather Bureau began releasing what it referred to as "30-day outlooks," a bold move for a science so fraught with uncertainty.

Today the National Weather Service (the U.S. Weather Bureau changed its name in 1970 and is now part of the Commerce Department) is still pushing the envelope, trying to get more and better data and to predict weather more accurately than ever before. Weather satellites now orbit the earth, giving us spectacular bird's-eye views of spiraling hur-

In 1947, near Seattle, *Washington, meteorologist William Allyn sets up a mobile weather station.*

Willard Scott, NBC's *ebullient morning weatherman, prepared for anything.*

Some rain, some rest; fine weather isn't always best.

ricanes and cloud cover. On the cutting edge of today's technology are sophisticated ground radar systems that can interpret and give early warning of severe storms such as tornadoes. But the real advances in weather forecasting may come as the result of a third great technological breakthrough, one that has already had all the impact on our age that the telegraph did in the 1840s and the airplane did in the early part of this century. The computers of today and tomorrow — ever faster, ever smarter — will be the key to processing the staggering amount of weather observations collected every day in the atmosphere, in the oceans, and on land.

And yet, for all our supposed wisdom, we still have much to learn about both the mechanisms of storms and our environment as a whole — and it's often when our predictors fail and people are caught unawares that the worst natural disasters result. Nature can sometimes seem random or

Cloudy with a Chance of Suicide

DO YOU LOSE YOUR TEMper on humid days? Does a low-pressure front make you blue? Does your head ache just before a rainstorm? If you answered yes to any of these questions, you are probably "weather sensitive." An extra sensitivity to the weather means that subtle atmospheric changes affect your mood, reflexes, and attentiveness. These changes can even amplify the pain of rheumatism or arthritis. Don't worry; you're not alone. Some scientists believe that as many as 150 million people exhibit extrasensitivity to the weather.

It doesn't take a genius to figure out that people are happier when the sun shines, or that they might be a little cranky when the sky is dropping hailstones the size of Volkswagens. But the scientists who call themselves biometeorologists say that it's not quite that simple.

For example, a sudden drop in barometric pressure (the first physical sign of an approaching storm) may cause the cells in your body to exert an increased outward pressure — at least until they adjust — which causes a bloated feeling, a headache, or grumpiness. And a sudden change in temperature causes your brain some confusion as its internal thermoregulators try to catch up. But it gets worse. Studies have shown that suicide rates increase in the early months of spring when the weather is at its most schizophrenic. Industrial accidents increase during thunderstorms and unsettled weather. Cold fronts can cause migraines and impair circulation. High humidity depresses crime rates but leads to increased irritability.

Not surprisingly, people are more likely to be alert, calm, and comfortable in times of high and stable barometric pressure and minimal changes in temperature, as in late spring and early autumn. In other words, the best weather is no weather at all.

What are the most mood-altering conditions that nature has to offer? The scientists all agree on those end-of-summer days when thunderstorms are expected. Those days when the air is thick and sticky. Those days when it's too hot to move, so you sit and watch the dark clouds gather. You watch and you wait, but for some reason, the sky refuses to rain. You don't need a biometeorologist to tell you that a day like that brings out the worst in anybody.

Ida Lupino on a bad weather day.

Pale moon doth rain, red moon doth blow, white moon doth neither rain nor snow.

even perverse when it deviates from the patterns we think it should follow. As far as meteorology has come in the past 400 years, any honest weatherman will tell you that a successful forecast is the product of three things: information, experience, and a little bit of luck.

Author's Note: Readers wishing to learn more about the history of weather observation and forecasting in America should consult the following books, which are also gratefully acknowledged as the main reference sources for this chapter.

Fleming, James Rodger. *Meteorology in America, 1800–1870* (Baltimore: Johns Hopkins University Press, 1990).

Hughes, Patrick. *A Century of Weather Service* (New York: Gordon and Breach, 1970). ∎

A SURE-FIRE (?) WAY TO PREDICT THE WEATHER

Check Your Onions

HAVE YOU EVER HEARD someone say about a person that "he (or she) really knows his onions"? This compliment usually suggests that the person referred to is capable or savvy or just has business well in hand. Although the origins of the phrase are somewhat murky, one possible explanation might involve an old way of forecasting the weather.

In some parts of France, the interval between Christmas Day (December 25) and the Feast of the Epiphany (January 6) used to be called *Les jours des lots,* or "The days of fate." (We call them the Twelve Days of Christmas.) During these 12 days, French farmers used to follow a carefully prescribed ritual to determine what the weather would be like for the next 12 months.

On Christmas Day, 12 onions were placed in a row, with a pinch of salt placed on top of each. Beginning on the left, the first onion in the row represented January, the second one February, and so on down the line, with the onion on the far right standing for the following December.

On Epiphany, the onions were examined. If the salt on any one of them had melted, the theory went, the month with which it corresponded would be wet. If the salt had remained intact, the corresponding month would be dry.

Like most folk traditions, cromnyomancy (forecasting with onions) might be worth trying just for fun. In terms of accuracy, though, you would probably do just as well by guessing. Save your vegetables for something really important — like French onion soup.

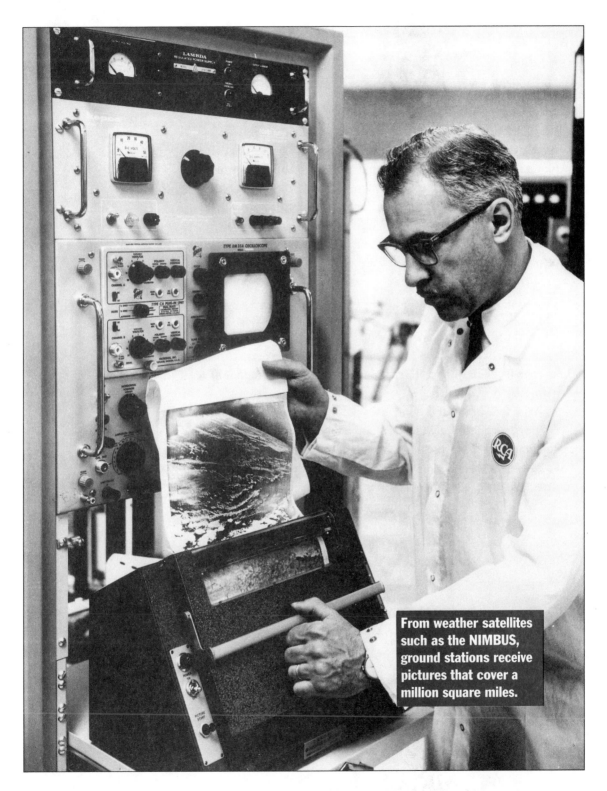

From weather satellites such as the NIMBUS, ground stations receive pictures that cover a million square miles.

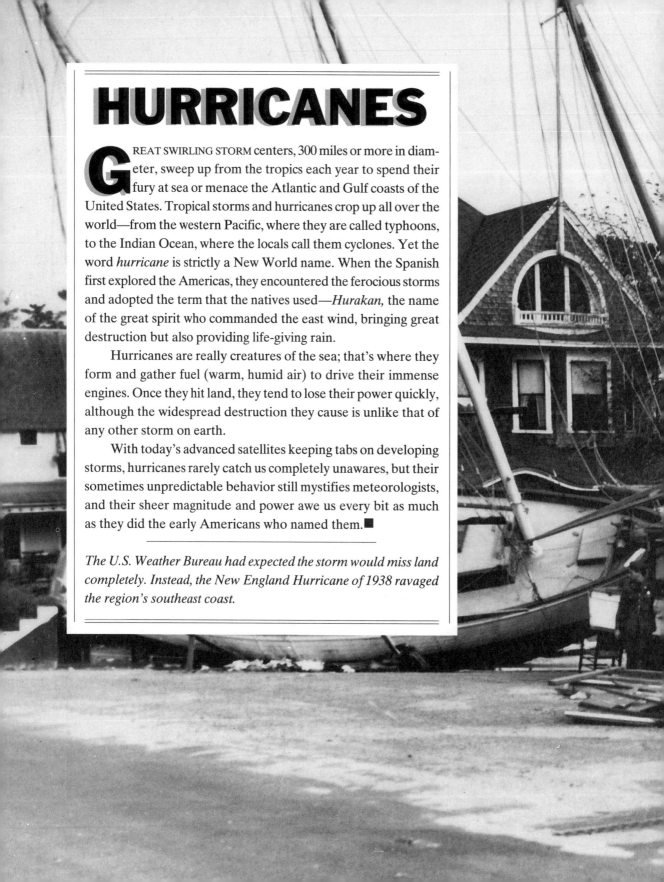

HURRICANES

GREAT SWIRLING STORM centers, 300 miles or more in diameter, sweep up from the tropics each year to spend their fury at sea or menace the Atlantic and Gulf coasts of the United States. Tropical storms and hurricanes crop up all over the world—from the western Pacific, where they are called typhoons, to the Indian Ocean, where the locals call them cyclones. Yet the word *hurricane* is strictly a New World name. When the Spanish first explored the Americas, they encountered the ferocious storms and adopted the term that the natives used—*Hurakan,* the name of the great spirit who commanded the east wind, bringing great destruction but also providing life-giving rain.

Hurricanes are really creatures of the sea; that's where they form and gather fuel (warm, humid air) to drive their immense engines. Once they hit land, they tend to lose their power quickly, although the widespread destruction they cause is unlike that of any other storm on earth.

With today's advanced satellites keeping tabs on developing storms, hurricanes rarely catch us completely unawares, but their sometimes unpredictable behavior still mystifies meteorologists, and their sheer magnitude and power awe us every bit as much as they did the early Americans who named them. ■

The U.S. Weather Bureau had expected the storm would miss land completely. Instead, the New England Hurricane of 1938 ravaged the region's southeast coast.

Galveston Harbor *as it looked before the big storm.*

Galveston's Night of Horror

Isaac Cline had tried to warn the skeptical citizens to head for higher ground. Now he was fighting for his own life against the rising tide.

B Y THE END OF THE NINETEENTH CENTURY, Galveston, Texas, had grown into one of the most attractive and prosperous cities in the country. Built atop the sands of a low-lying barrier island off the Gulf coast of Texas, Galveston boasted a warm climate and a protected harbor that had made it both a popular resort area and an important commercial port. By 1900, its population had swelled to 38,000.

Although Galveston had felt the wrath of hurricanes in the past (most recently in 1875), the long, gently sloping sea bottom that led to the city's beach had always provided a natural buffer against violent storms and serious flooding. Most residents felt that even if a hurricane hit, their city would be relatively safe from the storm's worst effects. But it took only one autumn day in 1900 to prove that this false sense of security was constructed, much like the city itself, on the shifting sands of reason.

Early on the morning of Saturday, September 8, 1900, Isaac Cline awoke and immediately started taking his first weather observations of the day. The barometer had fallen slightly overnight, but there were still some clear breaks in the clouds as the sun rose over the Gulf of Mexico. Cline was the chief of the U.S. Weather Bureau office at Galveston, and for the past few days, he had been monitoring the progress of a major hurricane that had crossed the Florida Keys on September 5 and entered the Gulf. On Friday the 7th, Cline had noticed heavy ocean swells rolling in from the southeast—a sure sign that the storm was on its way. By early Saturday morning, the huge surf was crashing high up onto the beaches and flooding the blocks nearest the Gulf with several inches of water. The odd thing was that the wind was blowing offshore from the north and should have been beating back the waves.

Around daylight, Cline decided to hitch up his horse and ride down to the beach to warn residents to head for higher ground. "Higher ground"

When men-of-war hawks fly high, it is a sign of a clear sky; when they fly low, prepare for a blow.

Twenty-fifth Street and Avenue P had been the site of a school. After the storm, only the desks, which were screwed to the floor, remained in order.

When the causeway over Galveston Bay washed out early in the storm, all links between Galveston and the mainland were severed.

When the hen crows, expect a storm within and without.

on Galveston Island meant the center of the city, but the highest point on the island was less than nine feet above sea level. When he reached the beach, Cline was surprised to find not only curious residents but many tourists as well, all having a grand time watching the thrilling sight of the enormous waves breaking on the shore. The weatherman rode up and down the beaches, warning people to leave the island or at least find some refuge before the storm arrived. Many people took his advice; others looked at him as though he were daft. They had seen storms before, and they thought that Cline was overstating the danger that faced Galveston.

The episode ended as a light rain began to fall, dampening the spirits of the beachgoers, and Cline headed for his office downtown, convinced that he had done what little he could to warn the population. By noon, the winds from the northeast had increased to 30 miles per hour and were still rising. At the same time, the rain became heavier and the barometer continued to drop. By this time, almost everyone in the city realized that a big storm was brewing, but there wasn't much they could do, since the flood waters had already risen alarmingly in the eastern and southern sections of town. By midafternoon, half of the city lay underwater, and residents were scrambling for higher ground. The high water in Galveston Bay had washed out the four bridges to the mainland, making escape from the island impossible. Come what might, people would have to contend with the hurricane on their own turf, which was rapidly being taken away from them as the flood tide rose higher by the minute.

At 2:30 P.M., the wind was blowing a gale from the northeast at 42 miles per hour, and Cline dashed off an advisory to the Weather Bureau in Washington. Cline's younger brother Joseph, who also worked for the Weather Bureau, took the message down the street to the Western Union office for transmission, but the telegraph operator told him that the key was dead, indicating that the wires had already come down in the storm. Joseph then went to the telephone office, and from there he managed to contact the weather office in Houston. He delivered Isaac's report, adding that relief should be sent as soon as possible. And that was the last thing anyone heard from Galveston. By the time the wind had reached hurricane force around 4 P.M., the telephone lines were dead, too, and the city was cut off from the outside world, left to face the longest night of its history alone.

As the wind howled, the water continued to rise, until that of the bay met that of the Gulf in the late afternoon, submerging all of Galveston. Even on the highest ground, the water rose a foot deep, and in the lower-lying areas, people struggled against the wind, slogging through chest-deep water in search of some safe haven. At 5:15, the anemometer on top of the Weather Bureau building blew away after recording a sustained wind speed of 84 miles per hour with gusts up to 100 miles per hour. By 7 P.M., the estimated wind speed had risen to 120 miles per hour or more.

Those wind speeds posed yet another hazard to people frantically seeking shelter from the storm. Because of a fire several years earlier, Galveston's building code required new houses to have heavy slate shingles, and as these were blown off roofs, they became lethal missiles that killed or wounded many unlucky refugees.

Isaac and Joseph Cline struggled home late in the afternoon to Isaac's house at 25th Street and Avenue Q. By 6:30 P.M., the flood waters had risen another four feet and stood waist deep on the first floor of the house. During the next hour, the tide rose five more feet, and Cline and his family headed upstairs, along with about 50 other people who had come to the house (one of the highest and best constructed in the neighborhood) seeking shelter. At 7:30 P.M., the wind suddenly shifted to the east, and the house began to capsize, pitching everyone into the swift-moving water. Joseph Cline grabbed the hands of his two older nieces, while Isaac, his wife, and his youngest daughter were carried underwater with the house. Isaac briefly lost con-

When the wind veers against the sun, trust it not, for back 'twill run.

Clara Barton, founder *of the American Red Cross and a Galveston relief worker.*

Birth of a Hurricane

A HURRICANE STARTS its life as something meteorologists call a *tropical disturbance,* a simple low-pressure area with light winds of less than 25 miles per hour. Hundreds of tropical disturbances form over the world's oceans, but only about 10 percent of these ever develop into full-fledged hurricanes.

Atmospheric scientists still have a lot to learn about how hurricanes behave, but they have discovered some of the conditions that are necessary for them to form, including the following:

• **Temperature.** Hurricanes form over warm ocean waters that have a surface temperature of 80°F or higher.

• **Location.** Hurricanes form in the tropics, between 5° and 30° north and south of the equator. (They don't form in the doldrums between 5° north and 5° south latitude because the Coriolis force, an atmospheric spin caused by the earth's rotation, is too weak in these latitudes to encourage a developing storm.)

• **Atmospheric conditions.** Important factors are high relative humidity; unstable air, allowing heat to rise from the ocean's surface; and low vertical wind shear (little change between wind speeds at different heights).

As towering cumulonimbus clouds form over the ocean, the moist, humid air rises and condenses into water vapor—releasing heat, creating updrafts, and lowering surface pressure. The center of the disturbance remains warmer than the outside air and begins to draw even more warm, moist air into its circulation. Eventually an "eye" forms around the area of lowest pressure, surrounded by a thick wall of rotating clouds. As the storm gets bigger and its wind speeds increase, it becomes known as a tropical depression, then a tropical storm, and finally a hurricane, the king of all storms.

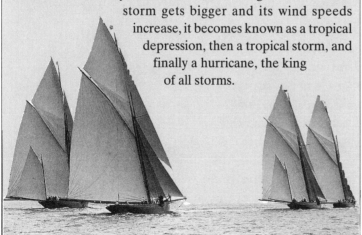

sciousness, and when he came to his senses a few minutes later, he found his young daughter and other family members nearby on the floating wreckage. His wife, Cora May, had disappeared.

For nearly three hours, the Cline brothers crouched with their backs to the wind, sheltering the three girls while the hurricane flung broken timbers and other debris through the air. As far as Isaac could tell, the wreckage they were riding headed seaward into the Gulf, then brought them back to Galveston, grounding them a mere 300 yards from where their house had stood just hours before.

A little before midnight, those people who had managed to reach higher ground noticed the water beginning to recede. At first this sight was a cause for celebration. It was as if the hurricane, like an unruly child, had grown tired of its vicious game. Even faster than it had come, the tide surged back through the city toward the ocean—causing almost as much death and destruction in its abrupt exit as it had on its arrival.

The great Galveston Storm had ended, but with the coming of dawn on Sunday, September 9, the full scope of the night's tragedy assaulted the eyes of the battered survivors. Thousands of homes had been ground to pieces in the hurricane and flood; only the business district had weathered the storm,

After the 1900 storm, *the city of Galveston constructed a massive sea wall. In this tourist postcard, the sea wall holds back the waves during the storm of August 13, 1932.*

protected by a semicircular wall of wrecked houses and other debris.

The almost complete destruction of Galveston—some $30 million in estimated damage—seems incredible in and of itself, but the real tragedy was the almost unimaginable loss of human life. Never before or since have more Americans died in any single natural disaster. The actual number of victims will never be known; the official death count stands at 6,000, but many suspect that the total might have been as high as 7,200 or even greater. In the western part of town, an estimated 1,200 people out of the 1,600 who lived there were thought to have perished in the storm. And the hand of death reached even beyond the city itself, claiming 1,000 victims in other towns along the Texas Gulf coast.

The stories of death and survival intertwined that Sunday morning in September, as the long job of clearing the wreckage and locating the dead and injured began. Most of the residents who had lived through the storm had survived by taking shelter in a few well-built or well-protected havens. The Ursuline Convent and Academy had taken in nearly 1,000 refugees who had washed up on the tide, and 400 more had huddled inside the Sacred Heart Church, which had lost its roof in the storm.

Sadly, tales of mass destruction were almost as common. The wind and waves had demolished St. Mary's Orphanage, near the beach west of town, killing 90 of the orphans and all 10 of the sisters; 3 other children had survived. The nuns had tied groups of children together with ropes in a desperate attempt to keep them

FOR THE RECORD

THE GALVESTON STORM OF 1900 resulted in the greatest loss of life of any U.S. natural disaster. But even the awful estimates of 6,000 to 7,200 dead pale in comparison with the figures from certain Asian storms. The greatest death toll from any single hurricane occurred along the coast of East Pakistan (now Bangladesh) on November 12–13, 1970. A great cyclone (the Indian Ocean name for a hurricane) swept into the Bay of Bengal, sending a wall of water more than 20 feet high over the low-lying islands, fields, and settlements in the Ganges Delta and drowning an estimated 300,000 people.

Silver Linings

ON THE NIGHT OF August 13, 1766, a powerful hurricane flattened the tiny village of Trois-Islets on the island of Martinique in the French West Indies. One of the island's wealthy planters, Joseph-Gaspard Tascher, was financially ruined by the storm. Thrown into poverty, his family was forced to make money the old-fashioned way: by marrying into it.

One of Tascher's young daughters, Marie Josephine Rose, later returned to France to seek her fortune. She married an army officer, the Vicomte de Beauharnais, who was guillotined in 1794. Two years later, she married another officer, one with a better head on his shoulders. And when her second husband, Napoleon Bonaparte, crowned himself in 1804, she suddenly became the Empress Josephine of France—and an inspiration to all social climbers.

together and bring them to safety. A report, perhaps apocryphal, of another desperate act involved a baby found on a rooftop in Galveston after the storm. Someone had driven a long metal nail through one of the child's wrists, securing him to the roof—a cruel act, perhaps, but one that saved the infant's life.

In his official report to the U.S. Weather Bureau, Cline wrote that "Sunday, September 9, 1900, revealed one of the most horrible sights that ever a civilized people looked upon." Yet once the appalling details of the tragedy had been absorbed, there was nothing for Galvestonians to do but begin the long job of clearing away the debris and starting over.

The sheer number of the dead and the oppressive heat that followed the passage of the hurricane left individual burial out of the question. At first, the bodies were taken out into the Gulf on a barge and weighted down for burial at sea. But then, compounding the existing horror, the corpses started to wash back onto the beach at Galveston. On Tuesday, the smoke began to rise from funeral pyres that would keep up the job of cremation for weeks to come.

Within only five days of the disaster, one of the railroad bridges to the Texas mainland had been repaired, and the first relief train arrived with much-needed assistance. Clara Barton, the founder of the American Red Cross, came to town herself to help feed the hurricane survivors.

After the first steps toward recovery had been taken, Galveston residents thought about what they should do to protect themselves against future disasters. In 1902, construction of a great sea wall began. When finished in July 1904, it stretched more than 3 miles and stood 17 feet above mean low tide. On August 16, 1915, when the next great hurricane hit Galveston, only eight people died, demonstrating the wall's effectiveness.

The body of Isaac Cline's wife, Cora May, was not found until October 3, 1900, nearly a month after the hurricane. She was discovered clinging to the underside of the same wall on which her husband and their youngest daughter had been riding that fateful night. Nearly every family in Galveston had lost at least one member, and many had been erased completely from the earth. Even in this, Isaac Cline shared with his neighbors the great tragedy that had befallen Galveston—a tragedy he had done everything in his power to prevent. ■

The Name Game

ONLY IN THE PAST FEW decades have tropical storms and hurricanes been dignified with official names. Before that time, storms were given more or less random monikers, often corresponding to the names of Catholic saints whose feast days fell on or near the date of the storm (like the two San Felipe hurricanes in 1876 and 1928) or commemorating individuals, ships, or cities affected by the storm. Perhaps the most whimsical handle was that given to North Carolina's Privy Hurricane of 1898, nicknamed in honor of a Weather Bureau outhouse destroyed by the storm.

In the last years of the nineteenth century, an Australian weatherman named Clement Wragge began giving female names to tropical storms (he also named several after politicians whom he particularly disliked). During World War II, meteorologists in the U.S. military picked up the practice, affectionately naming storms after their wives and girlfriends. (Who said romance is dead?)

By 1951, weather officials had decided to name storms using the phonetic alphabet (Able, Baker, Charlie, etc.).

But confusion arose here, too, and in 1953 the official use of female names became common practice in most of the Americas, with the first two hurricanes dubbed Alice and Barbara.

Needless to say, many women were less than thrilled by this decision, and complaints poured in to the Weather Bureau. But the practice continued until 1978, when hurricanes in the eastern Pacific were for the first time alternately named for men and women. In 1979, Atlantic hurricanes followed suit, with Hurricane Bob the first man in line.

In 1977, the World Meteorological Organization had developed six new, bisexual lists of official names for tropical storms, picking short, easy-to-remember ones from three languages: English (Arthur, Wanda); French (Henri, Claudette); and Spanish (Cesar, Paloma). To receive a name, a tropical low-pressure center must develop at least into a full-fledged tropical storm (with wind speeds

between 39 and 73 miles per hour). Every six years, the lists repeat themselves, except for the names of especially destructive storms, which are retired and enter a sort of Hurricane Hall of Fame. As of the end of 1991, ten storms had

received this dubious honor. (Score: males 6, females 4.)

As more and more names enter the record books, we could be in for a fiercely competitive Battle of the Sexes.

The Night the Florida Keys Almost Washed Away

As the relief train struggled south, the hurricane raced it to the islands—and won.

O N SUNDAY, SEPTEMBER 1, 1935—the day before Labor Day—a strong low-pressure center was reported just off Grand Turk island in the West Indies, bearing northwest toward the Straits of Florida and the southernmost tip of the United States. By 3:30 A.M. on September 2, officials had issued a weather advisory upgrading the storm to a hurricane and had posted storm warnings for all of southern Florida.

Wary of the power of tropical storms, the natives of the Florida Keys began their usual rituals of battening down—stocking up on fresh water, tying down boats or sinking them with their engines removed, and buying supplies of candles, kerosene, and canned food.

Soon the wind picked up, and palm trees groaned and genuflected. The day had turned gray and ominous, and the ground trembled from the pounding of the angry waves. The barometer fell steadily—to 29 inches, then 28, and then an incredibly low 27.15. The faces of people still outside in the elements were soon streaked with blood from the sharp, blowing sand.

Behind shuttered windows, the residents of the Keys could no longer see their Overseas Railroad, a triumph of engineering that some had called the Eighth Wonder of the World. Henry Flagler, a multimillionaire who had made his fortune with John D. Rockefeller, had begun construction of the railroad in 1905, leapfrogging it over a necklace of 29 islands for 156 miles, all the way from Miami to Key West. The most expensive short-line railroad in U.S. history, it had taken seven years to complete, and hundreds of lives had been lost building it. For 23 years, the bridges and trestles had weathered every storm, but the hurricane that was bearing down on the islands this Labor Day was no ordinary storm. It was a compact and incredibly powerful killer, one of only two Category 5 hurricanes ever to hit the United States (the other being Hurricane Camille in 1969).

The railroad and the local population weren't the only vulnerable things in the hurricane's path. In 1934, the federal government had assigned some 700 unemployed men, many of them World War I veterans, to work on building a highway that would

Multimillionaire *Henry M. Flagler built the Overseas Railroad, which linked the Florida Keys to the mainland—until 1935.*

Laborers pause near *the Islamorada siding on the railroad.*

parallel the railroad through the Keys. These men lived in flimsy shacks in camps located from Snake Creek to Lower Matecumbe Key. The Veterans Administration had set up a plan to evacuate these workers in case of a hurricane, and on Labor Day, with the storm's intensity building, an order went through to the Florida East Coast Railroad to send down a train from Homestead (on the mainland) to collect the workers and local residents and bring them to safety.

The only trouble was that no train was immediately available, and by the time a crew could be found in Miami and an 11-car train made up, it was already late in the day. The train finally left Homestead a little after 5 P.M., backing down toward the Keys along the single-track railroad and stopping frequently to clear away fallen trees and pick up hysterical evacuees.

At Snake Creek, a loose cable hooked the engine cab, and it took workers a full hour to free it. Three and a half hours after leaving Homestead, the train had traveled only 45 miles. Meanwhile, the highway work-

Laborers pause near *the Islamorada siding on the railroad.*

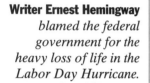

Writer Ernest Hemingway *blamed the federal government for the heavy loss of life in the Labor Day Hurricane.*

ers huddled beside the tracks with their bundles of belongings, waiting fearfully for the overdue train as the rain poured down and the storm shrieked all around them.

The wind picked up as the pressure fell even lower, reaching hurricane strength around 6:45 P.M. Later that evening, an aneroid barometer at Long Key registered an astounding low of 26.35 inches, the lowest barometric pressure ever recorded on land in the United States. The pressure became so intense that refrigerator doors popped open, glass jars exploded, windows burst, and small animals and fish died. Other animals were sandblasted to death by the incredible winds, which gusted to more than 200 miles per hour on the hurricane's eastern flank.

J.A. Duncan, the lighthouse keeper at Alligator Reef, looked up in terror as a wave at least 20 feet high rolled toward his 90-foot lighthouse. Clutching tightly to a ladder, he felt the surf crash over him and lap upward to the very top of the lighthouse.

This wasn't just a 20-foot surfer's wave; the whole ocean rolled in at a height 20 feet higher than normal. Many hurricane victims might have survived had it not been for this gigantic surge that washed over the islands,

At a makeshift funeral *pyre, a group of National Guardsmen prepare a rifle salute to victims of the hurricane.*

dashing almost everything to pieces in a path of total destruction some 30 miles wide. And the tremendous undertow that accompanied the moving wall of water sucked away people, wreckage, even whole islands.

Some people tied themselves to trees and hung on grimly while the wind and water lashed them mercilessly. Children floated by on beds, screaming in the night. On Windley Key, the Becom family watched their house being swept away, then fought their way through the storm to reach the comparative safety of their car. Turning on the headlights, they saw debris piling up on the windward side of the vehicle, forming a barrier that shielded them from the hurricane winds. Five other frantic survivors who saw the car's headlights crowded in with the seven Becoms and rode out the storm.

At Tavernier, Judge "Doc" Lowe, the justice of the peace, had built a special hurricane shelter by pouring a solid concrete foundation with a small concrete house over it anchored by two huge chains. When the hurricane hit, Doc led his family to the shelter. As they nestled in the fortresslike cubicle, a sudden gust lifted the whole structure—concrete, chain, and all—into the air, cracking it and pitching the family into the water. Swept against a small tree, Doc hung on while he strapped his belt around its trunk, his daughter's baby securely buttoned inside his coat. The rest of the family clung to each other around the tree, holding the children's heads above water. The wind howled and bent the tree in every direction

FOR THE RECORD

THE MOST ACTIVE YEAR FOR hurricanes in the North Atlantic Ocean, Gulf of Mexico, and Caribbean Sea was 1969. That year a total of 18 tropical storms formed, 12 of which developed into hurricanes. The 1933 season runs a close second, with 21 tropical storms producing 9 hurricanes.

The quietest year for storms was 1914, with only 1 tropical storm reported and no hurricane activity at all. But then, in 1914, with Europe already deeply involved in World War I, there was plenty of turmoil in the world already.

during the black night, but the tenacious family and the tiny tree rooted in the coral held fast.

One weather observer, J.E. Duane, was on the Keys during the hurricane and recorded what observations he could, even as he struggled himself for survival. Around 9 P.M., Duane noticed that the storm had abated,

'Tis the Season

THE OFFICIAL hurricane season in the Atlantic Ocean stretches from June 1 through November 30. On average, about ten tropical cyclones reach tropical storm strength each year, with six of these developing into full-fledged hurricanes.

The earliest hurricane of the season to strike the United States this century was Alma, which hit Florida's Gulf coast on June 9, 1966. The latest was an unnamed hurricane that made landfall near Tampa, Florida, on November 30, 1925.

A Memorial Day salute—to the start of hurricane season.

and he and 20 other refugees headed from a cottage where they had taken shelter to another, stronger building. The eye of the storm was passing over the islands, and the uneasy calm lasted some 40 minutes at Lower Matecumbe Key and 55 minutes at Long Key. During the lull, Duane's barometer read 27.20 inches. But around 10:15, another strong blast of wind came from the south-southwest and the pressure dropped again, to 26.90 inches. Just before he could get indoors, Duane was caught up by the rising storm tide and swept seaward. Riding the swell as best he could, Duane fetched up in a coconut palm and hung on until an unseen object flying through the darkness knocked him unconscious.

When the huge wall of water struck the rescue train at Islamorada late that evening, it uprooted the tracks and overturned ten of the cars. Only the 106-ton locomotive, the *Schenectady,* stood upright, its boilers flooded, sparing the lives of the engineer, fireman, and trainmaster. Thirteen passengers in the coaches managed to survive by holding themselves and their children out of the water all through the night.

By morning, everything was gone—trees, buildings, bridges, railroads, docks, and most of the highway workers and residents. J.E. Duane regained consciousness at 2:25 A.M. on September 3 and found himself still tangled in the palm tree, 20 feet above the ground. The hurricane winds continued until 5 A.M., but when dawn broke, Duane could see that all the water had receded and that the house containing his fellow refugees had made it through the storm, with everyone inside having survived.

Several communities on the Keys—tight enclaves where many people were interrelated—had been decimated. John Russell, the postmaster at Islamorada, had 79 relatives on the Keys before the hurricane struck. After the storm, only he and 10 others remained alive.

Some bodies were found hanging in the branches of uprooted trees. On one beach, Dr. G.C. Franklin of Coconut Grove came upon a hideous tableau of 39 men laid out in a windrow just as the wind had mowed them down in death. A few of the hurricane's victims had been

Hurricanes cause little corn-cern in the Plains states.

Why They Don't Have Hurricanes in Kansas

ONCE A HURRICANE makes landfall, it loses the main component that runs its engine—humid air above relatively warm waters—and it begins to weaken as it travels over the cooler and more irregular surface of the land. A typical hurricane loses about half its intensity and wind speed after traveling only 150 miles inland.

TEST YOUR HURRICANE KNOWLEDGE

1. **What percentage of all hurricanes that reach the United States strike the state of Florida?**
   a. 28   c. 55
   b. 39   d. 72
2. **Five of the 26 letters of the alphabet are not used to name hurricanes because of the scarcity of common names beginning with those letters. List them.**
3. **True or false: A hurricane can form only in tropical waters.**
4. **Most people know that the eye, or center, of a hurricane is the calmest area, with little or no wind or precipitation. In which quarter of the hurricane are the strongest and most damaging winds typically found?**
   a. left front
   b. left rear
   c. right front
   d. right rear

ANSWERS: 1. b. Also, two-thirds of the strongest U.S. hurricanes (Class 4 and Class 5 storms) strike either the Florida or Texas coast. 2. The letters Q, U, X, Y, and Z. 3. False, although all classic hurricanes are, by definition, tropical storms. So-called arctic hurricanes are small, intense cyclones that form in the winter just south of the ice sheets in far northern seas. Like their tropical cousins, these storms have a relatively warm center. 4. c. A hurricane rotates counterclockwise, and this motion, combined with the storm's forward speed, adds to the wind velocity on the right front flank, producing the strongest sustained winds and the greatest ocean swells.

sandblasted to death, their clothes and skin scoured away. Survivors described the electrostatic discharges that the flying grit gave off as it howled through the black night; to some it looked like millions of fireflies.

One man, still alive, leaned against a tree stump with a splintered two-by-four driven completely through him underneath his ribs. When doctors prepared to pull the wood out, the victim resisted. "When you pull it out, I'll die," he said. He then asked for two bottles of beer. When he had finished drinking them, he said, "Pull." The medics pulled, and the man died.

Some 577 bodies were found in the wake of the Labor Day Hurricane, but there are those who say that as many as 800 may have perished in the storm that night. Of these, 288 were federal highway workers from the three camps destroyed. The number could have been higher; 350 of the veterans from the camps had gone to see a ball game in Miami that day and were spared the fate of their coworkers.

One of the first relief workers to arrive on the scene was writer Ernest Hemingway. He owned a home on Key West, which had escaped the full force of the storm. Hemingway was one of many who were outraged by the high death toll among the highway workers and the government's alleged bungling of the evacuation. He later wrote an angry article titled "Who Murdered the Veterans?" Others blamed the railroad for the severity of the damage. The trouble with the railroad, many folks said, was that the high embankment for the tracks had blocked all channels between the Keys, giving the ocean no choice but to pound the islands.

Key West had heard its last train whistle, for the Overseas Railroad had died at sea, never to be rebuilt. But Henry Flagler had built well in spots; all of the concrete viaducts of the railroad's 34 bridges had withstood the hurricane, and today they support U.S. Route 1, the Key West Highway.

For years after the storm, skeletons were discovered in hidden recesses on the Keys. One rock pit yielded three autos with 1935 license plates and the bones of ten victims. And the skeletons still found occasionally in remote mangrove islands may bear further testament to the awesome power and destructiveness of the Labor Day Hurricane, which ranks as one of the United States' most violent natural disasters.   — RAYMOND SCHUESSLER ∎

Silver Linings

ON JULY 24, 1609, a fleet of nine ships carrying 500 colonists from England to Virginia encountered a hurricane near Bermuda. One ship sank, and the others were scattered, but seven of the ships managed to straggle into port at Jamestown. Only the flagship, the *Sea-Venture,* failed to appear, and after several weeks, it was given up for lost. For the colonists, the loss was an especially bitter one, as the new governor of Virginia, Sir Thomas Gates, had been aboard the flagship.

Giving up hope of seeing their comrades again, the Jamestown colonists settled down to work in their new home. Then, almost a year later, on May 23, 1610, most of the passengers and crew of the *Sea-Venture* arrived in Jamestown aboard two small pinnaces—much to the surprise and delight of their fellow settlers. Their ship had grounded on a reef while trying to land in Bermuda, but nearly everyone had come ashore safely. The castaways found Bermuda to be an island paradise, rather than the "Ile of Divels" most mariners thought it to be. They stayed there for nine months while building the two small ships they used to sail to Jamestown.

Later, back in England, a certain playwright read the account of the "miraculous" shipwreck and decided that some of its details might work well in his latest production. In 1611, William Shakespeare finished *The Tempest,* probably his last complete play and certainly the only comedy to have a hurricane in its very first scene (until "Gilligan's Island" debuted on television a few centuries later).

They Call It the Hurricane

THE WORD *HURRICANE* evokes such strong images of turmoil and destruction that it might be wasted if it were used only to describe a tropical cyclone. Luckily, many other things are called hurricanes, too. There are hurricane roses and hurricane lamps; even the upper deck of a ship is called the hurricane. But one hurricane, sold in the French Quarter of New Orleans and named solely for its ability to blow you away in one gulp, is the drink bartenders call the Hurricane. The recipe, according to purists, is as follows:

Combine 2 tablespoons lemon juice, 1 ounce rum (dark or light), and 1 tablespoon passion fruit juice.

Shake well with ice and strain into a tall glass. Fill the glass with soda water or 7UP and top with the rare and excruciating 151-proof rum.

Trio Con Brio

When they climbed trees to escape the flooding, some victims found that the water moccasins had got there first.

A coming storm
your shooting corns
presage,
and aches will
throb, your hollow
tooth will rage.

ACCORDING TO DATA from the National Hurricane Center in Coral Gables, Florida, a major hurricane (Category 4 or 5 on the Saffir/Simpson Damage Potential Scale of intensity) strikes the United States once every five years on average. Over the past 100 years, as the Atlantic and Gulf coasts have become more thickly settled, the probability of damage or fatalities from a hurricane in those areas has continued to rise. Since 1900, no fewer than 16 hurricanes (not all of them considered "intense" storms) have each resulted in 100 or more deaths in the United States. Along with the Galveston Storm of 1900 and the Labor Day Hurricane of 1935, the following three hurricanes represent some of the worst that nature has had to offer during this century.

• **The San Felipe Hurricane of 1928.** On the evening of Sunday, September 16, a powerful storm that had already dumped 30 inches of rain on parts of Puerto Rico, killing 300 there, struck the southern Florida coast near Palm Beach. As the hurricane raced across the southern tip of the state, it whipped the shallow waters of the great Lake Okeechobee into a frenzy, causing a massive flood that left water marks 25 feet high on some buildings. Residents of the southern lakeshore towns, trying to escape from their crumbling houses, were overtaken by the flood waters. Two hundred died along the road from Belle Glade to Pahokee alone.

In the aftermath of the storm, officials put the number of victims at 1,836, although the real death toll was almost certainly higher. Several persons died that night not from the hurricane or flooding, but from snakebite. By the time refugees began climbing into trees for safety, deadly water moccasins had already slithered up into the branches.

• **The New England Hurricane of 1938.** Many older Yankees still vividly remember this storm, the worst to hit the region in modern times. The Weather Bureau in Washington had been tracking the hurricane on Wednesday, September 21, but had forecast that it would track out into the North Atlantic, missing the Northeast entirely. Instead, the hurricane paralleled the Atlantic coast, barreling north at speeds of 60 miles per hour as it continued gathering strength. By the time the Weather Bureau could issue a warning at 3 P.M., it was too late; the storm had already made landfall on Fire Island and was racing across Long Island Sound toward the Connecticut coast.

Opposite: The tanker Phoenix *ran aground in Somerset, Massachusetts, during the New England Hurricane of 1938.*

In 1815, ships float down the main street of Providence.

All Hurricanes Are Not Created Equal

ANY TROPICAL STORM that packs winds of at least 74 miles per hour qualifies as a hurricane, but that general term covers a lot of ground and doesn't really describe the relative strength or destructive power of an individual storm. The two most intense hurricanes ever to strike the United States, the Labor Day Hurricane of 1935 and Hurricane Camille in August 1969, were both fairly small in size but carried a tremendous wallop that caused many deaths and considerable damage.

The Saffir/Simpson Damage Potential Scale places a hurricane in one of five categories, based on the barometric pressure in the storm's center (the lower, the stronger), sustained wind speeds, and height of storm surge. A hurricane gets classified only when it is expected to hit land within 72 hours.

Category	Barometric Pressure (in.)	Wind Speed (mph)	Surge (ft.)	Damage
1	28.94 or higher	74–95	4–5	Minimal
2	28.50–28.93	96–110	6–8	Moderate
3	27.91–28.49	111–130	9–12	Extensive
4	27.17–27.90	131–155	13–18	Extreme
5	Lower than 27.17	More than 155	More than 18	Catastrophic

Towns along the bays and rivers of coastal New England suffered most from the storm. At Providence, Rhode Island, the water rose to 13 feet 8½ inches in the downtown streets, deeper than in the famous September Gale of 1815, when sailing ships had floated through the business district. But even inland, the storm caused great damage as it raced up the Connecticut River valley and crossed Vermont's Green Mountains. Gusts as high as 100 miles per hour snapped or uprooted some 275 million trees in the forests of central New England.

In all, some 600 people died as a result of this storm, which caused $306 million in damage on Long Island and throughout New England. Most of the victims lived along the southeastern coast of New England and might have been saved if they had received adequate warning and had had a chance to escape inland.

• **Hurricane Camille, 1969.** One of the two most intense hurricanes ever to strike the U.S. mainland (the other Category 5 storm being the 1935 Labor Day Hurricane), Hurricane Camille was a compact, violent storm that made landfall along the Mississippi coast around 11:30 P.M. on August 17. The hurricane packed winds estimated at between 175 and200 miles per hour, and the storm surge that hit the shore along with the eye of the storm peaked at 24.2 feet at Pass Christian, Mississippi.

A total of 256 people lost their lives as Camille pounded Mississippi and Louisiana. The most famous tragedy occurred at Pass Christian, where some residents of the beachfront Richelieu Apartments were having a "hurricane party" when the storm came ashore. Since the U.S. Weather Bureau had predicted that Camille would make landfall on the Florida Panhandle, some 100 miles east, the partygoers didn't think that there was any risk in staying at home. But when the storm surge hit, the water rushed around the building, breaking in through the second-story windows and collapsing the apartment complex. Of the two dozen people in the building, only one—Mary Ann Gerlach—survived. As the water rose toward the ceiling of her apartment, she swam out a window and clung to some wreckage. Rescuers found her the next morning in a tree 5 miles away. They estimated that in the course of the night she had drifted back and forth some 12 miles on the storm tide.

Total damage from Camille amounted to more than $1.42 billion, about three-quarters of it in the state of Mississippi alone. The storm was one of the most powerful and awesome in U.S. history, featuring wind gusts officially clocked at 172 miles per hour and one of the lowest barometric pressures ever—26.73 inches, recorded in the Gulf of Mexico. ■

The Richelieu Apartments, *before and after Hurricane Camille.*

The Man Who Went Looking for Trouble

Colonel Joe Duckworth *took a bumpy ride into aviation history.*

Joseph Duckworth flew into the eye of a hurricane and survived. Then all he had to do was get back out.

ON THE MORNING OF JULY 27, 1943, Colonel Joseph B. Duckworth, commander of the U.S. Air Force's instrument flight training school at Bryan, Texas, heard a weather advisory stating that a hurricane was headed for Galveston. Duckworth, a veteran pilot for Eastern Airlines before the war, had started his career in aviation when visual flying was the only way to go: When the weather was bad, you stayed on the ground. But he had become a passionate exponent of instrument flying and maintained that a pilot could fly safely through just about any kind of weather by relying on instruments alone. Now he set out to prove just that.

Taking along the base navigator, Lieutenant Ralph O'Hair, as his copilot, Duckworth lifted off from Bryan Field just after noon in a single-engine AT-6 trainer with no special equipment aboard. The mission he had set for himself was simple—find the hurricane and fly straight through it.

No one had ever intentionally flown into the eye of a hurricane before (at least no one who had lived to tell the tale). But Duckworth climbed to 4,000 feet, then made radio contact with Houston controllers and informed them of his unusual flight plan—just before static from the storm cut him off.

As Duckworth and O'Hair entered the outer fringes of the hurricane, they flew blindly through bands of torrential rain, the plane bucking in the turbulence, climbing and diving uncontrollably for thousands of feet as it encountered incredibly strong updrafts and downdrafts. The heavy rain made both men nervous, since the water was rapidly cooling the cylinder heads of the single engine. If that engine cut out, there would be nothing to do but bail out into the storm and hope for the best.

Suddenly the plane broke through the eye wall of the hurricane and entered the calm central eye. Above, the two men saw patches of blue sky, and below they could see the ground. All around them towered the white walls of the circular eye, a sight no human had ever observed up close.

Having had enough of the bumpy trip, Duckworth dove and looked for a place to land, but the winds near the surface were much too violent for that. The only way out was back through the hurricane. The two men braced themselves and flew once more into the furious storm, with Duckworth keeping his eyes glued to the glowing instrument panel. Several hours later, with only a few cuts and bruises to show for their wild ride, Duckworth and O'Hair landed safely back at Bryan Field, the first two men to fly through a hurricane. Then Duckworth went back up and did it all over again. On his second historic flight, he took along the base's weather officer, Lieutenant William Jones-Burdick, who became the first person ever to gather meteorological data from a plane flying inside a hurricane.

Some of Duckworth's superiors didn't approve of his barnstorming flights that day, taken wholly on his own initiative, but others recognized the importance of the mission and its implications for weather forecasters. Duckworth received the Air Medal for his pluck, and within a year the U.S. Army and Navy had assigned crews to fly hurricane duty in the Atlantic, Pacific, and Caribbean theaters. Duckworth's historic flight marked the beginning of military and civilian flights aimed at measuring the size and intensity of hurricanes and relaying that information back to forecasters, who could then keep tabs on any tropical storm that threatened the mainland.

Even today, with sophisticated weather satellites orbiting the earth, the National Hurricane Center in Coral Gables, Florida, routinely sends out planes to check on developing storm centers. As with any good idea, though, someone had to be first, and Joseph Duckworth ensured his place in aviation history by trusting to his instruments and daring to do the impossible. ■

A U.S. Air Force *"Storm Tracker" in the air over the Gulf of Mexico. These aircraft provide important information on developing storms to the National Hurricane Center in Coral Gables, Florida.*

FOR THE RECORD

IT IS COMMON FOR MORE THAN one tropical storm center to develop in the North Atlantic at one time. The record number of hurricanes occurring at the same time is four, as observed on August 22, 1893. A few days later, one of these storms struck South Carolina and Georgia, killing between 1,000 and 2,000 people in one of the highest-fatality weather disasters in U.S. history.

Follow That Swan

ACCORDING TO weather folk-lore, if a swan flies against the wind, it is a certain sign of a hurricane within 24 hours, and generally within 12 hours. If you don't happen to have any swans in your neighborhood, you might look for other typical signs of a strong storm approaching: a hazy quality to the atmosphere, unseasonable humidity, high patches of cirrocumulus clouds, and (at the shore) unusually high tides or deep ocean swells, usually coming from the southeast.

Apia Harbor in Samoa, where a storm kept the peace.

Silver Linings

THE DESTRUCTIVE EFFECTS of hurricanes are well known to everyone. What most people don't know is that a hurricane halfway around the world may have kept the United States out of a war.

In 1888, the United States and Germany were on opposite sides of a diplomatic battle over the Samoa Islands. Plots and counterplots proliferated, and minor incidents became international events when fanned by the flames of the jingoistic press at home. By early 1889, three German, three American, and one British warship (the Brits were looking out for their national interests as well) were all stationed in the harbor at Apia, looking down the barrels of their guns at one another.

Then, on March 16, 1889, a great hurricane struck the poorly protected harbor. All six of the American and German gunboats were wrecked, sunk, or grounded in the storm. Only the British vessel, the *Calliope,* managed to limp safely out to sea, to the cheers of American seamen aboard the USS *Trenton.*

Although 150 sailors lost their lives in the hurricane, the newfound camaraderie among the seamen of all three nations helped defuse the potentially explosive situation. As the *New York World* put it: "Men and nations must bow before the decrees of nature. . . . Surely the awful devastation wrought in the harbor of Apia makes our recent quarrel with Germany appear petty and unnatural."

The common loss eventually led to peace, and later that same year the dispute over Samoa was settled (for a while, at least) in the Treaty of Berlin.

Some Days You'd Rather Be Wrong

I T'S THE KIND OF PREDICTION the editors of *The Old Farmer's Almanac* hope to be wrong about. On page 156 of the 1992 edition, the Almanac predicted that a hurricane would cross the southern tip of Florida at the end of August. Hurricane Andrew, which leveled much of southern Dade County on August 24, is now considered the costliest hurricane in U.S. history. More than 1 million people fled their homes in advance of the storm. Hundreds of thousands

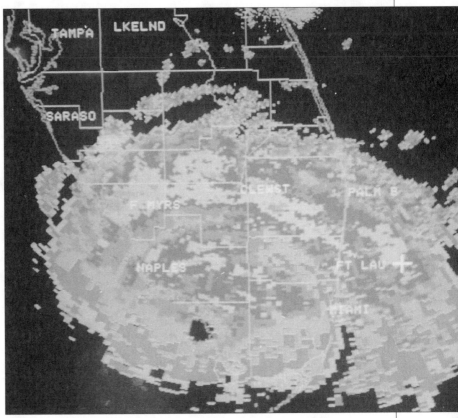

Above: *A computer image of 1992's Hurricane Andrew.*
Left: The Old Farmer's Almanac *prediction.*

will be slightly cooler than normal with a few isolated regions, such as the southwestern Great Plains and the far Northwest, being well below normal. Precipitation will be slightly below normal in the western third of the country. Isolated pockets of below-normal precipitation will also exist in southern New England, the Ohio River Valley from the lower Great Lakes to the east-central Great Plains, Oklahoma, and northern Texas. A possible hurricane crossing southern Florida at the end of August and a tropical disturbance entering Texas in early September would bring well above normal precipitation to the Gulf and South.
EARLY FALL will be warmer and drier than normal over the eastern two-thirds of the country except for the possible influence of another tropical storm or

returned to piles of rubble. Everglades National Park, often called the nation's richest and most biologically diverse ecosystem, became a swamp of uprooted trees and dying wildlife. Damage estimates quickly soared to more than $30 billion, making Andrew ten times worse than Hurricane Agnes, long considered the standard of destruction. And the only fact more shocking than these is the certainty that a costlier storm will someday strike.

For people who live on the Atlantic Coast, and for their friends and relatives, each year's hurricane season brings a familiar feeling of dread. That helplessness is shared by scientists and meteorologists, who know that although they can predict with growing accuracy, they still cannot prevent.

TORNADOES

WHEREVER THUNDERCLOUDS gather, tornadoes are a possibility. All 50 states have reported twisters at one time or another, although they are rare in the West and in other mountainous regions of the country. But nowhere in the world do tornadoes form as frequently as they do in the central and southern Great Plains, where geography, winds, and weather patterns all conspire to put a deadly cyclonic spin on the most innocent clouds, creating a monster that can flatten a building or an entire town in a matter of seconds.

A severe tornado packs the strongest winds found anywhere on earth, with speeds reaching 300 miles per hour in some cases. Moderate winds that are drawn into the vortex of the storm revolve faster and faster around a central core. It's the same principle that makes a figure skater like Kristi Yamaguchi spin faster when she pulls in her arms and legs.

Tornadoes fascinate us for many reasons: their power, their rarity, and the fact that they are dashing and free-spirited rogues, appearing to move over the landscape with an inscrutable will of their own. Hard to avoid and even harder to predict, tornadoes (like most rogues) command our respect and even a grudging admiration—as long as they don't get too close. ■

A tornado's dramatic funnel cloud threatens a barn on the Texas Panhandle.

The Tri-State Terror

Few even saw it coming, but suddenly they were in the middle of the deadliest tornado in U.S. history. The next thing they knew, their town was gone.

Cruel storms do not blow in a right course.

MARCH 18, 1925, WAS a dark, gloomy day in Gorham, a town of 500 people in southwestern Illinois near the banks of the Mississippi River. The morning air hung like a damp cloth, muggy and oppressive with not a breath of wind. A light drizzle was falling, but it offered no relief from the early-season humidity. Around 2:30 in the afternoon, the drizzle increased to a downpour and the sky suddenly turned as black as night. And then, without warning, the world turned upside-down.

In the local schoolhouse, children ran to the windows to look at the angry sky, until the teacher ordered them all to return to their desks. A moment later, a terrific wind struck the school, and the building began to

crumble. One schoolgirl who survived remembered the scene: "The walls seemed to fall in, all around us. Then the floor at one end of the building gave way. We all slipped or slid in that direction. If it hadn't been for the seats it would have been like sliding down a cellar door."

The storm that had dealt Gorham such a savage and sudden blow that afternoon came to be known as the Tri-State Tornado. Almost unequaled in the length of its destructive path—219 miles, from Ellington, Missouri, to Petersburg, Indiana—this powerful twister still ranks as the deadliest single tornado in U.S. history.

As the storm left Gorham and moved northeast toward other unsuspecting settlements, it left 37 people dead in its wake. In only five minutes' time, the town of Gorham had been almost completely destroyed. All communication lines with the outside world had been severed, and it was not until eight o'clock that evening that the first medical help arrived to treat the wounded.

Even before it reached Gorham, the Tri-State Tornado had done considerable damage in Missouri. Touching down around 12:55 P.M. near the

The great Tri-State Tornado *of 1925 destroyed the mining town of West Frankfort, Illinois. Only the strongest steel structures survived, including Peabody Coal Mine No. 9 (in the background).*

Desks in this Illinois *schoolroom bear silent witness to the destructive force of the tornado, which killed 689 people and caused more than $16.5 million in damage.*

FOR THE RECORD

THE LONGEST CONTINUOUS track ever recorded for a single tornado was 293 miles. The record belongs to the Mattoon-Charleston (or Long Path) Tornado of May 26, 1917, which killed 101 people and injured nearly 600 more as it tore through central Illinois and Indiana. This tornado also holds the record for the longest duration of a single twister—nearly 7 hours.

town of Ellington, the twister claimed its first four victims in the tiny Ozark village of Annapolis. Another four people lost their lives in the farming community of Biehle as the tornado, by now a quarter of a mile wide, blasted through town. Damage from two separate funnels was later noticed on the ground, but no one in Biehle reported having seen the funnel clouds. In fact, along most of its course, the tornado looked like a huge, amorphous cloud that people took for just another thunderstorm. What they were really seeing, though, was the huge inverted cone of the funnel, growing in strength as it left Missouri behind and crossed the Mississippi River into Illinois.

Growing to between one-half and one mile in width, the tornado slowed after crossing the river. In Missouri, it had barreled along at between 67 and 72 miles per hour, nearly twice as fast as a typical tornado. But as it left Gorham, the cloud began to chase the center of low pressure that fed it, swirling along at 60 miles per hour through southern Illinois and advancing on the manufacturing center of Murphysboro, ten miles away.

A few minutes after leaving Gorham, the tornado steamrollered its way into Murphysboro and reduced 100 blocks of the city to rubble, sparking fires in the residential area that destroyed another 70 blocks there, as firemen failed to coax any water pressure from damaged hydrants. In the end, the tornado destroyed 40 percent of Murphysboro, killing 234 of the city's residents.

Paralleling the railroad line, the storm continued northeastward, following its now-familiar modus operandi by sneaking up unsuspected on coal-mining and railroad towns like De Soto and West Frankfort and then delivering its crushing blow. Sixty-nine people were killed at De Soto, and the *St. Louis Post-Dispatch* reported:

> Only a dozen houses remain standing and all of these are damaged with roofs and porches missing. Piles of brick and timbers fill the streets, trees are split and uprooted. The scene resembles that of a World War battlefield, except that on a battlefield the victims are men. Here they are mostly women and children. Many of the men escaped through the fact that they were away from home, mostly at work in the coal mines, and were out of the tornado's path.

At West Frankfort, too, many of the men were working underground in the mines when the tornado hit. With electric power cut, the miners had to abandon the elevators and make the long climb up out of the shafts to return home—hoping that they still had homes to return to, and someone waiting for them there. A total of 148 people died in West Frankfort, and more than 400 were injured, many suffering permanent disabilities because medical relief did not arrive for more than eight hours.

Before the tornado quit Illinois, it smashed through the small town of Parrish, leaving only three buildings standing in the northwest corner of town—the church, the schoolhouse, and a home belonging to Clarence Lowman. Lowman, who ran the town's general store, saw the funnel of the tornado bearing down on the town and started to run the two blocks toward his home, but the tornado overtook him. He survived by throwing himself on the railroad track and hanging on to a rail for dear life. Buffeted by the incredible winds, Lowman hung on grimly, but the buffeting broke his shoulder, his arm, and several ribs.

As the storm approached Parrish and the sky darkened, the town's schoolmaster, Delmar Perryman, locked the doors of the schoolhouse and prevented the 50 or 60 students from leaving. The tornado missed the building, and Perryman's quick action was one of the few that saved lives that day.

After the whirlwind had flattened the town, hailstones half the size of apples began to fall, and then the sun broke through the clouds above scenes

TEST YOUR TORNADO KNOWLEDGE

1. **Which month has the greatest average number of tornadoes per year?**
   a. March   c. May
   b. April   d. July

2. **On a rough scale of destructiveness, how much more damaging is a 300-mile-per-hour wind than a 30-mile-per-hour wind?**
   a. 10 times
   b. 50 times
   c. 100 times
   d. 1,000 times

3. **What is the velocity (forward speed, not wind speed) of an average tornado?**
   a. 20 to 25 miles per hour
   b. 35 to 40 miles per hour
   c. 50 to 55 miles per hour
   d. 60 to 65 miles per hour

ANSWERS: 1. c. May tops the list with an average of 143 tornadoes per year. January is the least likely month for a twister, with an annual average of only 14.5. 2. c. 3. b.

of utter desolation. Mrs. Ivory Williams, the wife of the stationmaster at Parrish, was returning home by train with her two children. As she left the train, the first thing she saw was the body of her husband, crushed and burned beneath the wires of a telegraph pole. Searchers found the body of farmer William Rainey in a clump of trees more than a mile from his

Why Large Bathrooms & Walk-in Closets Are Safety Features

IF YOU'RE BUYING A NEW HOUSE in tornado country, look for one with bathrooms big enough to hold the whole family at once. Because of the extra structural protection of metal plumbing, a bathroom probably ranks as the second best place (next to the basement) to take shelter inside a house when a tornado is approaching. Interior closets also are good hideouts, so if you can't find a house with a large bathroom, the next best thing is one with a walk-in closet. Finances permitting, avoid buying a mobile home; more people die in these than anywhere else during tornadoes. If you're in a mobile home when a tornado warning is issued, evacuate immediately. And head for a house, not your car. An automobile, whether moving or not, is extremely vulnerable in the high winds and hail that accompany a tornado. If you're driving when a warning is issued, take shelter immediately.

Every home's tornado shelter.

house; both of his legs and his neck were broken, his right arm was severed, and there was a large hole in his head. Mrs. Lem Lounis was found a quarter of a mile from her home, but her remains were so mangled that relatives could identify the body only by her distinctive red hair.

Crossing the Wabash River into Indiana, the tornado's swirling cloud of mud and debris swept through Griffin, claiming 25 more lives and destroying the town. Just east of Griffin, the storm turned slightly north from the straight track it had followed up to this point, as if the tornado had a mind of its own—a grim intention to kill again. Near the town of Owensville, the twister flattened the Waters farm and killed Richard Waters, 70, as well as his son, Lemuel, 35, and his 6-year-old grandson, Dudie—three generations gone in a single stroke.

For six miles between Griffin and Owensville, witnesses reported sighting three separate funnels, as the tornado again began to pick up speed, racing along at 73 miles per hour. But soon the funnels disappeared once more into the shapeless black cloud that raced toward Princeton, slamming into the Baldwin Heights neighborhood and wiping out a quarter of the town. Amazingly, people in downtown Princeton didn't know for some time that the rolling black cloud they saw nearby had wreaked such havoc on their city and killed 45 of their neighbors.

Finally, some 16 miles northeast of Princeton, in a field outside Petersburg, the great Tri-State Tornado caught up with the low-pressure center it had been trailing and quickly disappeared. Three and a half hours and 219 miles after it had started, the storm had left 689 dead along its route—more than twice the number ever killed before by a single tornado. Nearly 2,000 people suffered serious injuries, and property damage from the storm topped $16.5 million.

Reconstruction in all of the major towns began almost immediately after the cleanup and rescue had ceased, and volunteer relief agencies such as the Red Cross and the Salvation Army soon entered the stricken area. In Murphysboro, the storm had left some 8,000 people homeless, and the National Guard erected tent cities for the survivors there, as well as in other devastated towns such as De Soto and Griffin.

Severe tornadoes occur with some regularity in the area whipped by the Tri-State Tornado, but nothing like the tragic scope of that storm has

Silver Linings

I N THE GREAT TRI-STATE TORNADO of 1925, Joe Boston, a policeman in Murphysboro, Illinois, lost a bond for a deed that had been locked inside a safe in his home. Somehow the bond was sucked out of the safe and transported to the town of Lawrenceville—125 miles northeast of Murphysboro—where it was later found and returned to Mr. Boston by mail.

About the same time, 130 miles away from Murphysboro in Robinson, Illinois, one lucky farmer watched a $10 and a $20 bill drop right out of the sky, along with other articles that the tornado had swiped from Murphysboro. Proving once (and possibly twice) the truth of that old proverb: Easy come, easy go.

Ringing in the ear at night indicates a change of wind.

ever been seen before or since that fateful day in 1925. An unlucky set of weather conditions created both the ground-hugging, "invisible" tornado that gave no warning to most of its victims and the leading low-pressure area that pulled the twister along on its long and extraordinary path. Some people claim that today, with our improved communications and tornado warning systems, a disaster on the scale of the Tri-State Tornado could never occur. We can only hope that they're correct—but never is a very long time. ■

Sleep Tight—But Don't Try To Sneak in an Afternoon Nap

SINCE TORNADOES ARE spawned within powerful thunderstorms, it should come as no great surprise that about 60 percent strike between noon and sunset, the time when towering cumulonimbus clouds tend to form. The hours between 3 and 5 A.M. are considered the least likely for a tornado, although twisters have been known to touch down at any time of the day or night.

Dagwood Bumstead, catching 40 winks.

We Don't Do Windows

FOR MANY YEARS, tornado safety instructions invariably included this piece of advice: When a tornado warning is issued for your area, open the windows on the windward side of your house (the side toward the approaching storm) so that if the tornado strikes, the air pressure inside the house will match the air pressure outside.

In theory, this was terrific. Better to have a wet floor and a few crooked pictures than to have your home explode, which is what almost everyone thought would happen during a severe tornado: The air pressure inside the house would be greater than the air pressure outside in the partial vacuum of the tornado, causing the walls and roof of the house to push outward and collapse.

In the past few years, though, scientists have debunked the time-honored explosion theory. For one thing, most houses today aren't built so tight that air can't readily escape before blowing the whole structure apart. And after going over many damage sites, tornado researchers began to notice that only three walls had fallen outward in most cases, not all four as you would expect if the houses had exploded. Generally, the windward wall had blown inward, suggesting that the strong winds associated with tornadoes, not the sudden drop in barometric pressure, were what had caused most of the structures to collapse.

The real reason that a house falls in a strong tornado is due to a principle called the Bernoulli effect—the same thing that causes an airplane to fly. When wind strikes the leading edge of a wing, it causes a reduction in pressure above the wing and an increase in pressure below, creating an upward lift. When the strong winds of a tornado strike a house, the wall forces the wind up over the roof and around the sides of the building, creating zones of reduced pressure that cause the roof to lift and the side walls to pull outward.

So what good does opening your windows do? Absolutely none—in fact, it may cause the wind to exert more force on the roof and walls from inside, making the house even more likely to collapse. In the event of a tornado warning, head for your basement, a shelter, or another safe place at once—and don't get caught with your sash up.

In 1953, young Senator *John F. Kennedy inspects tornado damage in Shrewsbury, Massachusetts. Experts say that opening the windows probably wouldn't have saved the house on the left.*

Outbreak!

ONE OF THE MOST DANgerous aspects of tornadoes is that they frequently strike in batches, sometimes with dozens of funnel clouds descending to earth in a single day over a large portion of the country. Although people tend to recall the single killer tornadoes that devastate only one or two towns or cities, some of the deadliest tornado tragedies in U.S. history have been played out on a much larger scale by groups of separate twisters. These are some of the most spectacular and deadly outbreaks in modern times:

• **February 19, 1884.** The Great Southern Outbreak spawned 60 tornadoes between 10 A.M. and midnight, moving from Mississippi to Virginia. The towns of Leeds, Alabama, and Columbus, Georgia, suffered heavy damage. Because of a question about the actual death toll (accounts over the years have ranged from a low of 182 to a high of 1,200 or more), this event has also been dubbed the Enigma Outbreak.

• **May 27, 1896.** Of the 18 tornadoes reported on this date, by far the most famous and deadly was the Great St. Louis Tornado, which claimed

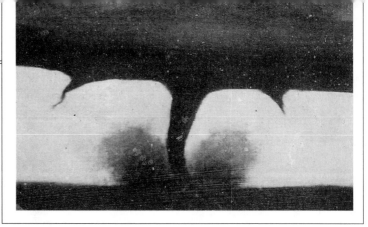

This 1884 tornado was the first ever captured on film.

137 lives in the city itself and 118 across the Mississippi River in East St. Louis, Illinois. A barometer in St. Louis recorded a 2.41-inch drop in air pressure as the storm passed, and winds associated with the twister have been estimated at almost 200 miles per hour, strong enough to have driven a two-by-eight-inch plank into a steel girder on a local bridge. The 18 tornadoes killed a total of 306 people and caused $15 million in damage.

• **April 24–25, 1908.** In two days another 18 tornadoes wreaked havoc from Louisiana to Georgia, killing 310 persons in all. One of the longest and deadliest twisters of all time traveled 158 miles, from Weiss, Louisiana, to the eastern border of Mississippi, near Winchester. In the path of that one tornado, 143 people lost their lives.

• **April 5–6, 1936.** The second deadliest outbreak on record began on the evening of April 5 and continued into the next morning, with 17 tornadoes sweeping from Tupelo, Mississippi, to the western Carolinas. Tupelo itself was hardest hit, with 216 fatalities, and Gainesville, Georgia, lost 203 residents in the whirlwind there. Overall, the storms claimed 446 lives and caused some $18 million in damage.

• **April 11–12, 1965.** The first funnel cloud of the famous Palm Sunday Outbreak touched down in eastern Iowa around one o'clock on the afternoon of April 11. Over the next 12 hours, a total of 51 tornadoes would take 256 lives throughout the Upper Midwest, causing more than $200 million in damage over six states. The worst single tornado of the day descended near Culver, Indiana, and followed a track 84 miles long, killing 72. Another deadly storm in southern Michigan traveled 92 miles on the ground, leaving 44 people dead.

What's Worse Than a Tornado? How About 148 Tornadoes?

WITH AN INCREDIBLE 148 tornadoes striking in 13 states and Canada, April 3–4, 1974, ranks as the most active 24-hour period for tornadoes in American history. Most people hope that record stands for a good long while. Spread out over a land area of 490,000 square miles, the twisters—known collectively as the Super Outbreak—destroyed more than 600 square miles along three major squall lines, killing 315 people and causing more than $500 million in damage. Eleven states reported fatalities, and parts of ten states were declared federal disaster areas in the wake of the storms.

The city of Xenia, Ohio, was hardest hit, with 34 deaths and many close calls. One of the narrowest escapes involved members of the high school drama club, who rushed to safety in a hallway just moments before a tornado deposited two school buses on the stage where the students had been rehearsing.

An aerial view shows damage to the Arrowhead section of Xenia, Ohio, where the tornado first touched down.

On a Scale from Zero to Incredible

The Fujita Scale makes sense. A few shattered windows are considered light damage. But when your car blows away and then your house goes, too . . .

UNTIL THE LATE 1960s, no widely accepted standard existed for classifying tornadoes based on their relative strengths. Tornadoes can wreak terrific havoc but typically do their worst in a very localized area. The average twister is only 140 yards wide, less than one and a half times the length of a football field. And damage from a storm can be even more selective and difficult to describe. Trees on the edge of a tornado track may be stripped of leaves and bark on one side and left perfectly unharmed on the other.

The man who put things in perspective was T. Theodore Fujita, a Japanese physics professor who in 1945 surveyed the devastation following the nuclear bombing of Hiroshima. After coming to the University of Chicago in 1953, Fujita logged many hours in the air and on the ground, surveying the natural damage caused by tornadoes. Looking at the aftermath of the Super Outbreak of 1974 reminded him of the mass destruction he had seen in World War II.

Today the Fujita Tornado Intensity Scale remains the best gauge of a tornado's power. It is based on observed damage and fits a tornado into one of six categories, labeled F0 (the weakest) to F5 (the strongest). At one time, it was thought that winds inside a tornado might approach the speed of sound (around 738 miles per hour), but all observations indicate that even the strongest tornadoes top out at around 300 miles per hour.

Only two percent of all tornadoes fall into the F4 or F5 category.

Fujita Number	Wind Speed (mph)	Observed Damage
F0 (very weak)	40–72	Light damage; twigs and branches broken off trees; some damage to chimneys and TV antennas; signboards damaged; some windows shattered
F1 (weak)	73–112	Moderate damage; surface peeled off roofs; mobile homes pushed off foundations; trees snapped; outbuildings destroyed; moving cars pushed off road
F2 (strong)	113–157	Considerable damage; roofs torn off frame houses; some buildings lifted and moved off their foundations; large trees snapped and uprooted; small objects become projectiles
F3 (severe)	158–206	Severe damage; roofs and walls destroyed; trees in forest uprooted; cars and heavy objects lifted off ground and rolled; metal and masonry structures damaged or destroyed
F4 (devastating)	207–260	Devastating damage; well-built houses destroyed; cars thrown and destroyed; trees debarked by flying debris; sandy soil eroded; large objects become projectiles
F5 (incredible)	261–318	Incredible damage; well-built houses lifted and carried away; car-size projectiles blown 300 feet or more; "incredible" phenomena occur (such as straws penetrating tree trunks) ∎

Tornado in a Bottle

TAKING THE SHIP-IN-A-bottle theme one step further, Burnham and Associates, a toy company in Salem, Massachusetts, has unveiled the Tornado Tube—an inexpensive product that allows a child to bring a tornado into his or her own home. The tube is really just a coupling device. You attach an empty two-liter soda bottle to one end and another soda bottle, partially filled with water, to the other end. Then you turn it over. And over. And over. The tube functions like a liquid hourglass. Inside, the draining water creates a vortex that looks and acts like a tornado—except, of course, it doesn't tear down buildings or throw cattle across state lines. It's the safest way for aspiring weather watchers to check out something like the real thing.

Natchez Landing as it looked around 1835. After the tornado of 1840, only one house was left standing. In the background is Natchez-on-the-Hill.

Nightmare at Natchez

The tornado didn't last long, and it's a good thing. At the peak of the twister's fury, damages averaged $1 million a minute.

JUST BEFORE TWO O'CLOCK on the afternoon of May 7, 1840, the citizens of Natchez, Mississippi, were sitting down to their midday meals. The masses of black thunderclouds that had gathered over the past hour rumbled and flashed, casting the beautiful city on the bluffs and its landing on the river into a profound and pitchy darkness. In the hotels on the hill, though, no one seemed overly concerned about the gloomy weather, and candles were quickly brought out for the benefit of dinner guests.

A few minutes later, the skies opened up, pouring down a storm more violent than anyone had ever seen before. And then a tornado struck with such fury that most people could not hear or even see the destruction that rained down all around them. In five minutes, the worst was over, although the tornado continued to sweep through the city and its environs for nearly half an hour.

When the storm abated, the residents of the city emerged to see what had happened, and they were met by an appalling sight. In the upper city, called Natchez-on-the-Hill, almost every house had sustained severe damage. William Parker's three-story Mississippi Hotel, described by some as the best hostelry in the state, lay in ruins. But Natchez Landing, at the foot of the bluffs, had suffered even more. According to one witness, Horatio Eustis, "The force of the wind was incredible. Iron spikes were borne by the blast with such force and direction as to be driven up to their heads, into the walls of houses. Other walls were pierced (even interior partitions) by pieces of shingles lanced from roofs a hundred rods distant. Men who were able to clutch hold of something firmer, were stripped perfectly naked."

The greatest death toll took place on the river itself. Fifty or 60 flatboats had been tied up at the landing that day, and only 6 survived the tornado and the six- to eight-foot storm wave that surged in off the Mississippi. Of the 317 estimated dead at Natchez, some 100 were boatmen. One steamboat that had been docked at Natchez Landing when the tornado hit was discovered two weeks later near Baton Rouge, Louisiana—a drifting ghost ship with 51 corpses aboard.

The Natchez Tornado ranks as one of the worst weather disasters in America's early history. The width of the tornado's path was phenomenal; it completely engulfed the mile-wide city of Natchez and stretched another mile across the river to simultaneously strike Vidalia, Louisiana, destroying the courthouse, the jail, and other buildings there. Although the port at Natchez soon hummed with activity again, it took years for the city to rebuild and recover from the staggering $5 million loss that the tornado had inflicted in only five minutes. ∎

The sharper the blast, the sooner 'tis past.

FOR THE RECORD

TWO OF THE THREE DEADLIest individual tornadoes in recent years occurred within only one day of each other. On June 8, 1953, a whirlwind struck Flint, Michigan, taking 116 lives. On the very next day, June 9, New England's deadliest tornado pounded Worcester, Massachusetts, and the surrounding towns, killing 90 people and injuring more than 1,300. The damage from the Worcester County Tornado—some $53 million—made it, at the time, the most costly single tornado in U.S. history.

And . . . action! The camera *was rolling as soon as storm chasers from the National Severe Storms Laboratory caught up to this tornado near Altus, Oklahoma, on May 11, 1982.*

Chasing the Wind

Some folks are always looking for trouble.

EACH SPRING, AMATEUR STORM CHASERS from all over the country descend on Tornado Alley, the most active breeding ground in the world for tornadoes. Running from northern Texas to southern Iowa, the flat southern plains offer the perfect conditions for the formation of "supercells," the severe thunderstorms that spawn tornadoes. During the spring months, cold, dry air descending from the Rockies frequently meets a "moisture tongue" of humid air drawn north from the Gulf of Mexico. The two collide along a boundary called the *dryline.* As billowy cumulus clouds form and rise throughout the day, they bump their heads against a low ceiling of relatively warm air 5,000 to 10,000 feet high called a *capped inversion,* which temporarily prevents them from rising any higher. But when the humid air finally does break through, it can create an updraft more than 40,000 feet high that acts like a giant chimney, sucking up moist air from the ground and sending it aloft. There the air cools and condenses, releasing even more energy into the growing cloud formation. Add a pinch of instability and some wind shear to the equation, and you have all the ingredients for a first class tornado.

So who in the world would want to chase a twister? Actually, the term "chase" is a little misleading. The men and women who drive all over creation in search of severe storms are more like private detectives than hunters. Their day starts early, as they check out reports of weather conditions on the ground and in the atmosphere, either from the National Weather Service or from private forecasting services. Experienced chasers know the kinds of morning weather conditions that are likely to lead to tornadoes in the afternoon. In the same way that the National Weather Service issues a tornado watch for a particular area, these amateur forecasters pick out the most promising areas for tornado activity. Then it's time to hit the road.

According to Tim Marshall, editor of *Stormtrack* (a bimonthly magazine for storm chasers), an average chase requires about seven hours and 475 miles of driving—getting to the predicted storm area, driving around to search for telltale cloud formations, and (all too often) driving home empty-handed.

Some storm chasers have yet to see their first tornado, even after years of tracking. The most promising thunderstorms can yield nothing, and even the most seasoned forecasters are often foiled. During the 1970s and 1980s, the Tornado Intercept Project run by the National Severe Storms Laboratory (NSSL) in Norman, Oklahoma, encountered tornadoes on only about one out of every seven chases—underscoring the difficulty of predicting tornadoes, even with up-to-the-minute forecasts and sophisticated equipment.

The region known as *Tornado Alley (shaded area on map) presents ideal conditions for the formation of tornadoes. Dry air collides with warm, humid air from the Gulf along a dryline, creating the severe storms that can spawn twisters.*

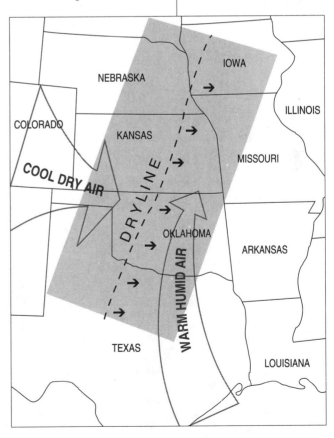

Never Mind Gray Skies— Watch Out for Green Ones

AS ANY WEATHER forecaster will tell you, few natural phenomena are harder to predict than tornadoes, which often strike suddenly and without warning. Folk wisdom, however, insists that "a pale green sky means the wind is high"—in other words, the sky turns green just before a tornado forms. There is some scientific validity to this belief. The clouds capable of producing funnels are often so thick and so low that the only available light underneath may be that reflected from the leaves on the trees. Another possibility is that when clouds are really dark, they simply look green instead of black. Whatever the reason, many people still insist that the sky's eerie emerald tint gives a distinct—and accurate—impression of impending doom.

Beware of green skies and anvil-topped clouds.

The real question is why anyone would want to spend his or her vacation driving through Oklahoma or Texas in search of something as fickle as a tornado. Well, for one thing, the field data and photographs collected by volunteers have proved useful to scientists studying tornadoes and to the National Weather Service, which uses videotapes to train storm spotters. But for most chasers, the ultimate thrill comes in the few minutes of adrenaline rush they feel when the cameras are set up, a tornado actually descends, and the most fleeting and elusive storm on earth is captured on film forever. Successful chasing combines equal parts skill and luck, and seeing a twister touch down only a mile or two away is, to a storm chaser, like hitting a grand slam and winning the lottery all at the same time. ∎

If Ever a Wonderful Twister There Was . . .

THE MOST FAMOUS TOR-nado ever to hit Hollywood was the one that propelled Dorothy and Toto from the Gale farm in Kansas to the land of Oz. The 1939 film, which was way ahead of its time in the use of special effects, featured a 35-foot muslin windsock as the offending twister. That effect alone cost $12,000, which, ironically, makes it the smallest and least expensive tornado in history.

"Look, Tin Man, it's another amazing special effect."

A SURE-FIRE (?) WAY TO PREDICT A TORNADO

For Couch Potatoes Only

1. Turn on your television set.
2. Turn down the brightness control all the way, until the screen is black.
3. Switch to Channel 2.
4. If the screen glows white, a severe thunderstorm capable of producing tornadoes is within 25 miles of your location.

This technique does have a basis in electrical science, since the electromagnetic radiation released by strong thunderstorms has a frequency close to that of television's Channel 2. But don't assume you're safe if the screen stays black. If a tornado warning is issued, seek shelter at once.

BLIZZARDS & WINTRY WEATHER

LIKE BEAUTY, A BLIZZARD is in the eye of the beholder. Someone living in southern California might consider even a light dusting cause for concern. After all, Los Angeles's all-time record snowstorm back in 1932 brought only two inches. In contrast, a resident of the western mountains or Michigan's Upper Peninsula sees so much snow in the course of a season that anything less than a foot is only a minor inconvenience, barely worth mentioning.

The National Weather Service defines a blizzard as a cyclonic storm system packing winds of at least 35 miles per hour, accompanied by temperatures below 20°F, and with ground visibility of less than one-quarter mile. Weather researchers say that a truly great and widespread blizzard strikes the country only once each century; many of the winter storms that make city folks and weathercasters shake in their boots (or Gucci loafers) just don't make the grade as bona fide blizzards. Still, until the next big one hits, nature will surely provide us with plenty of free entertainment—and more snow than anyone could ever need. ∎

A true blizzard can paralyze even the hardiest systems of transportation. Here, a locomotive labors through towering snowdrifts.

The Great White Embargo of 1888

The biggest snowstorm of the past 400 years brought the Northeast's largest cities to a screeching halt and put millions of lives on hold.

ON SATURDAY, MARCH 10, 1888, the weather in New York City was sunny and mild, with high temperatures in the mid-40s. Buds swelled on the trees in Central Park, and precocious spring flowers such as crocuses and daffodils added splashes of color around the city. After a mild winter, everyone was looking forward to an early spring.

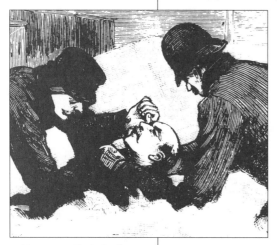

Rescuers find the frozen *body of George Baremore, a New York City merchant who collapsed in a snowdrift while on his way to work.*

Many of the city's department stores had gotten into the act, designating Monday, March 12, as the date of their grand spring opening. Only Edward Ridley & Sons on Grand Street seemed hopelessly out of step with the season. John J. Meisinger, the store's buyer, had recently taken a lot of good-natured ribbing for laying in a consignment of 1,800 wooden snow shovels. But when Monday morning rolled around, it would be Meisinger's turn to snicker.

If Meisinger had a premonition about the weather that spring, the experts didn't. The chief weather official in New York was Elias "Farmer" Dunn, one of the observers connected with the Signal Service in Washington, the precursor of the U.S. Weather Bureau. On Saturday, as the usual telegraphed weather bulletins came in to the Signal Service from around the country, they indicated nothing unusual—some snow in the South, a few rainstorms. Deciding that any major storm systems would probably dissipate or head out to sea, Dunn made the prediction that would run in the *New York Tribune*—"Clearing and cooler, preceded by light snow"—and closed up shop for the weekend. The forecast in the *Times* read, "Colder, fresh to brisk winds, fair weather."

On Sunday afternoon, March 11, a cold, hard rain began to fall from Washington, D.C., north to New England. In New York, the wind rose and temperatures dropped through the 30s. Then, a little past midnight on Monday, March 12, the rain changed over to snow.

When the city awakened on Monday morning, startled citizens looked out their windows at 10 inches of snow blowing around in a strong northwest wind. The sidewalks on the south side of many streets were bare, while across the way snow drifted up to 20 feet high, reaching the second sto-

Snow and ice cover telegraph wires on Wall Street. The storm brought most business in New York's financial district to a standstill.

ries of many buildings. People reluctantly headed out into the stinging snow in an attempt to get to work, even as the storm grew in intensity. Winds gusting to 70 miles per hour lashed pedestrians and knocked grown men off their feet. The scene resembled the worst aspects of a blizzard on the western plains—cruel winds and icy daggers of drifting snow—plunked down in the heart of Manhattan.

For a short time, people tried to carry out their normal routines despite the appalling weather. But soon the city's horse-drawn trolley system shut down completely, and cars stood idle or were knocked on their sides by the powerful wind. Trains bound in and out of the city foundered in drifted snow along the lines, paralyzing the rail system and virtually isolating New York from the rest of the Northeast. Commuters waited in vain on elevated train platforms. Two trains collided on the icy tracks of the Third Avenue El near 76th Street; one of the engineers was killed and 20 passengers injured. A train on the Sixth Avenue line traveled only two blocks in six and a half hours before finally stalling between stations. Passengers descended from the elevated tracks by means of ladders provided by enterprising gypsies, who charged a dollar apiece for the short trip down to the street. Elsewhere, a few of the city's hardiest cabbies ventured out into the blizzard with their hacks, charging fares of up to $40 a trip.

Most commuters who managed the perilous journey to work found nothing to do there and were soon faced with the unwelcome prospect of either heading home in the teeth of the storm or finding some shelter in the city. Hotels and saloons did a land-office business. At the Astor House, the 450 regular rooms quickly filled up, and workers set up cots in ballrooms, bathrooms, and almost anywhere else they would fit. Storm-tossed refugees also found shelter in the city's public buildings. Some bedded down on cots in the city's jails, while 300 others slept on benches in Grand Central Station, which was otherwise conspicuously empty and inactive.

With ferry crossings rendered impossible due to rough waters, the Brooklyn Bridge became Manhattan's last fragile link with the outside world. On Monday morning, local officials closed the bridge to foot and wagon traffic after receiving reports of pedestrians clinging to the railings and pulling themselves across hand over hand against the howling wind. Cable cars on the bridge crept along bravely between Manhattan and Brooklyn throughout the storm, though one car jumped the tracks on Monday morning, blocking them for nearly two hours. On Tuesday morning,

FOR THE RECORD

WHEN IT COMES TO SNOW, the western states hold more than their share of national records. Here are a few of the superlatives:

• **Greatest snowfall in a single storm:** 189 inches at California's Mount Shasta Ski Bowl, February 13–19, 1959

• **Greatest snowfall in a single calendar month:** 390 inches at Tamarack, California, in January 1911

• **Greatest 12-month snowfall:** 1,224.5 inches at the Rainier Paradise Ranger Station in Washington State, from February 19, 1971, through February 18, 1972

• **Most snow accumulation in a single 24-hour period:** 75.8 inches at Silver Lake, Colorado, April 14–15, 1921

• **Greatest depth of snow cover:** 451 inches at Tamarack, California, in March 1911

some foolhardy souls managed to make their way over the East River after large ice floes wedged together south of the bridge to form a tenuous crossing. When the tide went out later that day, the ice broke up, and more than 100 persons trapped on the floes narrowly escaped a watery grave.

All day long on Monday, the storm raged unabated, with temperatures falling through the night. Most theaters canceled their performances due to the weather, but roughly 100 dedicated patrons made it to Daly's Theatre in time to catch a performance of Shakespeare's *A Midsummer Night's Dream* (an ironic title if there ever was one).

By early Tuesday morning, March 13, the snow had tapered off in the city, and residents emerged from their homes to begin the long process of digging out. The blizzard had dumped 21 inches of snow on New York—not much compared with other locations such as New Haven, Connecticut, which had a whopping 45 inches, but more than enough to stymie vehicular traffic for days. The force of the wind had packed the snow into hardened drifts, which the plunging temperatures rendered even more solid and unyielding. (On Tuesday, the mercury fell to 5°F, a record low for the date in New York.) In many cases, street cleaners had to use axes

A young student at *Miss Porter's School pauses on a sidewalk in Farmington, Connecticut. The only way to make streets and sidewalks passable after the blizzard was to cut tunnels through the huge drifts.*

and picks instead of shovels to make any impression on the hard-packed dunes. Men and boys went to work on the drifts, earning between two and ten dollars a day for shoveling people out. Meanwhile, Ridley's buyer, John Meisinger, gladly peddled his wooden snow shovels for a dollar apiece, realizing a quick $600 profit for the store.

With all the New York stories from the Blizzard of '88, it's easy to lose sight of the fact that the storm paralyzed the entire Northeast, from Maryland to Maine, and affected nearly one-quarter of the nation's population. Like New York, Washington, D.C., was cut off from the rest of the country, as high winds from the storm toppled telegraph poles all the way to Philadelphia, blocking the rail lines. Early Monday morning, an ice storm glazed the streets in Philadelphia, laying a slippery foundation for the ten inches of snow that the storm would later deposit on that city.

North of New York, the blizzard wrapped beleaguered towns in a mantle of snow and ice. Of the major eastern cities, only Boston managed to avoid the worst of the storm. On Monday, the snow alternated with sleet and rain throughout the day, with a 12-inch accumulation isolating the city but not shutting it down completely. Other towns to the west and north of Boston didn't fare so well. In New Hampshire, Monday was Town Meeting Day, but attendance at town halls was so poor that many local officials postponed business until the following week. In Keene, New Hampshire, 3 feet of snow blanketed the ground, and nearby hill towns such as Dublin recorded as much as 42 inches.

All over the Northeast, the blizzard immobilized everyone and everything. New York's state capital of Albany picked up 47 inches of snow, while nearby Troy recorded 55 inches, perhaps the most of any large community. When the snow finally ended, many towns contented themselves with shoveling the white drifts off the sidewalks and into the middle of the street. Officials considered it ludicrous to try to remove that much snow. Workers laboriously shoveled pathways and tunnels from one side of the street to the other, then people just sat back and waited for the great white mountains to melt.

In New York, folks didn't have long to wait. On Wednesday, March 14, the sun reappeared over New York City, and temperatures climbed into the mid-30s. Over the next few days, life in the city slowly regained its usual rhythm, as 700 wagons and 1,000 workers began the her-

New York State's *Republican party leader, Roscoe Conkling, collapsed from exhaustion and ultimately died from his exposure to the blizzard.*

GOOD HEAVENS FRIEND HOW CAN YOU WEAR AN OVERCOAT AND LOOK SO COOL THIS WARM WEATHER?
I ALWAYS BRING MY OVERCOAT DOWN TOWN, AS I FIND AFTER DRINKING A GLASS OF "BLAKELY'S BLIZZARD SODA," DRAWN FROM HIS "ARCTIC FOUNTAIN," THAT I AM COLD THE BALANCE OF THE DAY.

culean task of snow removal on Broadway and other main thoroughfares. Load after load of snow traveled down to the East River piers, to be unceremoniously dumped into the harbor. After the cleanup, indignant New Yorkers complained about the huge public bill for dealing with the snow—a whopping $25,000.

The Great Blizzard *inspired all sorts of creative enterprises, including "Blakely's Blizzard Soda."*

It would be days before the real costs of the blizzard could be esti-mated. The death toll from the storm topped 400, with 200 dead in New York City alone. Searchers discovered the body of a 12-year-old boy in a snowdrift at the intersection of Cypress and Fulton avenues in East New York. In Brooklyn, more than 20 postmen were pulled from the snow unconscious. The most famous casualty was New York's Republican party leader, Roscoe Conkling, who had struggled nearly two and a half miles from Wall Street to his club at Union Square, collapsing from exhaustion at the end of his journey. After his harrowing experience in the storm, the hale and hearty Conkling took sick and died on April 18, the final victim of the Blizzard of '88.

When around the moon there's a ring, the weather it will sting.

A SURE-FIRE (?) WAY TO PREDICT A LONG WINTER

Always Observe Candlemas

This semireliable weather forecaster casts a long shadow.

THE OLD PROVERB GOES: "If Candlemas Day be fair and clear, there'll be two winters in the year." In the United States, Can-dlemas (February 2) is called Groundhog Day, and we still honor this old forecasting formula in our superstition concerning whether a groundhog emerging from hibernation will see its shadow. If it does, it supposedly will scamper back underground, and we can expect six more weeks of winter. If the day is cloudy and the groundhog casts no shadow, we can start planning for an early spring.

Home heating oil delivery, circa 1922.

Heating by Degrees

THE NEXT TIME a prolonged cold snap hits your area, chances are you'll scuttle down to the basement to check your fuel tank and wonder when the oil company will be by with your next delivery. The driver always seems to arrive right on time, and there's a good reason for that: The company is keeping track of how many heating degree days it's been since your last delivery.

Figuring out how many heating degree days occur for each day of the year is a cinch. All the figure represents is the difference between the daily mean temperature for your location (add the daily high and the daily low, then divide by 2) and 65°F, which is considered the normal mean. The theory is that when it's 65°F outside, most people feel comfortable in their homes and don't need to use the heat.

Say that on a particular date, the high temperature in your area was 45°F and the low 25°F. The mean temperature for that date would then be 35°F, which is 30 degrees less than 65. The number of heating degree days for that date would be 30. By adding the number for that date to the previous heating degree days for the year, you can keep a running total, just as the National Weather Service does.

The number of days the last snow remains on the ground indicates the number of snowstorms that will occur during the following winter.

THE MOST SOUTHERLY snowfall in American weather history occurred at Homestead, Florida, where a trace was recorded on January 19, 1977. Homestead lies south of Miami at 25° 29' north latitude—about as far south as you can travel on the U.S. mainland.

Similar tales of factory workers and farmers collapsing on their doorsteps or children freezing to death only a few yards from home filled the papers. A lesser-known tragedy played itself out along the eastern seaboard, where the storm's hurricane-force winds wrecked more than 200 vessels, killing more than 100 seamen and littering the coast from the Chesapeake and Delaware bays to New England.

Some of the most colorful stories of survival concerned the many people stuck aboard trains, which had stalled in huge drifts all over the Northeast. As the arctic winds howled outside, passengers broke up seats and other furnishings to burn in the small car stoves. Marooned travelers subsisted on whatever food they could find in the baggage cars or buy from local farmers and entrepreneurs, who sold, for a dollar or more, sandwiches that would normally cost a nickel.

By almost any reckoning, the Blizzard of '88 richly deserves its reputation as one of the worst storms in U.S. history. Millions of people over a huge geographic area watched helplessly as the storm's ferocious blast played havoc with all outdoor activity and turned metropolitan centers into isolated burgs. Some good did come from the storm: The U.S. Congress and other legislative bodies decided that the Northeast's vital communications network must never again be severed, and workers began the long and arduous task of moving telegraph and telephone lines (as well as public transit routes) underground.

Meteorologists claim that a storm the size of the Blizzard of '88 hits the Northeast only once every four or five hundred years, but don't trust too much in the law of averages. After all, no one in 1888 expected the blizzard that seemed to strike out of nowhere. ∎

A SURE-FIRE (?) WAY TO PREDICT THE WEATHER

Watch a Good Weathervane

LOOK AT THE WEATHERCOCK at 12 noon on St. Thomas's Day (December 21) and note in which quarter the wind lies. Weather tradition says it will keep blowing from that direction for the next three months.

Shovel Off to Buffalo

DEPENDING ON WHICH FIGURES you'd like to quote, Buffalo, New York, may have the dubious honor of being the snowiest city in the United States. According to the National Weather Service, Buffalo's snowfall total for the 1970s (an extremely snowy decade) topped out at 1,109.8 inches. Rochester, New York, took second place, recording 1,074.2 inches during the same period. No other city even came close. Salt Lake City, Utah, the third-place finisher, trailed the leaders with only 818.3 inches. Because of the high population density of the Snow Belt (which stretches around the southern and eastern sides of Lake Ontario, from Buffalo to Syracuse and north to Watertown), probably more people are hampered by heavy snowfalls in that area than in any other part of the country.

These statistics, based on snowfall totals from only the top 50 metropolitan areas, tell just part of the story. If you dig a little deeper, you'll find plenty of places around the country that make Buffalo look, in the words of one local booster, like "the Miami of the North." During the 1970s, Syracuse outstripped Buffalo with 1,198.3 inches of snow, and the town of Caribou, in northern Maine, received a whopping 1,257.5 inches during the decade.

Such comparisons may not be reassuring when those bone-chilling winds come off Lake Erie, but then again, the citizens of Buffalo will take whatever cold comfort they can get.

The Miami of the North?

The Blizzard Hall of Fame

- **February 27, 1717.** The Great Snow of 1717 was actually a series of four storms that lasted until March 7 and dumped up to five feet of snow on some parts of New England. Around 95 percent of New England's deer population died as a result of the snow, and John Winthrop reported that one farm on Fishers Island in Long Island Sound lost 1,100 sheep. Twenty-eight days after the storm, two surviving sheep were dug out of a 16-foot-high snowdrift, where they had stayed alive by eating the wool of their frozen companions.
- **December 26, 1778.** The Hessian Storm, named for nine German mercenaries who froze at their posts in Newport, Rhode Island, struck southern New England in 1778. More than 50 persons reportedly froze to death in the subzero temperatures that accompanied the 18-inch snowfall. Great gales offshore wrecked many ships, most notably the American brig *General Arnold* (nearly 100 dead) off Plymouth, Massachusetts, and 28 vessels that beached on Staten Island.
- **January 14–15, 1831.** This was the heaviest and most

Chivalry in action in New York City, 1947.

extensive snowstorm on record prior to the Blizzard of '88. Several inches of snow fell as far south as Georgia and as far west as the Ohio Valley. Gettysburg, Pennsylvania, recorded 30 inches on the ground, and Pittsburgh had 22 inches.

- **January 18–19, 1857.** The Great Cold Storm brought heavy snow, subzero temperatures, and gale-force winds to the East and South, with temperatures dipping to –40°F at Watertown, New York, and as low as 16°F in Jacksonville, Florida. All rail traffic into and out of New York City was stalled as a 12-foot snowbank blocked the tracks in Bergen Cut. Washington, D.C., had nearly two feet of fresh snow, and even Athens, Georgia, received eight inches.

- **January 12, 1888.** The *First Great Blizzard of 1888* was largely overshadowed by its eastern counterpart, which struck two months later, but in the western states, the first storm was the year's big one. Following a morning of springlike temperatures, the storm spread swiftly and without warning from the Dakotas down to Texas, catching many schoolchildren and settlers out-of-doors and claiming many lives.
- **January 22, 1922.** The Knickerbocker Storm dumped 28 inches of snow on Washington, D.C., immobilizing the city and causing the roof of the Knickerbocker Theater to collapse under the weight of the snow, killing 100 moviegoers.
- **November 11, 1940.** The Armistice Day Storm struck

the Great Lakes and the Upper Midwest with howling winds. Muskegon, Michigan, recorded a wind speed of 67 miles per hour, and many vessels on Lake Superior and Lake Michigan were wrecked, with the loss of 59 sailors. In Iowa, 17 inches of snow fell, and in Minnesota alone 49 people died as a result of the storm.

• **March 15, 1941.** One of the worst blizzards of modern times struck the northern plains on Saturday night, when many people were out on the town. In North Dakota, 39 people died in the storm; 32 succumbed in Minnesota. Observers in Grand Forks, North Dakota, measured an 85-mile-per-hour wind, and those in Duluth, Minnesota, clocked wind speeds up to 75 miles per hour.

• **December 26, 1947.** New York City's deepest snowfall left 27 inches of new snow on the ground in Central Park in only 24 hours' time. The death toll from the storm also was 27, and costs for snow removal soared to $8 million.

• **January 2, 1949.** The most savage series of blizzards since the settlement of the Great Plains began, raging almost without pause for seven weeks. During breaks in the heavy snowfall, winds gusting to 80 miles per hour drove the fine, powdery snow into massive drifts and filled deep gullies and cuts to the brim. Temperatures plummeted again and again, as low as –50°F. Amazingly, the death toll didn't exceed 200, but livestock losses were staggering. An estimated 125,000 sheep and 25,000 cattle died on the range.

• **January 10, 1975.** A blizzard described as a "100-year storm" in Minnesota blew in, with the wind-chill factor as low as –80°F. Up to two feet of snow fell, and there were 35 storm-related fatalities.

• **February 6–7, 1978.** The biggest blizzard in southern New England's modern history struck Boston and the coast with full fury, following another storm on January 20 that had deposited up to two feet of snow. Thousands of motorists were forced to abandon their cars on Route 128 west of Boston when two tractor-trailers jackknifed during the storm; many sought shelter in churches. For the first time in 106 years, the *Boston Globe* was unable to deliver its papers. Traffic came to a complete standstill for nearly five days, as more than 27 inches of snow accumulated in Boston.

Catching some rays while waiting for a plow, 1978.

Hell Without the Heat

*If you think the cowboy's life was a romantic one,
you should have been there in 1886.*

In his drawing,
*"Waiting for a
Chinook," cowboy artist
Charles M. Russell
immortalized the Big
Die-up of 1886.*

BY THE MIDDLE OF THE 1880s, the brief and glorious years of the great cattle drives had begun to draw to a close. Only 20 years earlier, in 1866, cowboys had driven the first of the wild breed known as Texas longhorns north—crossing the Red River into what is now Oklahoma—to railhead cattle towns such as Abilene and Dodge City, Kansas,

and onto new rangeland where they could graze before heading to markets in the East. At the height of the drives, in 1883 and 1884, some 500,000 head passed through the town of Ogallala, Nebraska, alone. But with the coming of the railroads, homesteaders began to settle the newly opened land, and the Texas Trail stretched even farther north, to the northernmost plains of Wyoming and Montana, in a never-ending search for new and bigger pastures.

The end of the summer of 1886 brought fine weather to the northern range, with hot, sunny days and frost-free nights extending well into October. As the balmy autumn days wore on, cattlemen along Montana's Missouri River noticed that the wild geese and songbirds were flying south much earlier than usual. Not only that, but the beavers were working overtime, storing away great quantities of willow brush, and the muskrats' coats had grown extra thick. Granville Stuart, the legendary cattle boss, noticed arctic owls for the first time on the range that fall. Older Indians who saw the white birds took them as an ominous sign of a long, cold winter ahead.

On November 16, the temperature dipped below zero in the Rockies, and a brisk northwest wind started to blow—the harbinger of snow on the Great Plains. Six inches of fine snow drifted over the dry, overstocked range. More snow followed in late November, but the two weeks before Christmas brought fine, sunny weather, and the few cowboys who had been kept on past the autumn months to protect the cattle still hoped for a moderate winter.

The famous cowboy known as Teddy Blue was working for Granville Stuart that winter in the Little Rocky Mountains of Montana. He described his experiences in his classic book, *We Pointed Them North:*

> On Christmas Eve it started to storm and never really let up for sixty days. It got colder and colder. I have a cutting from the post paper at Fort Keogh that reads that on January 14 it was sixty below zero at that place and snow two feet deep. The latter part of January it started a chinook—just enough to melt the snow on top. But it turned cold, and on February 3 and 4 the worst blizzard I ever saw set in. The snow crusted and it was hell without the heat.

Some Native Americans call the month of January the Month of Cold-Exploding Trees, and January 1887 certainly lived up to that name. In the Yellowstone country of Wyoming, a steady snow began falling on January 9 and continued, an inch an hour, for the next ten days. By midmonth, the temperature stood at –46°F. And the worst was yet to come.

Top: Rancher Granville *Stuart.* Bottom: *Cowboy E.C. "Teddy Blue" Abbott. Teddy Blue's reports to Stuart brought home the devastation of an incredible winter.*

How Cold Was It?

ON JANUARY 23, 1971, Prospect Creek Camp in Alaska (at 66° 48' north latitude) recorded a temperature of –79.8°F, the lowest in U.S. weather history. The lowest temperature for the Lower 48 states is –69.7°F, recorded at Rogers Pass in Montana on January 20, 1954.

The lowest average winter temperature for the United States is –15.6°F, on Alaska's Barter Island. And the weather station at Barrow, on Alaska's North Slope, has the dubious distinction of having not only the lowest average annual temperature in the nation (9.6°F) but also the lowest average temperature for its three summer months (36.7°F). Not the kind of place you'd want to grow tomatoes.

When the first chinook arrived in January, Teddy Blue wrote to his boss that the loss of cattle from the storms would probably not exceed 10 percent. Ten days later, he estimated that 75 percent of the herd wouldn't make it through the winter. On January 28, the greatest blizzard of the season struck the northwest plains, howling for three days as the icy needles of wind-driven snow lashed everything in sight. In the wake of the storm, millions of cattle lay scattered over the open range, many already frozen stiff and buried in huge snowdrifts, many more weakened and dying from starvation and exposure.

The cowboys were not faring much better than the cows. Trying to round up stray cattle under these conditions—the drifts shoulder high, the temperatures 50° to 60° below in the howling wind—sapped a man's energy. Horses stumbled through the deep snow, fighting every step of the way. Their feet were cut by the sharp, crusted surface, which also scraped the hair and hide off steers as far up as their knees and hocks.

For the cowboys, the task of driving scattered bands of cattle back toward the hills seemed never ending. Many cattle drifted down from the range and onto the rivers and died there by the thousands as they fell through air holes in the ice. When the spring thaw finally came, their carcasses littered the streambeds.

Cowboys faced the very real possibility of getting lost on the range, as the loose, blowing snow created ground blizzards that blotted out all familiar landmarks. The coulees (shallow ravines or gullies) had long since drifted full of snow and lay even with the surface of the plain, offering no shelter from the penetrating winds. Teddy Blue recalled that just to make camp for the night, he and his partner had to shovel out a drift in a coulee, then cut pine boughs to use for bedding, building a huge sagebrush fire to take some of the edge off the cold.

To protect themselves from the frigid winds and subzero temperatures, these winter herders sometimes created outlandish, if highly practical, costumes. Teddy Blue donned "two pairs of wool socks, a pair of moccasins, a pair of Dutch socks that came up to the knees, a pair of government overshoes, two suits of heavy underwear, pants, overalls, chaps and a big heavy shirt." He also cut sleeves from a pair of women's stockings and wore wool gloves, heavy mittens, a blanket-lined overcoat, and a huge sealskin cap. He must have made quite a sight riding over the plains, looking more like a hardy horseman of the central Asian steppe than what we think of as a cowpoke.

Despite all their precautions, many cowboys died on the range that winter. Many homesteaders in Montana and the western Dakota Territory also died, their cabins buried under drifting snow. In some cases, whole families were found frozen to death, entombed inside their homes.

After the brief chinook at the end of January, the frigid air returned, freezing the surface of the snow and preventing the cattle from foraging for the brown grass underneath. Ranchers didn't supply range cattle with hay in those days, and there would have been no way to get the hay to them even if it had been available. Some cattle starved and others weakened, making them easy prey for wolves and coyotes. They browsed on whatever they could find, mostly bitter sagebrush or other twigs. One cowboy reported finding a dead steer the next spring high up in the crotch of a tree, where it had apparently gotten caught while foraging on top of a high drift.

In the town of Great Falls, Montana, 5,000 hungry steers rampaged through the streets, eating everything in sight. In the eastern Dakota town of Medora, hundreds of bellowing cattle ate the tarpaper off the sides of shacks until they sickened and died. Residents had to nail boards over their windows to prevent the cows from punching them in. And along the railroad lines, the starving herds stared at passing trains as if looking for a handout—or a lift south.

The weather finally broke on March 2 as the skies cleared and a warm chinook blew down from the mountains. By the middle of the month, the trickling snow melt in the draws and coulees had become a roar, and the Little Missouri and other rivers began to flood. Down on the flats, the ice chunks scoured the bark off the tops of tall cottonwood trees, and the river's turbid waters carried

TEST YOUR WINTER KNOWLEDGE

1. If you've been out in the cold and are afraid that you have frostbite, you should rub the affected area with snow. True or false?

2. How many sides does a regular snow crystal have?
   a. four   c. six
   b. five   d. eight

3. Car A and Car B are traveling down ice-glazed roads in two different locations. The temperature where Car A is traveling is 30°F; the temperature where Car B is traveling is 0°F. The drivers of both cars hit the brakes at exactly the same moment. If both cars and the roads they travel are otherwise identical, which car will come to a stop first? (Hint: Hitting a tree doesn't count.)

4. We've all heard of snow blindness, a condition caused by sunlight reflecting off snow. But what percentage of the sun's rays is actually reflected back from freshly fallen snow?

ANSWERS: 1. False. Frozen skin tissue can easily be damaged by rubbing. A better alternative is to heat the frostbitten area quickly in warm, but not hot, water. 2. c. Even if they look irregular, all snow crystals start with an underlying six-sided structure. 3. Car B will stop before Car A. The car driving on ice at 30°F needs a braking distance twice as long as the car driving on ice at 0°F, since ice is slipperier near the freezing point than at lower temperatures. 4. The albedo, or reflective property, of fresh snow is typically around 87 percent.

Baby, It's Cold All Over!

WITH AN average mean temperature of only 22.8°F, January 1979 stands as the coldest month on record for the United States as a whole. As opposed to most cold spells, which hit one region while leaving another one untouched, the January deep freeze of that year caused below-normal temperatures at around 98 percent of the weather stations reporting. Based on satellite photographs, the snow and ice cover over the United States was the most extensive since such records have been kept.

the frozen remains of cattle downstream. A man named Lincoln Lang described the grisly spectacle:

Countless carcasses of cattle [were] going down with the ice, rolling over and over as they went, so that at times all four of the stiffened legs of a carcass would point skyward, as it turned under the impulsion of the swiftly moving icecakes. Now and then a carcass would become pinched between two ice-floes, and either go down entirely or be forced out on top of the ice, to be rafted along.

The loss of livestock was appalling. Granville Stuart's men had branded 10,000 calves in the spring and fall of 1886, but in the '87 spring roundup, they counted only 100 yearlings. A big roundup on Timber Creek netted only 1 steer. According to Teddy Blue, at least 60 percent of the cattle in Montana had died by March 15. When asked by a friend how his cattle were doing, cowboy artist Charles M. Russell drew a picture of a starving cow faced by a pack of anxiously waiting wolves. Russell called the drawing "Waiting for a Chinook, or, The Last of Five Thousand," and it became perhaps the most famous and graphic reminder of the terrible winter.

For many cattlemen, the huge financial losses of 1886 and 1887 meant the end of the line. A few survived, but the years that followed the "Big Die-up" saw homesteading increase, as smaller ranchers fenced the range and started to feed hay to their cattle in times of hard weather. The big trail drives grew smaller and smaller, until in 1895 the XIT Ranch brought the last three herds north. The days of the Texas Trail were soon part of American history and folklore.

About the only people who profited from the awful winter of 1886–87 were the bone pickers who descended on the plains to gather the chalky remains of dead steers (as they had done years before with the buffalo) and ship them off to be ground up into fertilizer. Even though the physical reminders have disappeared, the Great Plains will never forget the winter of the Big Die-up. The words of one old cowboy song expressed it best:

I may not see a hundred
Before I see the Styx,
But, coal or ember, I'll remember
Eighteen eighty-six.

The stiff heaps in the coulee,
The dead eyes in the camp,
And the wind about, blowing fortunes out
As a woman blows out a lamp. ■

Open wide and say "Brrr!"

Now That's a High Temperature

THE WORLD'S LARGEST thermometer is located in International Falls, Minnesota—a perennial cold spot—and stands 30 feet high. The world's smallest thermometer, called an ultra-microthermometer, was developed by Dr. Frederich Sachs, a biophysicist at the State University of New York at Buffalo. Its tip measures one micron in diameter. (An average human hair has a diameter of about 50 microns.) Scientists use this Lilliputian thermometer to take the temperature of a single living cell.

Watch the Thermometer

WHEAT FARMERS and commodity futures traders could probably do worse than to take the advice of an old Belgian proverb that ties the price of grain in the coming year to the weather on the previous winter solstice. According to tradition, if there's a freeze on the solstice, the price of grain will fall; if the weather is mild, the price will go up.

Sounds just about as sure-fire as some of the theories we've heard from Wall Street lately.

What a Shame They Melted Before Anyone Could Double-Check

ACCORDING TO a 1915 issue of the *Monthly Weather Review,* the largest snowflakes ever recorded fell in Montana on January 28, 1887. Witnesses described the monstrous flakes, which fell over an area of several square miles, as being "larger than milk pans." When measured, they were found to be 15 inches across and 8 inches thick. (No wonder Montana's license plate says "Big Sky Country"!)

If You Go to South Dakota, Pack Your Fur Coat & Bikini

THE MOST REMARKABLE temperature fluctuations ever recorded took place at Spearfish, South Dakota, on January 22, 1943. At 7:30 A.M., the thermometer stood at −4°F. Just two minutes later, it registered 45°F, a meteoric rise of 49 degrees.

This record alone would have made the day remarkable, but later that same morning, the mercury plunged almost as rapidly as it had shot up. At 9 A.M., the temperature at Spearfish was a balmy 54°F, but at 9:27, it had dipped to −4°F again, exactly where it had stood before the chinook blew in two hours earlier.

Super Frosty

ACCORDING TO THE *Guinness Book of World Records*, the world's largest snowman was one that once towered over Anchorage, Alaska, at 63½ feet. It was built in March 1988 by Myron L. Ace and eight of his friends, who used a crane to pile 8-inch blocks of snow in the shape of a snowman. The giant sculpture, which they named "Super Frosty," took three weeks to complete. After the group had finished, the city was hit by a 70-mile-per-hour dust storm, turning the snowy masterpiece into a black work of art.

A Flake by Any Other Name

ONE OF THE MOST PERSISTENT (and unfounded) pieces of weather folklore concerns the hundreds of names that Eskimos have supposedly invented to distinguish between the many forms of snow—though nobody seems to be able to list more than half a dozen. In fact, Inuit and other Native languages may not be all that different from English when it comes to words for snow. English has *snow* (usually on the ground) and *flake* (usually in the air)—the same basic distinction that's found in the vocabularies of most northern Native Americans. Add a few extra words such as *flurry* and *blizzard,* and our winter vocabulary can match that of any other language—except perhaps Russian. How can we pretend to have won the Cold War when the Russians have six words *(vyuga, myatel, kurritsya, ponosukha, buran,* and *pozemka)* describing different kinds of blowing or drifting snow? Apparently, we should have been spending less on defense and more on dictionaries.

In wintertime, Russians never find themselves at a loss for words.

DROUGHT, DUST & CONFLAGRATION

TURN ON ALMOST ANY television newscast, and you're likely to see some weathercaster taking the credit for warm and clear weather—or the blame for not producing it. Almost everyone enjoys sunny, settled weather, but too much of it (like any good thing) can be a problem.

Rain is the lifeblood that nourishes our planet, and when it doesn't fall—and fall on a regular basis—most plants and people wither. Lawns turn brown, reservoirs shrink, and people pray for rain. In the driest years, the soil itself cracks open and starts to blow away, as it did in the Dust Bowl of the 1930s.

Droughts and forest fires have more in common than the fact that one often makes the other possible. Both are natural cycles in nature. Both profoundly affect humans, and vice versa. And both are phenomena that we understand very little and can control even less. ■

A dust storm turns day into night along this road in north Texas. Even headlights don't do much to make driving through the gritty mess easier.

Gone with the Wind

Crops withered. The parched earth cried for rain. Life in the Dust Bowl was hard enough—and then the black rollers started moving in.

Farmers settled the *southern plains in a time when rainfall was relatively abundant. So they were completely unprepared for the long years of drought that created the Dust Bowl.*

THE OLD JOKE GOES something like this. A farmer was standing on a street corner in town, staring up at the sky during a strong windstorm.

"What's the attraction?" a friend of his inquired.

"I may be crazy," the farmer said, "but I think I just saw a quarter section of my land blowing over town."

To the thousands of farmers who lived through the Dust Bowl of the 1930s, this story was all too familiar. Strong winds and drought that fol-

lowed years of unwise tillage blew away miles of fertile topsoil from the plains—and with it the prospects of an entire generation. Humor, religion, federal assistance, and pure cussedness were just about the only things that kept people going.

Geographically, some 97 million acres of land made up the heart of the Dust Bowl. This included the Texas and Oklahoma panhandles, along with parts of Kansas, Colorado, and New Mexico. Even before the 1930s, the region had had a long history of dust storms, as the weather cycled between wet and dry periods lasting several years. In 1860, during a protracted drought, black snow had fallen as far east as Oberlin, Ohio, and black rain at Syracuse, New York—both the result of dust clouds blowing in from the West.

Using a one-way disk plow *near Canyon, Texas, in 1917. The combination of drought, wind, and overworked soil would soon spell financial ruin for farmers in the Dust Bowl states.*

On April 5, 1895, settlers first experienced what they would later call a snuster, a combination of snow and dust driven by strong, cold winds. Men working to clear train tracks east of Denver had to cover their faces, and still the wind-driven sand cut through the cloth and lacerated their skin. The violent storm raged for 40 hours. When it was over, the carcasses of dead cattle littered the riverbanks, and three children who had been out gathering stock were found dead.

But by 1905, it seemed that the dry years had finally ended, and over the next quarter century, farmers settled the plains in increasing numbers, following the railroad lines. Even after 1929, as the rest of the country slipped into economic depression, the plains farmers prospered. In 1915, there were only 3,000 tractors in the entire state of Kansas. By 1930, there were more than 60,000, as farmers began to mechanize so they could plant more

It is not easy for man to understand that it takes but little less rainfall than normal over a very few years to change the face of the land.

winter wheat, which had become the major cash crop. In one good year, a wheat farmer could make as much profit as a stockman could make from his cattle in a decade. It made sense to plow up as much land as possible, and the tractors ran day and night, turning over millions of acres of rangeland that had never before grown anything but native grasses. No one could argue with the results: In 1926, the wheat harvest was the biggest one the area had ever seen.

Then, beginning in 1930, the most severe drought in U.S. history struck the eastern and northern plains. Ironically, the period began with a flood, as heavy rains washed out bridges in the Oklahoma Panhandle. As soon as the rains subsided, a damaging windstorm began, eroding topsoil and providing a small taste of things to come.

A dust storm begins when a particle of soil breaks loose in the wind. When it strikes another clump of dirt, it scatters more particles, much like a cue ball breaking a rack in pool. This kind of chain reaction rolls across the field, sending more and more dirt swirling into the air. By 1930, much of the soil in the Dust Bowl region had been pulverized to a fine powder by the new one-way disk plows that farmers were using to till the soil, so it didn't take much to spread the dust. Over the next few years, the combination of drought, wind, and overworked soil would spell financial disaster for most of the Dust Bowl's farmers.

The harvest of 1933 was the worst of the decade. The grain elevators at Texhoma, Oklahoma, had handled between 2 and 3 million bushels of wheat in 1931. In 1933, only 200 bushels were sold. Stockmen gathered wild plants such as Russian thistle and soapweed to feed their cattle. By the end of the year, 70 dust storms had been reported in Oklahoma, and in mid-November, high winds from a storm in Nebraska carried dust to the East Coast, sprinkling it all the way from New York to Georgia.

Along with the foul weather, the people of the Dust Bowl had to cope with plagues of almost biblical proportions. During the drought, hordes of spiders, grasshoppers, and jack rabbits invaded the fields, eating everything in sight. Rabbit drives became a popular diversion during the winter months. As many as 2,000 people—men, women, and children—would act as beaters, encircling an area of up to five square miles and driving jack rabbits toward the wings of a wire fence and into a central pen. A large drive could net as many as 5,000 to 6,000 rabbits, and after they were killed, the meat was shipped to New York City and sold for food.

On April 14, 1935, nearly 300 people had driven out to Two Buttes Reservoir in southeastern Colorado to enjoy a sunny, pleasant spring day

Now That's Some Dust Bunny

A LARGE DUST storm about 315 miles in diameter can carry around 100 million tons of dust in the air.

A dust storm strikes *Elkhart, Kansas, on May 21, 1937. Just two minutes elapsed from the time that the "black roller" first appeared* (top left) *until the dust cloud completely engulfed the town* (bottom).

A farmer in Cimarron *County, Oklahoma, raises a fence to keep it from being buried in drifting dirt.*

fishing and picnicking. Around 3 P.M., they saw a long, black cloud rolling in from the north. Everyone knew that such a black roller represented the approaching front of a dust storm, and they ran for their cars. Before they could drive away, however, the cloud had overtaken them, plunging the area into darkness. In the midst of the storm, people had to hold lights directly in front of their faces to see anything.

At about 4 P.M., the storm approached a rabbit drive that was being held near Hooker, Oklahoma. One eyewitness, Mrs. Emma Love, described the black cloud as a beautiful and strangely colorful sight as it rolled in across the prairie: "At the top of the storm were plumes that danced in the sunlight and emblazoned the colors of the rainbow across the sky before plunging savagely toward the ground."

The dust storm of April 14 became the most notorious of the decade. When the storm struck Pampa, Texas, singer Woody Guthrie began writing the song "So Long, It's Been Good to Know You," one of the many Dust Bowl ballads he would compose. The storm even inspired the term *Dust Bowl* itself, which was coined by Associated Press reporter Robert Geiger, writing from Guymon, Oklahoma.

A severe hailstorm buffeted Cimarron County, Oklahoma, on April 14, dropping hail the size of billiard balls that broke windows and killed many head of livestock. At Cap Williams's farm near Felt, Oklahoma, the school bus was forced to stop, and Williams ran out into the hail with a blanket, covering one child at a time and escorting each to the safety of his house. A little punchy by the time he was done, Williams picked up what he thought was the last child on the bus, only to discover a pet greyhound when he opened the blanket inside. The hail still lay so thick on the roads the next morning that parents had to drive tractors to Williams's house to pick up their children. The dust that had settled on top of the hail formed a layer of insulation that prevented it from melting for a week.

The storm of April 14 became known as The Black Blizzard, and it was only the first of many dust storms that would make a big impression on the people of the East Coast. In 1935, huge black dust clouds floated for the first time over Washington, D.C., giving the nation's lawmakers a brief glimpse of what was happening all over the Dust Bowl region. Oceangoing ships reported sighting low, gritty clouds far out into the Atlantic and in the Gulf of Mexico.

No one who has never seen a black roller in person can truly appreciate the awesome sight. It starts with the finely pulverized soil, or blow dirt, that lifts off the ground in the slightest breeze. As more soil rises, the cloud continues to build, becoming thicker and thicker, until at last the visibility within the storm is reduced to 1,000 yards or less. Once the wind picks up to 40 or 50 miles per hour, the dust cuts visibility to 50 yards or less.

The dust cloud appears banked like a cumulus cloud, but jet-black instead of white, and it hugs the ground as it rolls over on itself like a breaking wave. Birds of all kinds try to escape before the storm, but only the strongest fliers survive. Small birds fly until they are exhausted, then fall and are smothered by the dust—like most of the animals on the ground that can't avoid the storm.

During the Dust Bowl years, traveling often proved perilous in the midst of a black blizzard. Static electricity filled the air from the friction of the dust particles, and the ignition systems of cars and other vehicles often refused to work until after the storm had passed. Thunder and lightning frequently accompanied the storms, and electrical wires, according to one account, looked like "a line of bright red fire glowing in the darkness." Even headlights were not much help to a driver in the midst of a dust storm. The reflection from the particles of dust just threw the light back into the driver's eyes.

Whether you were indoors or out, the dust was inescapable. The fine particles of silt somehow managed to find their way through every crack

Top: Woody Guthrie, *Dust Bowl balladeer.* Above: *Newspaper editor John L. McCarty advised his neighbors to "grab a root and growl."*

Dust Busters

CONTRARY TO the image created by John Steinbeck's *The Grapes of Wrath*, not all Dust Bowl residents left their farms. Large areas of Oklahoma and Texas lost only a few thousand residents in that infamous decade. And one 27-county area of southwestern Kansas actually gained population between 1930 and 1935. These Dust Bowl farmers owned their own land and had too much invested to leave.

Henry Fonda and cast in The Grapes of Wrath.

and chink around doors and windows, and it was common to find dust drifting an inch deep inside the house. Every morsel of food, every drink of water carried a thin coating of grit. Many people tried to filter out the dust by breathing through a wet shirt or towel, but even when they used the dry filter masks issued by the Red Cross, the moisture from their breath was enough to form a muddy scum between mouth and the mask.

During the worst years of the dust storms, nearly everyone suffered from some form of dust-related illness. The majority of people admitted to hospitals complained of respiratory ailments, generally called dust pneumonia. In many families, two or more people died from the prolonged effects of breathing dust.

One farmer who lived near Johnson, Kansas, went to see his doctor, complaining of weight loss and shortness of breath. The doctor discovered that one of the man's lungs had not been functioning for some time, and he began therapy to loosen up his bronchial tube. The following day, the farmer coughed up several pieces of solid dirt, each three to four inches long and the diameter of a pencil. He eventually regained his health, but others who had been exposed to the dust were not so lucky.

By the mid-1930s, thousands of farm families who had stuck it out in hopes of a better crop next year decided to move on, and the great Okie migration began in earnest. Not all of these migrants came from the heart of the Dust Bowl, although the government estimated that during the summer of 1936, roughly 50,000 refugees a month left the Great Plains, many of them traveling to find migrant farm work on the West Coast. Between mid-June of 1935 and the end of 1937, the California Department of Agriculture counted some 221,000 persons entering the state to look for jobs; 84 percent of these migrants came from Dust Bowl states. The population of Elkhart, Kansas (to take just one example), dwindled from 1,700 to only 300 residents.

Given all of the good reasons for quitting, the indefatigable spirit of the people who remained is nothing short of amazing. John L. McCarty, the editor of the *Dalhart Texan,* advised his neighbors to "grab a root and growl" and hang on to what was left of their land. McCarty organized the Last Man's Club, which was open to anyone who pledged to be the last person to leave the Dust Bowl.

Finally, in the fall of 1938, gentle rains and generally good weather prevailed over the Dust Bowl, and farmers at last had some reason to hope for better days ahead. The harvest of 1939 brought a million bushels of wheat to the elevators at Texhoma, prompting the *Texhoma Times* to declare that " 'Dust Bowl' is a term to be discarded and forgotten."

The obstinate refusal of Dust Bowl residents to be defeated by the drought recalls another story that came out of the 1930s. A tourist from the West Coast stopped at a gas station in Liberal, Kansas. While the attendant was filling his tank, the tourist started

FOR THE RECORD

THE DROUGHT OF THE "Dirty Thirties," though severe, was only part of the weather story in the Dust Bowl. Almost every conceivable kind of extreme weather struck the region during the period—much of it very wet.

On June 12, 1932, severe thunderstorms dumped eight inches of rain on Baca County, Colorado, washing one bridge more than 50 miles downstream to Johnson, Kansas. And on May 6, 1933, aviator Charles A. Lindbergh canceled a flight across the Texas Panhandle because of heavy downpours.

At each of five weather stations in the Oklahoma Panhandle, some measurable rainfall was reported for every month but five during the decade of the 1930s, and no two consecutive months were rainless.

telling him about the drive he had just made through Death Valley. Then he looked around at the barren Kansas landscape and exclaimed, "Why, this place is nothing but a desert!"

The attendant, somewhat insulted, remarked, "You went through a lot worse desert back there in California."

"Yes," the tourist replied, "but there aren't any damn fools out there trying to farm it!" ■

The peasant prays for rain, the traveler longs for sunshine, but God gives each what is best.

The Little Dust Bowl

IN 1950, WHEN MEMORIES of the Dust Bowl in the Plains states had begun to fade, another drought began. This one, which became known as the Little Dust Bowl, stretched far beyond the boundaries of the 1930s Dust Bowl to include portions of Arizona, Missouri, Nebraska, Nevada, and Wyoming.

The dry conditions lasted through 1956, but one of the drought's most famous events—a massive black blizzard—occurred on March 31, 1955. By coincidence, Robb Sagendorph, then editor of *The Old Farmer's Almanac,* was in the region when the dust storm hit. Here's how he described it in the 1956 edition:

"Here was a huge churning mass of some 500,000 square miles of black dust, sand, rain, snow, and hail traveling for some thirty-six hours at speeds ranging from forty to seventy-five miles per hour. We hung a washed-out shirt to dry on the doorknob of a motel room in Albuquerque, New Mexico. In less than twenty minutes, dust seeped through cracks through which even light could not pass in the door. It streaked that shirt with prison bars of black and our lungs with a coating of umber. Out-of-doors, from the Santa Fe Railroad's *Chief* next day (all day) through Colorado, and Oklahoma, and Kansas, we watched, in the intervals in which we could see at all, bluebirds flying for their lives scarcely inches from the ground; trains standing on sidetracks cleaned of their paint and left with ominous grooves and gouges seared into their metal sides. Nothing living walked abroad in an atmosphere in which only the arch [fiends] of destruction laid their wands . . . upon the face of our land."

Birds, too, found pickings slim during the Dust Bowl. This nest was actually built of barbed wire.

What Kind of Weather Causes Drought?

METEOROLOGISTS RECOGNIZE A number of different weather patterns that can lead to prolonged dry weather, but all of them have something to do with stationary systems that prevent the usual ebb and flow of weather and block the normal pattern of rainfall in a particular region.

In the eastern and central United States, drought conditions often result when a ridge in the jet stream becomes stationary over the middle of the country. If the ridge pushes the jet stream too far north, upper-level winds become light and hotter, and drier weather generally prevails.

On the West Coast, much of the annual rainfall occurs during the winter months. During the winter, the Hawaiian high-pressure system normally moves south and allows frontal systems to bring rain to the western United States. If the high remains in the North, the winter (and hence the whole year) tends to be drier in the West.

Another factor that enters into this equation is the imperfectly understood El Niño effect, which warms ocean waters off the Pacific coast of South America. (*El Niño* means "the little boy" in Spanish; the effect is named after the Christ Child, since the phenomenon tends to appear around Christmas.) The unusually warm ocean temperatures not only reduce the catch of Peruvian fishermen but are thought to shift storm tracks and disrupt normal weather patterns as well, bringing excessive rain or snow to some regions and dry winters to others. Every few years, when a particularly strong El Niño occurs, it tends to bring wet weather to southern California and the southern United States and drier conditions to the North.

El Niño, named for the *Christ Child, causes unusual weather patterns around Christmas.*

Baptized by Fire

The message was as brief as the time it had taken to wipe Peshtigo from the face of the earth. "We are on fire," it read. "Send help quick."

O N SUNDAY MORNING, October 8, 1871, a copper-colored sun rose over the town of Peshtigo, Wisconsin. The early autumn day felt warm and dry as many of the town's 2,000 residents made their way to church. A trainload of 200 railroad workers was just pulling in from Peshtigo Harbor, located six miles down the Peshtigo River on the western shores of Green Bay. The men would have this one day of liberty before they began laying track for the Chicago and North Western Railroad, which was building the first rail line into town—and they weren't headed to church. In a matter of minutes, they had disembarked, making straight for the doors of Peshtigo's 14 saloons.

In 1871, Peshtigo was a prosperous frontier town, shipping lumber and wooden products out at an impressive rate. Every day the woodenware factory manufactured some 600 pails, 170 tubs, 5,000 broom handles, and 45,000 shingles. Locals proudly claimed that it was the largest factory of its kind in the world. By mid-September, the Peshtigo Company sawmill at Peshtigo Harbor had already cut nearly 5.7 million board feet of lumber for the year. The factory, the mills, and the 60 logging camps in the area employed around 800 men, and with the coming of the railroad, everyone expected that business would only get better.

A person who climbed to the top of a tall tree in Peshtigo could look out over a seemingly endless forest of white pine stretching out for hundreds of miles. Around Peshtigo, the dense forest was

Fire burns and loosens the heavy forest floor, warms and releases seeds to light and life, and feeds them its ash. Our redwoods and Douglas firs are forests from fire.

People ran for their lives *to the river, the only haven in the fiery storm that consumed Peshtigo.*

MADISON DAILY

MADISON, WIS., FRIDAY EVENING, OCT. 13,

7.

DEMOCRAT.

ILY AND WEEKLY BY
INSON & CO.

PER YEAR.
: : Weekly, $2.00.

Nominations.

OOLITTLE, of Racine

CE, of Waukesha.

gomery, of Monroe.

s, of Brown.

of Fond du Lac.

missioner—
nson, of La Fayette.
r Public Instruction
r, of Rock.
Immigration
en of Dodge.
ably—2d district
E, Madison.

Discussion.

and places of meeting have
the Joint discussion between
en. Washburn;
lay, Oct. 10.
y, Oct. 14.
y, Oct. 19.
y, Oct. 21.
ct. 23.
nesday, Oct. 25.
Oct. 27.

BURNT DISTRICT OF WISCONSIN.

MICH

MARATHON

OCONTO

SHAWANO

WAUPACA

OUTAGAMIE

BROWN

KEWAUNEE

MANITOWOC

WINN

DOOR

GREEN BAY

LAKE MICH

BY E. PLACKETT, OF MADISON.
The Dark Portion of the Map is the Burnt District.

1. 2. Marinette 3. Williamsonville. 4. Two Creeks. 5. Two Rivers. 6. Ahnapee.

TELEGRAPHIC!

WISCONSIN.

APPALLING FROM PESHTIGO.

Worst Reports True

325 Burned Bodies Recovered.

As Many More not yet Found.

FEARFUL DESTITUTION OF THE SURVIVORS.

Food And Clothing Must be Sent.

TWENTY FOUR THOUSAND DOLLARS ORDERED TO BE DRAWN FROM THE STATE TREASURY.

CHICAGO.

Newspapers to Re-

The Tribune in an
build the City," says
$400,000,000 worth
destroyed, Chicago
not a mere collection
lumber; these were
the power which pr
They were but the
high courage, un
strong faith, and
which have built
metropolis. The grea
all in existence. Th
the spacious harbor
production, extendi
Pacific the great out
the Oceans, the 36 l
necting the city wi
continent, these the
and commerce all r
diminished and all re
sumption.

What therefore ha
lost the accumulate
years of growth, we
trade on land the
have lost money, bu
health vigor and i
dozen grain elevato
have material on ha
have lost. We have
the whole country to
plies of every deser
two weeks from the
merchants can fill a
merchandise that ma
credit of Chicago
whole country has
confidence in us ther
in Chicago itself. T
the city can be rene

With all telegraph lines *down, it took several days for the horrible reports of Peshtigo's tragedy to reach the outside world.*

punctuated only by an occasional clearing where a lumber camp or an isolated homestead stood—though a few miles west of town, three areas of half-cleared farms and hardwood stands, dubbed the Upper, Middle, and Lower Sugar Bush, interrupted an otherwise solid sea of timber.

In these early days of settlement, fires had become almost commonplace for the people who lived and worked in the woods and in the sawmill towns they surrounded. In times of drought, many farmers routinely plowed deep furrows around their homesteads as firebreaks. Train workers patrolled the tracks regularly, dousing any small fires they found. Still, many fires burned unchecked in the woods—left to their own devices until they threatened a settlement or a mill. Then the townspeople would turn out in force to defend their property from the encroaching flames.

Since 1871 had so far proven to be the driest year in memory, no one expected the fires to be any less frequent. Drought conditions had prevailed from early May through September, broken only by a shower on July 8 and an even lighter sprinkle on September 5. The summer and fall had been so dry that railroad workers laying track to Peshtigo found the going easy. The swamps had dried as hard as pavement, and the only problem foremen faced was finding enough drinking water for the men. For loggers, too, work went on. But few of the trees they cut ever made the journey downstream, as the rivers were too low to transport them. Millions of board feet of lumber were stacked along riverbanks awaiting the winter freeze, when they could be hauled out on sledges over icy trails.

Since the supply of timber seemed infinite, lumber bosses showed little concern for getting the most out of each tree. Loggers wasted nearly one-quarter of all the wood cut, leaving it behind in the woods as slash—and as potential fuel for the fires that seemed to break out everywhere.

By late September, many small fires were smoldering in the woods in an area 100 miles long and 70 miles wide. The single telegraph line that connected the towns of the region had been destroyed, isolating the area north of Green Bay from the rest of the state. Franklin Tilton, an editor from Green Bay who watched the flames encircle the town of Oconto, described ground fires that gnawed at the roots of giant trees "as a cancer eats away the life of a man." When the wind rose, the towering pines would topple, their desiccated trunks and leaves instantly alive with flames. As accustomed to fire as they were, most people couldn't help feeling uneasy as they looked around at the dense, suffocating smoke that filled the air.

By noon on October 8, a sickly yellow light had washed over Peshtigo. It seemed to emanate from everywhere and nowhere, since the disk of the sun had long since vanished in the haze. Around suppertime, black and white ashes began to flurry down from the sky, and as evening fell, an angry red glow over the treetops marked clearly where the fire was burning—a slumbering dragon that was coming to life just southwest of town.

Father Pernin, the Roman Catholic priest for Peshtigo and Marinette, had been watching the sky nervously all afternoon. From across the street, he could hear the sounds of drunken laughter in a tavern where railroad men were still carousing, either unaware of or unconcerned by the closeness of this latest fire. As night came on, Father Pernin began digging a six-foot trench in his garden to bury the church's valuables. His next-door neighbors, who were having a dinner party, looked on with much amusement.

Around 9 P.M., the air was filled with a low moaning, which soon became a deep roar. Some survivors described the noise as sounding like a great waterfall. Suddenly, slabs of fire began to rain out of the sky, the advance front of a fiery storm that was racing

Dust rising in dry weather is a sign of approaching change.

FOR THE RECORD

ONLY ONE INFERNO IN ALL of history has claimed more lives than the Peshtigo Fire of 1871. In May 1845, a fire erupted in a theater in Canton, China, killing 1,670 people. Taken as a whole, however, the separate blazes that swept through Wisconsin (1,100 to 1,200 dead), Chicago (250 dead), and Michigan (100 to 200 dead) on October 8, 1871, rank alongside the Canton fire as the worst the world has ever seen.

How Smokey the Bear Edged Out Hitler

I N 1942, THE UNITED STATES found itself at war, and the newly formed Wartime Advertising Council began spearheading the propaganda battle on the home front. Included in its campaign was a stern message about the danger of forest fires. As FDR's secretary of agriculture, Claude R. Wickard, put it, "Every fire in our fields or forests this year is an enemy fire."

Accordingly, the first fire-prevention posters pictured the flame-lit faces of Hitler and Hirohito smirking fiendishly above messages such as "Careless Matches Aid the Axis" and "Your Match, Their Secret Weapon." But by 1944, the war effort was going well, and the Ad Council decided to soften its approach by playing on the public's sympathy for woodland creatures. In their search for a symbol, the advertisers went through squirrels, monkeys, and a host of other animals. They finally settled on one—a bear.

Albert Staehle did the first drawings of a uniformed bear with a somewhat world-weary and knowing expression, and, in 1945, Smokey the Bear was born. (His name—officially, it's Smokey Bear, with no "the" in the middle—was said to have been inspired by New York City fireman "Smokey Joe" Martin.) In 1947, Smokey's trademark slogan, "Only You Can Prevent Forest Fires," was added, and Smokey found a radio voice—courtesy of Washington disk jockey Jackson Weaver. In 1948, a Forest Service artist named Rudy Wendelin started drawing Smokey; his version is the one most of us are familiar with today.

The promotion spread like, well, wildfire. In 1952, Congress passed the Smokey Bear Act, which regulated the commercial use of Smokey's increasingly popular name and image. And in 1968, a survey revealed that Smokey had become the most popular symbol in the United States, with more name recognition than the President. (Sorry, LBJ.)

toward Peshtigo. The firebrands burned in the streets, which had been paved with sawdust to keep down the dust, and they ignited the pine-plank sidewalks. By 9:30 P.M., the southwest wind had become so strong that it was difficult for a man to stand. A frightened deer bounded out of the woods and stood in the middle of the street, surrounded by a pack of local dogs. Strangely, the dogs hardly seemed to notice.

As the fire storm approached the town, residents began to seek refuge wherever they could. About 40 people ran into the Peshtigo Company's boarding house, a substantial, three-story building that they evidently believed might survive. It was a fatal mistake. Workers had tried to wet down the building with the company's fire engine, but its hose had quickly burned through. Around 10 P.M., the fire jumped the Peshtigo River and struck the boarding house. Five minutes later, the building collapsed, killing everyone inside. Only 12-year-old Peter England, a young farmboy, managed to escape. He had been standing in the open door of the building.

Almost everyone else was heading for the safety of the Peshtigo River, which ran through the middle of town. Father Pernin had already set his horse loose, so the priest himself pulled a light wagon containing the church's tabernacle, chalice, and other artifacts he hadn't had time to bury. His home was only two and a half blocks west of the river, but the journey seemed to take forever. In the priest's own words, "People seemed stricken dumb with terror. They jostled each other without exchanging look, word, or counsel. The silence of the tomb reigned among the living. Nature alone lifted up its voice and spoke."

By the time he reached the river, all the buildings on the west bank were ablaze, as was the wooden bridge, which was clogged with people and animals, all frantically trying to escape. With the searing heat close behind him, Father Pernin pushed his wagon into the river as far as it would go. Then, retreating to the riverbank, he looked out upon a hellish scene illuminated by fire that was brighter than daylight:

> The banks of the river as far as the eye could reach were covered with people standing there, motionless as statues, some with eyes upturned towards heaven and tongues protruded. The greater number seemed to have no idea of taking any steps to procure their safety, imagining—as many afterwards acknowledged to me—that the end of the world had arrived and that there was nothing for them but silent submission to their fate.

Father Pernin wasn't so sure that the end had come. He began pushing the people into the water, then jumped in himself.

The river provided almost the only safe haven from the fire, which by now had begun to roll and curl like breaking waves over the ground, mowing down everyone and everything in sight. Yet even the water was not without its dangers. Some of the people standing in the river were knocked off their feet and swept to their deaths under the falling timbers of the bridge or against the burning dam downstream. A five-year-old girl named Carrie Heidenworth escaped drowning by grabbing the horn of a cow that was swimming past her.

Burning logs from the factory floated downriver past the frightened refugees. Tongues of flame licked across the water, and even people standing up to their necks were not safe. Some people had brought quilts and blankets, which they soaked repeatedly and placed over their heads for protection from the searing heat. Almost as soon as they were lifted from the water, though, the coverings dried out and began to catch fire.

Many townspeople who lived far from the river sought shelter on open ground. The members of three families, 21 people in all, ran into a field with

Mrs. Lucius Fairchild, *wife of Wisconsin's governor, kept a cool head in her husband's absence and diverted emergency supplies to fire victims.*

TEST YOUR FOREST FIRE KNOWLEDGE

1. **Most wildfires are caused by**
   a. lightning c. arson
   b. carelessness

2. **The safest way to light a kerosene lantern or portable stove at a campsite is to**
   a. bring it inside your tent and away from any flammable vegetation
   b. set the lantern in a shaded area, under a tree or bush
   c. light it in a spot cleared of vegetation

3. **The best way to extinguish a campfire is to**
   a. cover it with rocks
   b. pour water on it
   c. cover it with dirt

4. **To be sure that coals have been extinguished, you should**
   a. check carefully for smoke
   b. break them apart to look for embers
   c. feel them with your bare hands

ANSWERS: 1. b. Lightning accounts for only 14 percent of all wild-fires. Arsonists set another 26 percent. Still, more than 50 per-cent of fires are started by carelessness in the home or garden, at campsites, or with electrical equipment. **2. c.** Never light a stove or lantern inside a tent or camper. Before bringing a lantern inside, be sure to check for proper ventilation. Never light a camp-fire or stove near overhanging vegetation. Low branches, bushes, and tall grasses are called ladder fuels and can lift even a small campfire to the treetops, sending it quickly out of control. **3. b.** Drown it with water. Once all sticks, coals, and embers are wet, stir the remains. Add more water and stir again. Move the rocks surrounding the fire to check for hidden embers. Do not leave the campsite until all embers are extinguished and cooled. **4. c.** Coals should be cold enough to touch before you leave your campsite.

only a single quilt to protect them. The smaller children crawled on top of the women underneath the quilt, and the men stayed out in the open, wetting down the fabric. All the men died that night, but everyone under the charred quilt survived. Not so lucky were the 68 people who died in a corn field outside of town. There the heat was so intense that a boulder five feet high cracked in two.

People who had no other refuge dropped to the ground with their faces in the dirt, desperately hoping to avoid the flames. But the fire seemed to follow no logical pattern; some people hiding in shallow wells survived the holocaust, whereas others who took shelter in similar spots were suffocated or cremated.

In less than half an hour after the first building caught fire (and some say within ten minutes), the entire town was in flames. The woodenware factory exploded, shooting blazing tubs and pails through the air like fireworks. Within an hour, the worst of the fire was over, simply because there was nothing left to burn. Every-thing had been consumed in the furnacelike heat.

Leaving Peshtigo, the fire raced northward, toward the towns of Marinette, Wisconsin, and Menominee, Michigan. The only thing that saved these two towns from the same fate as Peshtigo was the low glacial hills that formed a barrier between them and the fire and forced the flames to split in two. Around midnight, the east wing of the fire claimed its last victims as it roared through the village of Birch Creek, Michigan. Of the 100 people living there, 22 died.

At the same time that the Peshtigo Fire was ravaging north-ern Wisconsin, other massive fires were blowing up throughout the Great Lakes region. All across Michigan, fires had broken out in the afternoon, early enough so that evacuation, aided by daylight, was still possible in most towns. At the southern end of Lake Michigan, the Great Chicago Fire started at almost the same moment that Peshtigo burst into flame. And on the eastern shore of Green Bay, the Door-Kewaunee County peninsula burned from the city limits of Green Bay 30 miles north to Sturgeon Bay. The fire there destroyed Rosiere, Williamsonville, Brussels, New Franken, and other settlements, as the death count rose to at least 75. Because of the timing, many people later thought—incorrectly, it now appears—that this fire was an offshoot of the one that had struck Peshtigo and that it had somehow jumped across the 30-mile-wide bay.

Back in Peshtigo, it was around 3:30 A.M. on October 9 before Father Pernin and the other survivors thought it safe to leave the river. Nothing remained of their town but a few blackened posts, and the face of death lay everywhere. James Monahan, a Peshtigo mill worker, described the horrible scene they encountered:

Here and there over this great field of ashes lay the blackened corpses of the dead and the carcasses of animals. The stench rising that morning was so powerful that we could not bear it. The smell of burned flesh was so sickening that many of the women, after escaping from the river, fainted.

In the burned-over area, the ash had fallen so heavily in creeks and rivers that dead fish floated on the surface, and the water tasted strongly of lye.

As morning dawned on October 9, no one except the Peshtigo survivors knew of the town's ordeal. The telegraph line had been down for weeks, and there was no way to summon help or to communicate with the outside world. John Mulligan, a logging-camp foreman, was one of the first to spread the alarm. Mulligan rode a singed horse into Menominee, Michigan, and told his boss, Isaac Stephenson, that Peshtigo had been wiped out. Stephenson hastily scribbled a note and gave it to Captain Thomas Hawley of the steamer *Union,* telling him to send it by telegraph to the governor as

How Your Flower Bed Can Save You

GARDENERS, TAKE NOTE. THE plants and trees close to your home can either slow an approaching wildfire (defined as any fire that's burning out of control) or help deliver it to your house. Eucalyptus trees all over Oakland exploded into flames as the 1991 residential fires in that city spread. Because of their high resin and oil content, the trees served as living torches, igniting the houses and vegetation around them. Similarly, pine and juniper trees—and any other dry plants that regularly drop their leaves—will provide fuel for an oncoming fire. But that doesn't mean you should give up on landscaping altogether. Fire-prevention experts suggest that you provide a fire-break by planting only succulents (plants that retain water) within 30 feet of your home. Cacti, yuccas, euphorbias, some members of the lily family, aloes, kalanchoes, and sedums are all examples of succulents, which will help to slow the course of a wildfire.

Pour a Glass of Water

IN YEARS PAST, A CUSTOM among the country people of Belgium, Germany, and Bohemia (part of modern Czechoslovakia) used to help them foretell how dry or wet the coming year would be. If you'd like to try it yourself, here's how to do it: On the evening before St. Andrew's Day (November 30), fill a glass to the brim with water and let it stand all night on the grass. If on the next morning any water has spilled over the top of the glass, expect a wet year to come. If none has spilled, a dry year is almost certain to follow.

Anxiously awaiting next year's forecast.

soon as the *Union* reached Green Bay. The message was imperative and terse: "We are burning up. Send help quick."

By the time Stephenson's telegram finally reached Governor Lucius Fairchild's office in Madison on Tuesday morning, October 10, the governor had already left for Chicago to lend assistance to the survivors of that city's tragedy. But the governor's wife ordered the diversion of a supply train that was ready to leave for Chicago, sending it north to Green Bay instead. In the days after the fire, two men were posted at the dock in Menominee and told to lift and drop heavy boards; amid the dense smoke from the burning forest, the continued thudding of the planks was the only way that steamers bringing relief supplies could find the port.

Nearly 1,200 people died in the Peshtigo Fire, about 600 in Peshtigo alone. The sawmill at Peshtigo Harbor, which had survived unscathed, began sending up rough boards so that coffins could be made to bury the dead. Some of the victims had suffocated and died untouched by the flames. Others could be identified only by some personal effect—a penknife, perhaps, or a watch—that lay beside a charred piece of bone or amid a little pile of ashes.

One of Father Pernin's parishioners came up to him after the fire and told him that he had found the tabernacle floating safely on a log in the river. When the priest retrieved the box, he discovered that the flames had not damaged it at all, a fact that many of his flock considered a miracle. In the trying days that followed, there was a need to believe in God's mercy; too many people had already witnessed what could only be described as His wrath. And the image of Father Pernin pushing people into the river in a kind of forced baptism seemed to make the words of John the Baptist frighteningly real: "I indeed baptize you with water unto repentance: but he that cometh after me is mightier than I . . . he shall baptize you with the Holy Ghost, and with fire." ■

Too Hot to Handle: America's Deadliest Forest Fires

• **October 7, 1825.** The worst fire in Canadian history roared through New Brunswick's Miramichi River valley and destroyed the provincial capital of Fredericton. Many lumberjacks saved themselves by riding huge log booms downriver through a searing tunnel of fire. In Maine, fires stretched from Moosehead Lake to the Penobscot River, burning a swath 40 miles long and 6 miles wide. Estimates of deaths ran as high as 500, but only 130 bodies were found.

• **September 1, 1894.** A wave of fire obliterated the towns of Hinckley, Pokegama, Mission Creek, Sandstone, and Partridge in eastern Minnesota, killing 418 people. Railroad engineer Jim Root and his crew saved some 300 refugees by backing Train Number Four, the Duluth Limited, six miles north of Hinckley to Skunk Lake.

• **August 20–21, 1910.** The Big Blowup in the Northwest scattered firefighters and townspeople in Idaho and Montana. Gale-force winds from the southwest swept dozens of fires over mountains and rivers, destroying the towns of Taft, Deborgia, Haugan, and Tuscor in Montana. By the time early-winter rains quenched the flames, more than 3 million acres had burned—some 7 to 8 billion feet of marketable timber.

• **October 12, 1918.** Hurricane-force winds strewed flaming planks and hay over the sawmills at Cloquet, Minnesota, destroying most of the town and burning more than 250,000 acres. One estimate put the death toll as high as 538, with property damage around $30 million.

• **August 14, 1933.** Fires broke out in western Oregon, igniting the great Tillamook Burn. A huge blowup on August 24 destroyed 200,000 acres in less than a day, as a strong east wind whipped flames 1,600 feet high. After the fire storm, pastures in Tillamook County lay buried under three feet of ash.

• **May 20, 1963.** To the residents of New Jersey's Pine Barrens, this is known as Black Saturday. Near the Lebanon State Forest, flames moved nine miles in only six hours. The fire continued for 11 days, by the end of which the flames had consumed more than 200,000 acres, killing seven people and leaving nearly a thousand homeless.

Carl Pretzel
Gone where
the
Woodbine twineth
How ub for High
VAS DOT.
Dooken A Shmall
Vonce
REST
Dots ZO.

Jno. C.W. Bailey & Co
SOCIETY RECALIA &c
AND
OFFICE VOICE & MASONRY
160 WARREN AV.

The Forge That Shaped Chicago

The Great Chicago Fire of 1871 burned its way through four miles of the city and into American history.

IN THE DAYS IMMEDIATELY following the massive Peshtigo Fire, the eyes of the nation were fixed not on the Wisconsin woods, but on Chicago, Illinois. At roughly the same time that Peshtigo was being destroyed, a fire began in Chicago that burned more than 2,100 acres (including the downtown commercial district), killing more than 250 people and driving nearly 100,000 others from their homes.

By 1871, Chicago had some 334,000 residents and was growing fast; it was well on its way to becoming the "Queen of the Midwest." But from the Fourth of July to the night of October 8, only two and a half inches of rain had fallen, less than one-third the normal precipitation. As in the Wisconsin and Michigan woods, the summer's drought had made everything tinder dry, especially in the sprawling districts to the southwest of the city center, where wood-frame buildings and stables formed a labyrinth of narrow streets and lanes—all highly susceptible to fire. The only thing missing was the spark.

A serious fire had already swept the western district of the city on Saturday, October 7, causing nearly a million dollars in damage. On the following day, city firemen were weary from their exhausting battle of the night before and little expected that another major blaze would break out soon.

But break out it did, a little after 9 P.M., in the vicinity of DeKoven and South Jefferson streets on the city's South Side. The traditional (though unsubstantiated) story is that the fire started when Mrs. Patrick O'Leary's cow kicked over a kerosene lantern, which ignited its stable. Whatever the fire's immediate cause, by the time the alarm could be sounded at a box several blocks away, two or three other buildings had already caught fire. Five minutes later, the whole neighborhood was ablaze.

Strong southwesterly winds (another feature that this blaze had in common with the Peshtigo Fire) spread the fire quickly and helped it to vault across the Chicago River around midnight. When the South Division Gasworks caught fire and the flames could not be extinguished, the fate of the whole commercial district was sealed.

By 3:30 A.M. on October 9, the main fire had split into two columns and again jumped the river. The first building north of the river to catch

Above: The Patrick O'Leary *home near the corner of DeKoven and South Jefferson streets in Chicago. Tradition has it that the family's cow started the Great Chicago Fire in the stable behind the house.* Left: *The Chicago Tribune Building as it looked before* (inset) *and after the fire.*

COPYRIGHT, 1915, BY
R. R. DONNELLEY & SONS CO.

A map of the burned-over *areas of Chicago shows the fire line advancing northward along the shores of Lake Michigan. Roughly 17,500 buildings were destroyed in the blaze, at an estimated loss of almost $200 million.*

fire was the engine house of the waterworks. With the city's main water supply cut off, all hope for stemming the inferno evaporated. Fanned by the gusting southwest wind, the fire gutted the supposedly fireproof buildings of brick and stone in the city's business district, destroying them almost as rapidly as it had the wooden structures on the South Side.

Pandemonium reigned in the streets, as people hurriedly dressed, grabbed whatever valuables they could, and tried to get away. Some fled to the few narrow strips of undeveloped land adjoining Lake Michigan. As the heat and smoke marched closer and the sparks fell in showers around them, the frightened refugees waded deeper into the chilly waters of the lake.

Many residents of Chicago's North Side had been looking at the fire from their windows and balconies in the early morning hours, when they suddenly realized with horror that the flames had nearly surrounded their

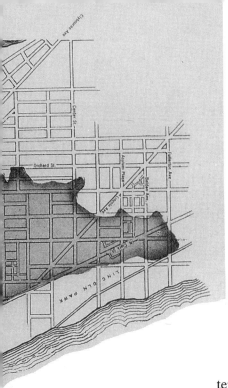

neighborhood. Some fled north to Lincoln Park, while others traveled west along Chicago Avenue, joining the sea of carts, wagons, and humanity heading for the open prairie.

All day long on Monday, October 9, the fire raged out of control on the North Side of the city. Policeman Richard Bellinger reportedly fought the fire himself by rationing his water, pouring only a ladleful on each spark as it landed on the shingles of his roof. By the time the last drop was gone, the embers still showered around him, but he remembered a barrel of cider in the cellar that he had just laid in for the winter. He ordered the cask drained and the contents brought to him. The combination of hard work and hard cider apparently did the trick, and Bellinger managed to save his house.

Late on October 9, the fire finally burned itself out around Fullerton Avenue in the northeast part of the city, halted only by a steady rain and the natural barrier of Lake Michigan. Almost as soon as the flames had petered out, pens started flying in an attempt to immortalize Chicago's apocalyptic nightmare and bring it to the world's attention. With all telegraph and rail links north of Green Bay severed, it would be days before the rest of the country would hear of the disaster that had struck Peshtigo and northern Wisconsin. But word of the Chicago fire was telegraphed to the rest of the world immediately. And in an age before the "instant book," the first comprehensive account of Chicago's ordeal, *Chicago and the Great Conflagration* by Elias Colbert and Everett Chamberlin, was published on December 1, 1871, less than two months after the fire.

The Great Chicago Fire, though nowhere near as deadly as the tragedy in Peshtigo, nevertheless cost the city dearly. Nearly 17,500 buildings had been

Assistance poured in *from all over the world. Here the mayor of Chicago accepts a contribution from a representative of the Empress of Germany.*

The fire set Chicago's *development back three years. However, the flames ushered in a period of massive urban renewal, and many people considered the blaze to some extent a blessing in disguise.*

destroyed, and property damage estimates topped $196 million. Although the fire set Chicago back nearly three years in its development, some dispassionate observers thought the inferno had actually done some good by sweeping away many unsafe wooden structures and hastening Chicago's transition from a frontier capital to "America's Second City."

In 1956, Mayor Richard J. Daley decided to build the Chicago Fire Department Academy near the site of Mrs. O'Leary's barn on DeKoven Street—perhaps the most fitting tribute imaginable to the memory of Chicago's greatest disaster. But it was author Bret Harte who best summed up, in just three lines, the swift growth and the even swifter destruction of nineteenth-century Chicago:

> *Like her own prairies by some chance seed sown,*
> *Like her own prairies in one brief day grown,*
> *Like her own prairies in one fierce night mown.* ∎

Was That a Cow or a Comet?

ALMOST EVERYONE HAS heard the story of Mrs. O'Leary's cow, who supposedly kicked over a lantern and started the Great Chicago Fire. For want of a better explanation, almost everyone accepts the story.

Everyone, that is, except Mel Waskin, a man who thinks the cow theory is a lot of bull and who believes a comet may have started it all.

Back in 1982, Waskin ran across an extraordinary book called *Ragnarok: The Age of Fire and Gravel,* which had been published almost 100 years earlier by an amateur scientist named Ignatius Donnelly. Donnelly had suggested that many of the catastrophic events in earth's history might have resulted from comets striking or coming close to

striking the earth. He thought the Great Chicago Fire might be just one more example.

Witnesses in Wisconsin described the fire as having come down from the sky in flaming balls. Were these the fragments of a comet that was brushing past the earth? Also, in Chicago, firemen reported that "basements were burning blue." Waskin suggested that the blue flames might have been caused by the methane and acetylene gases typically found in the frozen mass of a comet.

Waskin believes that he has even identified the rogue comet. In 1846, astronomers discovered that Biela's comet had split in its approach toward the sun, forming Biela I and Biela II. Waskin suggests that Biela II's elliptical orbit may have brought it into a collision course with the earth as it hurtled through

space at 30 miles a second.

"What probably happened," Waskin explains, "was that chunks of frozen gases broke away from the main body of the comet and were heated to their gaseous state as they plunged through the atmosphere, fueling existing fires or igniting new ones."

A far-fetched explanation? Maybe. Waskin himself says of his book, *Mrs. O'Leary's Cow,* that "the facts are all factual, but the speculations are highly speculative." But consider the accounts of survivors near Peshtigo, Wisconsin, who swore they saw a "great black, balloon-shaped object whirling through the air over the tops of trees, and which seemed to explode." At the time, the gas cloud was thought to have been swamp gas, otherwise known as methane. It might have come from a swamp. Then again . . .

The Wind That Sets L.A. on Edge

When the Santa Ana wind blows its hot, dry breath across southern California, it can topple power lines, fan huge brush fires, and give everyone the heebie-jeebies.

To the people who reside near the mountains and canyons south of Los Angeles, the Santa Ana wind comes, in the words of one unnamed Californian, as a "skin-drying, lip-cracking, unpleasant visitant," a devilish wind that threatens lives, property, and nerves. The irritating wind can blow at any time of year but is most common in the fall, when high pressure builds over the northern Rockies or the Desert Southwest and a low-pressure area stalls offshore in the Pacific. As the air moves from the high-pressure area toward the coast, it usually compresses and picks up heat. For every 1,000 feet of altitude it drops, it warms up by approximately 5°F, and by the time it reaches southern California, the wind may be 25° hotter than it was when it left the Great Basin.

California's narrow canyons (such as the Santa Ana Canyon in Orange County, which probably gave the wind its name) provide the only easy access for the wind through the mountains, and as the hot air squeezes through them, its speed increases. Santa Ana winds are normally clocked at around 35 to 40 miles per hour in the basins, but some of the windier locations, such as Cajon Pass, have recorded gusts of up to 100 miles per hour.

Almost no one has anything good to say about the Santa Ana wind. One of its most common and devastating effects is its ability to whip brush fires into raging infernos, which sometimes burn thousands of acres before they can be brought under control. In 1961, a windblown fire in Bel Air destroyed nearly 500 homes, including those owned by Cliff Robertson, Burt Lancaster, and Zsa Zsa Gabor. On April 21, 1982, a Santa Ana wind blew power lines together, igniting a fire that burned through a densely populated neighborhood in Anaheim, destroying $50 million in property and displacing 1,200 people.

One of the main reasons that the Santa Ana wind poses such a fire hazard stems, ironically, from the success in suppressing brush fires in southern California. As the region became more heavily settled, people weren't keen on having periodic wildfires barbecuing their backyards. With better fire control and fewer fires, the amount of brush in the nearby chaparral (a dense thicket of shrubby oak and manzanita) increased. In drought years, of which southern California has recently had plenty, the brush becomes an ideal fire starter, and the resinous leaves of the native shrubs add plenty of fuel to the flames. Factor in a hot, gusty Santa Ana wind (which can reduce the humidity of the air to 5 percent or less), and you have all the makings of a first-class forest fire.

The Santa Ana wind does have its more whimsical aspects—like the night of November 28, 1989, when it set off movement-sensitive burglar alarms all over Huntington Beach and caused a 30-foot pile of horse manure to spontaneously ignite, driving some none-too-happy residents from their homes in Irvine. Then there was the time, in February 1992,

Above: In 1982, Amy *Davidson, of Anaheim, California, gives her son a drink at a shelter for victims of an apartment-building fire.* Left: *Zsa Zsa Gabor digs through the remnants of her Bel Air home, destroyed by fire in 1961.*

No weather's ill if the wind be still.

when a 40-mile-per-hour Santa Ana wind blew countless ladybugs from the Laguna Mountains to the coast, much farther than they usually travel on their spring migration. Swarms of the beneficial insects covered beaches or were blown out to sea by the wind.

Most Californians, used to dealing with everything from earthquakes to mud slides, take this sort of thing in stride. But anecdotes abound linking the onset of the Santa Ana wind with violence, crime, and other mayhem. Author Joan Didion referred to it as "the season of suicide and divorce and prickly dread." And writer Raymond Chandler described the Santa Ana wind as a sensation that could "curl your hair and make your nerves jump and your skin itch. On nights like that . . . meek little wives feel the edge of the carving knife and study their husbands' necks. Anything can happen."

Despite all the folklore concerning the malevolent effects of the Santa Ana wind, most police officials and psychiatrists downplay its influence on human behavior. In fact, not all Santa Ana winds are even hot; those that originate in Canada actually bring cooler temperatures (and maybe cooler tempers). But none of this information makes Californians feel any less nervous when the temperature climbs and a hot wind starts to blow. ■

Gold Wasn't the Only Reason for Rushing

IN THE YEARS BETWEEN 1896 (the beginning of the Yukon Gold Rush) and 1940, it has been estimated that fires burned around 80 percent of the land in Alaska at least once. And in one later summer alone (1957), more than 5 million acres went up in smoke.

Alaska: Good weather didn't always pan out.

Another legend bites the dust: The famous 20-mule teams that crossed Death Valley actually had only 18.

Death Valley's Human Ice Cube

DEATH VALLEY'S COLORFUL HISTORY is peppered with bogus stories. There was the great silver fraud perpetrated by two Nevada senators, and then there was the fake town named Kasson, where the federal government decided to set up a post office—until postal inspectors couldn't find anyone living within 25 miles of where it was supposed to be.

One day in 1874, the editor of the Virginia City *Territorial Enterprise* evidently needed to fill some space, so he concocted the story of a scientist who had invented some "solar armor" that he planned to test in Death Valley. Covering himself with a spongelike material, the story said, the intrepid researcher saturated himself with water and set off across the desert.

According to the paper, the inventor was later found sitting on a rock, frozen solid. The rapid dehydration of the water had supposedly turned the sponge into ice. The unfortunate man's beard was covered with frost, and a foot-long icicle drooped down from the end of his nose.

As hoaxes go, this one was wildly successful. Newspapers all over the world reprinted the piece. It may have sounded somewhat less preposterous at the time because it had the aura of scientific fact. Perspiring *does* lower body temperature, and more people *have* died of dehydration in Death Valley than of heat stroke or other causes.

To our knowledge, no one has ever tried to duplicate the fake experiment for real. Just to be on the safe side, though, we wouldn't recommend that you suit up with sponges on your next trip through Death Valley—unless you have a cool head on your shoulders (and some good thermal underwear).

It Would Be All Right If Only You Could Keep Dry

DEATH VALLEY'S impressive credentials include three records that have confirmed its reputation as the lowest, hottest, and driest spot—not only in the United States but in the entire Western Hemisphere.

- **The lowest-lying piece of dry land:** Badwater Basin, at 282 feet below sea level
- **The highest official temperature:** 134°F, recorded at Greenland Ranch on July 10, 1913
- **The lowest average annual precipitation:** 1.66 inches

Despite this last statistic, roads in Death Valley are normally closed several times a year as a result of flash flooding, as rains sweep down the barren slopes of the surrounding mountains and into the valley.

FLOODS

FLOODS HAVE BEEN A MAJOR threat to humankind since the dawn of civilization, when nomadic peoples first started to settle down, farming and building their cities in the fertile river valleys. Today they cause more widespread destruction than any other kind of weather-related disaster. Hundreds of floods occur all across the United States every year, ranging from the seasonal swelling of mountain streams to the devastating aftermath of hurricanes and coastal storms. On average, more than 100 Americans are killed in floods each year, and some 75,000 are driven from their homes.

In the Bible, only Noah and his family survived the Flood to repopulate the earth and start anew. On a much smaller scale, all floods since that time have done pretty much the same thing—sweeping away the past but also clearing the slate for new works and new people. And, always, there are the survivors, who return to rebuild what nature has taken away. ■

In Fort Worth, Texas, folks took to their roofs to await rescue from this 1949 flood.

An Hour of Flood, a Night of Flame

People in Johnstown joked about the idea that the dam would ever burst. On May 31, 1889, they stopped laughing.

THE REVEREND H.L. CHAPMAN, minister of the Methodist Church in Johnstown, Pennsylvania, had just sat down to begin work on his next sermon. The text read, "But man dieth, and wasteth away: yea, man giveth up the ghost, and where is he?" The doorbell rang. He answered it and found his wife's cousin, Mrs. A.D. Brinker, standing on the front porch, agitated and soaking wet from the rain that had been falling all night.

Above: Although the corpse *was reportedly moved into this scene by the photographer for greater dramatic effect, the death and destruction at Johnstown itself were all too real.* Left: *Debris and water covered the landscape following the 1889 flood.*

Members of the famous *"Bosses Club" included* (top to bottom) *Andrew Mellon, Andrew Carnegie, and Philander Knox.*

The woman was terrified that the South Fork Dam would burst on account of the high water and that the town would be deluged. "Johnstown is going to be destroyed today!" she wailed.

The minister remained calm. "Well, Sister Brinker, you have been fearing this for years, and it's never yet happened," Chapman said. "I don't think there is much danger."

It was May 31, 1889, and Mrs. Brinker's prophecy, repeated so many times in the past that her neighbors laughed about it, was about to be fulfilled. Before the day was over, the dam would indeed burst, and most of Johnstown and several neighboring communities would be smashed, swamped, or burned. More than 2,200 persons would die in America's worst flood ever—a disaster at first seen as a visitation from God but later shown to have been manmade and avoidable.

The dam, 37 years old in 1889, held 450 acres of water suspended 450 feet above the streets of Johnstown, 14 miles of narrow river valley away. The dammed water was originally planned as a reservoir that would feed the Pennsylvania Canal, but the completion of a railroad line through the Allegheny Mountains had made it obsolete before it was finished. The reservoir was purchased in 1879 by the South Fork Fishing and Hunting Club, whose members included some of the wealthiest and most powerful men in the country: Andrew Carnegie, future treasury secretary Andrew Mellon, and future secretary of state Philander Knox. In Pittsburgh, where most of the members lived, it was known as the "Bosses Club."

The old dam had burst once before, in 1862, but the water level at that time had been low, and little damage had occurred. When the rich men of Pittsburgh took over, they ordered the dam repaired so that they could stock the reservoir with fish and ply its waters in sailboats. The materials dumped against the clay foundation of the dam included rock, mud, brush, hay, and horse manure. A fish screen was placed across the spillway to ensure that none of the black bass with which the lake had been stocked could slip downstream to be caught by nonmembers. There was no way that the water level could be lowered in an emergency.

Such an emergency seemed most unlikely, even though the two rivers that met at Johnstown—the Little Conemaugh and Stony Creek—ran high every spring, often inundating parts of the town. There had been floods in 1885, 1887, and 1888. Still, although everyone talked about the possibility of the dam letting go, it never had.

But an ecological catastrophe was in the making. The population of Johnstown had tripled to 30,000 after the Civil War, when it became a steel-making center. The steep hillsides had been stripped of timber, causing severe erosion. April of 1889 had been snowy, and a storm on the night of May 30 had dumped seven inches of rain on the barren slopes around the reservoir. The fish screen in the spillway was clogged with debris, reducing its flow to a trickle. Now the water began to rise, to lap over the top of the dam. Men worked frantically to stop it, but at ten minutes after three on the afternoon of the 31st, the dam gave way. Twenty million tons of water went rampaging down the Little Conemaugh Valley.

Legend says that a horseman named Daniel Peyton raced ahead of the angry waters, spreading the alarm. He never existed. But Johnstown had been warned. Three messages had been sent from the dam, by tele-

Propelled by the incredible *force of the water, a full-sized tree skewered this Johnstown home.*

FOR THE RECORD

AT LEAST UNTIL THE MISsissippi overflowed its banks in 1993, wiping out both towns and records, the most costly flooding in U.S. history took place in June 1972 as a result of Hurricane Agnes. One hundred five deaths and more than $4 billion in damage were reported. In Pennsylvania, the worst-hit state, damage from floods climbed to $2.8 billion for the year.

graph and by foot, saying that the flood was imminent. They were paid no more heed than Mrs. Brinker.

The huge wave smashed the little valley villages first: South Fork, Mineral Point, East Conemaugh, Woodvale. Their only warning came from a Pennsylvania Railroad engineer named John Hess, who heard a noise like a hurricane and saw "a commotion in the timber." He drove his engine toward East Conemaugh with the whistle shrieking and gave many people there the chance to scramble uphill. Hess wanted to go all the way into Johnstown, but the track wasn't clear. He jumped out of his cab to safety.

The people of Johnstown heard a rumble, a roar, a sound like "a lot of horses grinding oats." The few survivors who actually saw the 35-foot wall of water approaching said it looked like a hill covered with rubbish—rooftops, trees, pieces of houses—preceded by a black mist, "a mist of death."

Buildings went down like dominoes. Every tree in the city park was ripped out by the roots and flung, along with houses, freight cars, horses, cows, and people, against the mountainside on the other end of town. After the gigantic wave crashed against the hill, the backwash sped up the untouched valley of Stony Creek, dealing death and destruction. The center of the city was erased in ten minutes.

The wave had spent much of its force in hitting the hillside, so a stone bridge, downstream from the place where the Little Conemaugh and

Houses and parts of *houses lean against each other just as they washed up in the flood.*

Many homeless residents *of Johnstown picked through the flood's debris for materials to build makeshift shelters such as this one.*

Stony Creek joined, survived. As debris piled up around its arches, a new dam was formed, along with a lake 30 feet deep in places. The bridge saved hundreds of people who had ridden their houses or rooftops with the flood; they climbed, many of them naked and bleeding, over the wreckage to the roadway and from there fled to higher ground. But many were trapped inside the mound of rubbish, and they suffered the most hideous fate of all. As darkness fell, the whole twisted heap caught fire. It burned "with all the fury of hell," wrote one witness, throughout the night. Perhaps as many as 80 people were cremated alive.

The stories of those who survived verged on the miraculous. Six-year-old Gertrude Quinn was swept away on a mattress. There she bobbed along like a cork, until a man named Maxwell McAchren jumped off a floating rooftop and joined her. He managed to throw her from the little raft to rescuers in the window of a building that had been left standing. McAchren himself was pulled out of the water farther downstream.

Johnstown's Horror Revisited

ALMOST 90 YEARS AFTER the Johnstown Flood of 1889, the flood-control system in the Little Conemaugh Valley had been vastly improved, designed to withstand a 100-year flood. By 1977, officials had declared the city of 41,000 virtually flood-proof.

Then, on the night of July 19, it began to pour, and the stalled storm drenched the area for eight hours. In West Taylor Township, northwest of the city, 12 inches of rain fell, and the Laurel Run Dam gave way, sending a swirling tide down on Johnstown and leaving destruction in its wake.

In all, at least 77 people died in the second Johnstown Flood, which caused an estimated $325 million in damage in a seven-county area.

Later, an observer noticed a strange irony. On a hillside high above the city, rows of white crosses mark the graves of the unidentified dead from the great flood of 1889. The number of crosses there is 777, which corresponds exactly to the month and year of the second-worst flood in Johnstown's history.

In the days immediately following the disaster, it was feared that as many as 10,000 might have perished. The actual count came to 2,209, although bodies continued to be discovered as late as 1906. Fifty undertakers were needed to bury the victims. Property damage was estimated at $17 million.

The Johnstown Flood was the story of the decade. It occupied every inch of the front page of the *New York Times* for five days running. More than $3.7 million in private donations was sent to help the city rebuild, along with tons of food and clothing. Clara Barton showed up with her new organization, the American Red Cross, and stayed for five months, working every day.

Some of the millionaire members of the South Fork Fishing and Hunting Club gave generously to relief efforts. Some gave nothing at all. Neither the club nor any of its members paid a dime in damages. But a man named Isaac Reed, remembering the fish screen that had blocked the spillway of the South Fork Dam, wrote a poem that summarized the feelings of the nation:

An hour of flood, a night of flame,
A week of woe without a name . . .
All the horrors that hell could wish,
Such was the price that was paid—
*   for fish!*

— TIM CLARK ∎

The Worst Floods by a Dam Site

SOME OF THE MOST SERI-ous and deadly floods in history have been caused by the failure of dams as a result of heavy or prolonged downpours. Frequently the cause of these collapses can be traced, at least in part, to imperfect engineering or shoddy construction—as with the tragic Johnstown Flood of 1889. Here are a few of the worst floods in U.S. history in which dams have played a part.

• **May 16, 1874.** A poorly constructed dam in Williamsburg, Massachusetts, broke, killing 138 persons in the industrial Mill River valley.

• **March 12–13, 1928.** Just before midnight on March 12, the St. Francis Dam near Santa Paula, California, collapsed after less than two years of service, killing 450.

• **February 26, 1972.** Two coal-slag dams along Buffalo Creek in southern West Virginia broke, unleashing two miles of backed-up water and causing a lower dam, which had been smoldering for months, to explode. In the hollow below, 125 people died, hundreds of homes were swept away, and 4,000 were left homeless.

• **June 5, 1976.** The 305-foot Teton Dam in Idaho collapsed, releasing some 80 billion gallons of water into the farmland below and killing 11 persons.

• **November 6, 1977.** An earthen dam above the town of Toccoa Falls in northeast Georgia gave way in the early hours of a Sunday morning, inundating the town and killing 37 people.

A young survivor of the 1972 Buffalo Creek Flood.

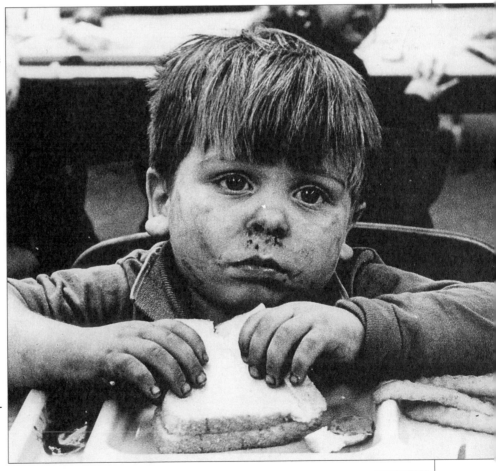

Rapid City's Hundred-Year Flood

Experts said the right conditions would occur no more than once in a hundred years. On June 9, 1972, Rapid City's hundred years were up.

IT WAS A WARM, HUMID, early-summer day in South Dakota. In Rapid City, located at the foot of the Black Hills just west of Mount Rushmore, inner tubers bobbed down Rapid Creek, its cool waters a welcome relief from the mugginess. Behind Canyon Lake Dam just west of town, a number of boaters and swimmers were enjoying the manmade lake and an early end to the workweek. Even Don Barnett, Rapid City's 29-year-old mayor, was playing a few holes of golf with a friend. It was Friday, June 9, 1972, and Barnett remembers shooting a 48 and finishing his round just as a light sprinkle started to fall.

Rapid Creek, the largest stream draining the Black Hills, snakes through the heart of this city of 43,000. Despite its long history of flooding (34 times since 1878), local officials had done little to discourage building near the creek. About 25 percent of the city lay within its flood plain—a crazy quilt of homes, businesses, hospitals, shopping centers, and car dealerships. After many years of false alarms, most folks took the threat of spring flooding pretty much in stride. But the events of this Friday night would write their own grim history and change forever the face of Rapid City and the lives of its people.

The National Weather Service forecast for Rapid City and the Black Hills called for "variable cloudiness with a chance of scattered showers and thunderstorms." In the upper atmosphere, however, a far more complex and unusual picture was emerging. A massive airflow, 3,000 feet thick and 78 miles wide, was pumping moisture-laden air toward the Black Hills. Normally when this occurs, the warm air rises, then cools, dropping

Following the flood cars *were stacked like dominoes along East Boulevard in Rapid City.*

A mother who had *watched the water carry away her home enjoys a tearful reunion with her son, whom she had feared lost.*

its moisture as rain or snow until the prevailing westerly winds push the clouds away from the Black Hills and eastward over the plains. This Friday, though, the upper-level winds from the west were unusually light. Under these extremely rare atmospheric conditions (a National Weather Service spokesman later characterized them as a "once in a hundred years" occurrence), a rainstorm striking the Black Hills would be trapped there until it ran out of moisture, drenching a very small area and bringing with it the potential for flash flooding.

For Mayor Barnett, the first uneasy feelings about the weather began around 8 P.M. as he was leaving the YMCA after a swim. An attendant said by way of conversation, "I guess we can expect some big rains on the creek." That comment, and the continuing heavy rainfall, made Barnett head for city hall. On the way, he radioed the police department and asked them to call Leonard Swanson, the city's director of public works. Once he reached city hall, Barnett decided to head for Canyon Lake with Swanson and police chief Ron Messer, to set up a command post below the dam and check for anything unusual. By this time, local radio stations were relaying alerts for high water in the Black Hills and along Rapid Creek in the city.

Up at Canyon Lake, Swanson and a parks department crew opened the dam's spillway gates to divert the rising water around the dam. They were trying to shove logs and other large pieces of debris through the gates when they noticed that the paddle-boat dock across the lake had broken loose and was drifting toward them. Unable to break up the dock, the men watched helplessly as it clogged the spillway gates. The water in the lake kept rising, lapping at the earthen top of the dam.

Checking out the area where the dock had broken free, Swanson's heart sank as he saw more signs of erosion, with water coursing around the north end of the dam and running hubcap deep in the road. Realizing the dam wouldn't hold much longer, Swanson radioed back to the crew on his walkie-talkie, ordering them to higher ground.

Mayor Barnett's evacuation order came at 10:40 P.M. Around 10:45, the dam gave way, adding to the already swollen waters of Rapid Creek. West of town, a wall of water five to ten feet high was already racing toward Canyon Lake. When the flood crest hit, around 11:15, the breached dam did little to hold back the raging tide, which raced furiously toward the nervous city.

At 3805 Riverdell Drive, Mr. and Mrs. Leo Hessman were watching TV around 11 P.M. when they heard the evacuation order for all residents on the south side of Jackson Boulevard. "The water hit us about three minutes later," Mrs. Hessman recalled in an interview with the *Rapid City Journal.* "We were preparing to leave in the Jeep when I told Leo, 'I've got to save Julie's [their daughter's] wedding dress.' I went back to put it on a high shelf, and by the time I got back to the door, the water was so high we couldn't get out. If we had left in the Jeep, we probably would have been washed away. The Jeep was cut in two."

The Hessmans, like many other residents, spent the night in their attic. Although their home was damaged, they (and the wedding dress) survived the flood unscathed.

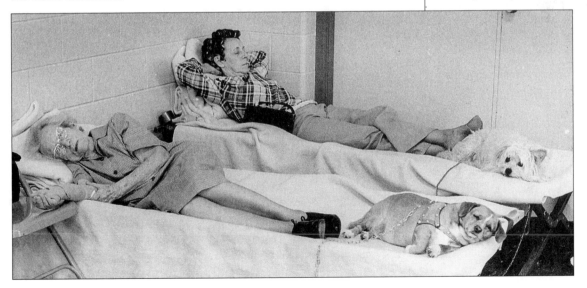

Two women who were *able to save their canine companions find refuge in a Rapid City shelter.*

By now the full force of the flood had hit the city, and everywhere in its path were confusion and calamity. Many houses and mobile homes were pushed from their foundations by the force of the water. As utility poles and power lines went down, most of the city lost electricity, and the streets were plunged into darkness. Utility crews scrambled to shut off gas mains, but many lines ruptured and ignited as houses were carried away. The resulting fires lent an eerie glow to the night. Firemen ignored the burning buildings, concentrating all their efforts on saving residents perched in trees or clinging desperately to rooftops.

About the same time the Hessmans were saving their daughter's wedding dress, Patrolman Sam Roach was turning back motorists at the corner of Jackson Boulevard and Mountain View Road. Suddenly he saw a great wave of water strike the side of the Clarkson–Mountain View Guest Home, knocking down a wall and endangering the lives of dozens of elderly residents. With all additional help cut off, Roach waded through the swirling waters alone, carrying survivors one by one to safety.

Shirley Hessman adjusts *the veil of her daughter Julie's wedding dress, which saved two lives in the Rapid City flood.*

He was later credited with having saved 41 lives.

Sometime before midnight, the rain began to diminish, but the high water that coursed through Rapid City didn't start to recede until after 2 A.M. The waves of thunderstorms that had buffeted the Black Hills had disgorged an estimated 143 billion gallons of water in only six hours. Rainfall totaled more than 10 inches in an area of only 60 square miles. At Nemo, 15 inches was recorded during the storm. Yet some locations on the nearby plains received only an inch or two.

After what seemed an almost endless night for rescuers and survivors, a thick fog cloaked the dawn on Saturday morning. The devastation was likened to the imagined aftermath of World War III. Cars were stacked like dominoes on East Boulevard. Mattresses, furniture, and clothing hung from the few trees left standing in the flood plain. A yellow

Volkswagen perched in the crotch of a cottonwood tree atop a heap of debris. Mangled bodies lay everywhere. The few people wandering the streets looked dazed. Everywhere the smell of propane escaping from ruptured tanks blended with the putrid smell of mud and debris. When the mud finally dried, it blew around in clouds of silty dust.

As the day wore on, the rescues continued. Thousands of people were missing, separated from their families during the night. The task of

Why You Should Always Clean Your Bathtub Before a Flood

AFTER A FLOOD, MUNICIpal water supplies may be contaminated or the loss of electricity may prevent well pumps from working. You can use a clean tubful of water for cooking or drinking until things are back to normal. So, in the event of flood warnings in your area, fill your bathtub—but be sure to clean it first.

The presidential profiles *atop Mount Rushmore bore mute witness to the deluge that raced toward Rapid City.*

locating bodies went on for days. In the end, the flood claimed 238 lives, and more than 2,800 families lost their homes. At the height of the flood, an estimated 375,000 gallons of water had raced through the city, and property damage was ultimately pegged at $165 million. Only 40 to 50 Rapid City households had carried flood insurance.

Some residents returned to their homes on Saturday to assess the damage and salvage what they could. Mrs. Leonard Roy Smith had watched her house at 3702 Franklin float away in the flood and come to rest a block away. When she returned, she found little damage; even the books in the bookcase were still in place. Another woman found an upper room of her house intact and was observed calmly going through her linen closet in the middle of Meadowbrook Golf Course, where the room had come to rest.

Many changes have been made in the years since the flood. Canyon Lake has been dammed again, but the flood plain along Rapid Creek is now a green swath of parkland, with golf courses and bike paths replacing the homes and businesses of 1972. If and when the next hundred-year flood strikes, such changes should minimize the damage.

Some people in Rapid City still refer to events as B.F. and A.F.—Before the Flood and After the Flood. In some way, this tragedy touched the lives of everyone there, townspeople and visitors alike. To Canadian tourists Derik Emery and his wife, one image came to symbolize their experience during the flood. On Saturday morning, as the couple finally made their way out of the campground area where they had been stranded, they looked up at the four presidential profiles on nearby Mount Rushmore. "Water was gushing down their stone faces," Derik Emery said, "and it looked exactly as if they were crying." ■

TEST YOUR FLOOD KNOWLEDGE

1. **Floods usually occur as a result of**
   a. heavy rains
   b. melting snow
   c. ice breakups on rivers
   d. any or all of the above

2. **When escaping from a flood on foot, you should never cross any moving water that rises above your**
   a. ankles   c. waist
   b. knees   d. chest

ANSWERS: 1. d, 2. b.

The Roar of Death

Water shot through the canyon like a runaway train . . .

FOUR YEARS AFTER the Rapid City flood, the same unusual atmospheric conditions that had caused flooding in the Black Hills—light upper-level winds from the west and a large, humid air mass feeding in from the southeast—contributed to another disastrous flash flood in Colorado's Big Thompson Canyon, about 50 miles northwest of Denver.

The July 31, 1976, flood occurred on a busy summer weekend, when the number of people in campgrounds, motels, and vacation homes had swelled to an estimated 3,000. The storm stalled for four hours over the eastern foothills of the Rockies, from 8:30 P.M. Saturday to 12:30 A.M. Sunday, dumping 10 to 12 inches of rain directly over the steep-sided canyon.

The huge volume of water roared through the 30-mile canyon like a runaway train, turning the Big Thompson River from an 18-inch-deep stream into a surging flood tide nearly 20 feet high, moving 25 feet per second and scouring everything in its path.

The flood killed 139 people, and the bodies of 6 other victims have never been found. More than 400 homes were destroyed, and damage was estimated at well over $35 million, making this flood one of the costliest, swiftest, and deadliest of recent times.

National Guardsmen help refugees cross Colorado's Big Thompson River.

If a hen crows, there'll be a flood.

Commercial Street in
Boston, covered with molasses and wreckage a few hours after the flood.
Inset: *The Purity Distilling tank looms in the background just before the tragedy.*

The Day Molasses Ran Through the Streets of Boston

For years, people said, on a hot summer night you could still catch a whiff of the strangest flood in American history.

O N JANUARY 15, 1919, the North End neighborhood of Boston was basking in the warmth of a real January thaw. On Sunday the 12th, the temperature had stood at 2°F, but by 12:30 P.M. on the 15th, the mercury had risen to 43°F, warm enough in the sun for the railroad freight handlers along Commercial Street to doff their heavy coats.

Running overhead and alongside the busy street, the tracks of the elevated rail line skirted houses, wharves, the paving division of the city's Public Works Department, and the freight sheds of the Boston & Worcester and the Eastern Massachusetts railroads. In the background, looming above the scene, stood the Purity Distilling Company's massive holding tank, 58 feet high and 90 feet across, which contained 2.3 million gallons of crude molasses waiting to be made into rum.

Inside the Boston & Worcester terminal, foreman Percy Smerage was directing the loading of a half-empty freight car when a low, deep rumble shook the building. Suddenly the sounds of popping bolts and ripping metal filled the air. A booming roar followed, as the bottom of the giant molasses tank split open, sending a geyser of amber fluid high into the air.

With a terrible sucking sound, the gooey liquid shot out of the tank under a pressure of two tons per square foot, smashing everything in its path. The half-loaded freight car was caught on the crest of an eight-foot wave and hurled through the metal walls of the terminal. Under the weight of the sticky tide, now five feet deep inside the shed, the floor gave way, suffocating many workers who tried in vain to escape.

On the elevated tracks above, a train filled with passengers was approaching the tank just as it ruptured. As the trestle snapped and the tracks sagged down to the street, the motorman threw his train in reverse, saving many lives in the process.

The great wall of molasses, 30 feet high, continued on its rampage, smothering five men who were eating their lunch inside the Public Works Department. Bridget Clougherty died when the front of her house was sheared off by the roaring wave, and rescuers later found the body of Maria Di Stasio, a little girl who had been gathering firewood underneath the freight cars just moments before the explosion.

Fireman William Connor was one of the fortunate survivors of the disaster. Playing cards inside the station house, he looked through the window at the rolling wall of molasses bearing down on him. "It came with the speed of a cyclone," he remembered later. "The flood of molasses at times flowed up to our ears. We bumped our heads on the floor above trying to keep our noses and mouths above the fluid." Fireman George Leahy wasn't so lucky. As the gigantic wave knocked the firehouse on its side, he was crushed beneath a billiard table.

In all, 21 people were killed and 150 injured in the Great Molasses Flood. Firemen began attacking the sticky mess with hoses the next day, but it would be weeks before the neighborhood got rid of the viscous goop, which frothed up in yellow suds as soon as the salt water from the fire hoses hit it.

Following the disaster, about 125 lawsuits were filed against Purity Distilling. Six years later, the court finally ruled that the tank had not been strong enough to withstand the enormous pressure of the 2.5 million gallons of molasses it was designed to hold. Purity Distilling ultimately paid over $1 million in damages.

A visitor to Boston today would see nothing unusual about the scene of the macabre events of January 15, 1919. But sometimes, on a warm summer night, older residents still surrender to the power of suggestion and catch just a whiff of the cloying sweetness that people say lingered for years. ∎

Winter thunder and summer's flood never boded any good.

A SURE-FIRE (?) WAY TO PREDICT A FLOOD

Pull Out a Calendar

ONE TRADITIONAL WAY to predict a flood involves knowing the day of the week on which the moon changes phase. Many people once believed that if the moon changed phase on a Sunday, a flood would occur before the end of the month. In the words of a popular weather rhyme:

A Saturday's change brings the boat to the door,
But a Sunday's change brings it up on mid floor.

Francis's Folly

There was, he said, only one flaw in the system.

His critics scoffed when *he built his Great Gate, but engineer James B. Francis had the last laugh.*

N 1848, THE CITY OF LOWELL, Massachusetts, was the booming center of the American textile industry. Thousands of people had been recruited to operate looms in the city's new mills, which converted bales of cotton into millions of yards of finished cloth.

Much of Lowell's industrial success resulted from the innovations of James Bicheno Francis, chief engineer of the locks and canals. Francis had built a five-mile system of canals that drew water from the mighty Merrimack River, providing an even, uninterrupted source of power to dozens of textile mills. Seasonal changes in the river level were controlled by a system of gates and locks that Francis had built into the canal network.

There was only one flaw in the system. Francis had compiled a history of floods on the Merrimack and had discovered that once, during a major flood in 1785, the river had crested above Pawtucket Falls at 13 feet 6 inches. Since the city of Lowell was sited 30 feet lower than the falls, Francis knew that if the river ever rose that high again, water would surge through the canals, destroying the heart of the city.

To prevent this from happening, Francis proposed building a massive portcullis-style gate that could be dropped in place to close off the entrance to the feeder canal in times of flood. The gate would be similar to those used to defend castles against invaders in medieval Europe, and Francis saw it being used in much the same way to deflect flood waters.

His contemporaries roundly ridiculed the plan. The Merrimack, they argued, had not reached such heights in more than 60 years. And even if it did, surely a flimsy gate would never hold the river back. But Francis's position of authority allowed him to override his critics, and he built the gate in the face of fierce opposition.

Completed in 1850, the wood-frame shelter housing the Great Gate was anchored to granite piers. Grooves two feet deep were notched in the solid granite to receive the gate and hold it fast. Suspended by a massive iron chain, the enormous gate hovered like a huge guillotine above the placid waters of the canal. To Francis's critics, it was a frivolous display of his poor judgment, and it soon became known as Francis's Folly.

But in April of 1852, as Francis maintained his annual spring vigil on the flooding Merrimack, he saw the waters rising steadily. Finally he decided it was time to lower the gate. In two years' time, the chain had rusted tight, and the huge iron links had to be cut with a hammer and chisel.

On April 22, 1852, the river crested at 14 feet 1 inch above Pawtucket Falls—7 inches higher than in the 1785 flood. The gate, snug in granite, held fast. Deflecting the flood waters, it saved Lowell from destruction.

The Great Gate was never used again in Francis's lifetime. But in 1936, more than 40 years after his death, the river again began to rise to dangerous heights. Fortunately, someone remembered the Great Gate, and on March 13 it was dropped for the second time in its history. Workers found the same hammer and chisel that had been used to cut the chain 84 years earlier still resting on top of the gate.

Less than 24 hours later, a 28-foot-high wall of water slammed against the stone-bound gate. Again the gate held. Lowell had been spared a second time by Francis's Folly.

More than 55 years have passed since the great flood of 1936. No one can predict when the river will flood again, but James B. Francis knew that history has a way of repeating itself. Until it is needed again, the Great Gate stands watch as it has for more than 140 years—a testament to its creator and a silent guardian of a city's existence.

— JOHN S. TRANT, SR. ■

There is a compulsion in man to build his dams. He is forever chained and may never know the untamed freedom of the river.

The Great Gate
kept the raging Merrimack River out of Lowell's canals and twice saved the city from a watery fate.

EARTHQUAKES

WE TEND TO THINK OF ROCK, both literally and metaphorically, as the firm foundation of our world. An investment company tries to create an image of financial security by suggesting that it's as "solid as the Rock of Gibraltar." Stony silence, an adamant refusal, or being petrified (with fear)—all of these expressions reflect our belief that rock is the most rigid, unyielding, and inflexible substance on earth.

But all rocks are flexible, to a degree. As the floating continents move over the earth's surface, great stresses accumulate in rock masses that lie along faults, fracture lines in the earth's crust. When a fault finally breaks under the strain, one of its sides moves and is displaced in relation to the other side. It's a lot like bending a pencil between your fingers. Bend it a little, and you'll have a curved pencil; bend it some more, and the stress will snap the pencil in two. On a vastly larger scale, that's what happens deep inside the earth's crust during an earthquake.

The ancient Japanese believed that earthquakes were caused by the *namazu*, a gigantic catfish that lived underground and thrashed around from time to time. Today's scientists know a lot more about what causes a quake, but they are almost as helpless as our ancestors when it comes to predicting exactly when and where a major one will strike. ∎

Following the earthquake and fire of 1906, billowing smoke rises above the city of San Francisco while shattered buildings litter its streets.

The Day the Mississippi Ran Backward

For three months near the small Missouri town of New Madrid, it seemed that the earth would never stop moving.

ASK ALMOST ANYONE TO name the greatest earthquake zone in the United States, and the answer will almost invariably be "California." Chances are the respondent will pass right over the middle of our country, a region that even seismologists consider, on the whole, quite stable. Yet buried deep beneath the bootheel region of southeastern Missouri lies the New Madrid Fault, a mighty rift zone 120 miles long. Until it made headlines a few years ago, this fault had been largely forgotten. But way back in the winter of 1811–12, in the earliest days of western settlement,

God keep me from still water; from rough I'll keep myself.

the worst series of earthquakes in U.S. history brought the name *New Madrid* to the lips of every citizen and schoolchild in the nation.

In December of 1811, the Scottish naturalist John Bradbury was exploring along the Mississippi River, collecting North American plants for the Botanical Society of Liverpool. He traveled in the manner of the time, on a flatboat ballasted with 30,000 pounds of lead. Even in the daytime, navigation could be tricky on the river, so on the evening of December 15, Bradbury and his French crew decided to moor at a small island for the night.

Around 2 A.M., a cacophony roused the boatmen from their sleep. The air seemed alive with the screaming of birds, the cracking of trees, and the sound of a violent windstorm—though they couldn't feel a breath of wind. Then, in the darkness and confusion of the night, there came an even more fearful and ominous sound, which Bradbury described as "equal to the

Many boatmen perished *when the first shocks near New Madrid plunged acres of riverbank into the Mississippi and whipped the Big Muddy into a boiling rage.*

After the shocks, the earth *rolled in waves, flinging settlers to the ground and collapsing even the sturdiest houses.*

loudest thunder, but more hollow and vibrating." New Madrid's long nightmare had begun with a bang.

Nestled in a horseshoe bend of the Mississippi, the youthful settlement of New Madrid had been built on a low-terraced ridge of sand and clay, perfectly sited to serve the busy river trade. By 1811, more than 3,000 settlers had come to New Madrid County to begin clearing the forests and draining the rich alluvial soil to make way for farms and homesteads. The first hard shock on the morning of December 16 brought an abrupt end to many settlers' dreams and ushered in a long winter of severe earthquakes that focused attention more on immediate survival than on any future plans.

In a letter first published in the *Lexington* (Kentucky) *Reporter,* one unnamed resident of New Madrid described in vivid detail the events of the morning of December 16:

About 2 o'clock this morning we were awakened by a most tremendous noise, while the house danced about and seemed as if it would fall on our heads. I soon conjectured the cause of our troubles, and cried out it was an Earthquake, and for the family to leave the house; which we found very difficult to do, owing to its rolling and jostling about. . . .

[Shocks continued for the next four and a half hours, but] at half past 6 o'clock in the morning. . . , believing the danger to be over I left home, to see what injury my neighbours had sustained. A few minutes after my departure there was another shock, extremely violent. I hurried home as fast as I could, but the agitation of the earth was so great that it was with much difficulty I kept my balance—the motion of the earth was about twelve inches to and fro. . . . The earth seemed convulsed—the houses shook very much—chimnies falling in every direction. The loud, hoarse roaring which attended the earthquake, together with the cries, screams, and yells of the people, seems still ringing in my ears.

The damage and consternation on the shore were extensive, but the toll from the shocks was greatest on the water. As dawn brought an end to their sleepless night, John Bradbury and his crew looked out on a river covered with foam. Huge trees stood planted in the channel between the island and the shore, flung by the force of the earthquake from the river's bank to lodge in its muddy bottom. Even more ominously, empty boats floated by, with no cargo and no crew.

Collapsing banks were nothing new to boatmen along the Mississippi; to them, the mighty river seemed to be continually involved in reshaping itself. But in this first series of shocks, witnesses saw acres of riverbank at a time crash into the channel in huge columns, raising swells seven or eight feet high that rose up like a wall in the middle of the stream, swamping boats and beating furiously against the banks. Because of this fierce wave action, many survivors reported that the Mississippi's current had for a time reversed—in other words, it had actually run backward.

On land as on the river, the laws of nature and reason alike seemed suspended. As earth waves rippled over the area, the ground resembled the ocean. When the swells burst, they threw up water, sand, and charcoal covered with a sulfurous substance. The earth was covered with holes that resembled the craters of volcanoes. Surrounding these sand blows, some of which were up to 30 feet in diameter, were rings of white sand, quite distinct from the mucky black topsoil and more carbonized wood or coal. In the words of a later visitor, James McBride, "All nature appeared in ruins, and seemed to mourn in solitude over her melancholy fate."

In 1811, Missouri was a remote backwater, and details of the tragedy

Look to the Heavens

ACCORDING TO THE Greek historian Pausanias, "previous to earthquakes, the orb of the sun is of an unusual color—remarkably red, or tending to black. Bodies are seen running in the heavens, accompanied with abundance of flame, and the stars appear of a shape different from that which they possessed before."

the first steamboat to ply the Mississippi, was on her maiden voyage down the river when the earthquake hit. Under a full head of steam, she crawled along, fighting her way against a river that seemed to run backward.

Change of weather finds discourse for fools.

spread slowly to the rest of the nation. But even before they got the news, almost everyone in the eastern United States already knew that something quite spectacular had happened. The tremors rang the bells of St. Philip's Church in Charleston, South Carolina, as well as those in Washington, D.C. The New Madrid Shocks became a national event, with the tremors being felt all the way up to Detroit, New England, and parts of Quebec. In all, the quake on December 16 (and the subsequent hard shocks of January 23 and February 7) was felt over a total land area of almost one million square miles.

Jared Brooks was an engineer and surveyor living in Louisville, Kentucky. Using a primitive, homemade seismograph, Brooks recorded 1,874 tremors between December 16, 1811, and March 15, 1812, most of them too light to be felt generally. A second sequence of shocks began in the vicinity of New Madrid on January 23, with a tremor that many witnesses believed to be as strong as the first on December 16. Between January 23 and February 4, one observer noted, "the earth was in continual agitation, visibly waving as a gentle sea." Then, on the 4th, the tremors began to increase in intensity, rising to a crescendo at 3 A.M. on February 7, in the great quake known as "the hard shock."

On its maiden voyage down the Mississippi, the steamboat *New Orleans* was somewhere south of New Madrid when the shock of February 7 hit. Moored for the night at Island #32, the crew found the three-mile-long island gone at daybreak, sunk entirely but still attached to the boat's hawser, which pointed straight down from the bow into the river. Once released from its mooring, the *New Orleans* was soon under power with a full head of steam, but had to fight its way toward Natchez, Mississippi, as

Gimme That Old-Time Religion

I N THE WAKE OF the New Madrid shocks, circuit-riding preachers flocked to the region from all over the western territories, anxious to instill the fear of God in the populace. In the words of one satisfied man of the cloth, "It was a time of great terror to sinners."

During 1811 and 1812, the Methodist church took full advantage of the bonanza, increasing its membership by 50 percent. But as the religious fervor gradually died down, many converts, who were contemptuously dubbed "Earthquake Christians," began backsliding into their old, sinful ways.

FOUR SURE-FIRE (?) WAYS TO PREDICT AN EARTHQUAKE

1. Look at your pet. Animals may sense in advance that a tremor is coming (perhaps by feeling or hearing foreshocks that humans can't detect). The naturalist John James Audubon was in Missouri during the New Madrid Shocks of 1811–12, and he reported that his horse stood stock-still in the middle of the road, legs outspread and braced, just before a tremor struck. Cats, dogs, and birds also behave strangely.

2. Keep your ears open. Many people have heard unexplained booming noises in the hours or days before a major earthquake or volcanic eruption. Other people have noticed a peculiar quality to sound itself, with sounds close at hand seeming far away and every noise being heard distinctly.

3. Look for weird lights in the sky. An electrical phenomenon called earthquake lights is said to precede some tremors. People have described these lights as huge columns that appear before sunrise on the eastern horizon, towering up into the sky and disappearing as rapidly as they come. The quality of light also can be affected, with the sun appearing dull and red in the sky.

4. Buy a copy of THE OLD FARMER'S ALMANAC. Then find the highest and lowest tides for the year. Some people claim that high tidal stresses can trigger a quake along a fault that's ready to pop.

Naturalist John James Audubon.

the river once again appeared to run backwards.

Theories regarding the cause of the New Madrid quakes abounded. Some observers pointed to the heavens, to the brilliant comet with a forked tail that had appeared suddenly in September of 1811 and that shone into the following year. They were convinced that the earth had been caught between the "horns" of the comet and that the shocks had been caused by its attempts to shake itself loose. Many Indians credited the great Shawnee chief Tecumseh with calling forth the quake as a warning to his enemies and a scourge to the white people.

The hard shock of February 7 marked the beginning of the end of New Madrid's long ordeal, although milder aftershocks continued to be felt for years. The New Madrid Fault is still active, still shaking the region periodically with small tremors. Seismologists predict another major quake in the region sometime in the next 50 years. (A few years ago, the late climatologist Iben Browning drew the nation's attention to the area when he predicted—falsely, as it turned out—that "sometime" would be within 48 hours of December 3, 1990.) But the New Madrid Shocks of 1811–12 will always be remembered as some of the most violent and prolonged in history. ■

Learning Your Scales

THE BEST KNOWN AND most commonly used index for measuring earthquakes is the Richter scale, developed by seismologist Charles F. Richter in 1935. The Richter scale measures the *magnitude* of an earthquake—the energy released at the quake's focus—and is determined by amplitudes recorded on a seismograph. The scale is open ended, but the highest magnitude ever recorded was 8.9 (the devastating Chilean Earthquake of 1960). To put things in perspective, seismologists consider a temblor that registers between 6.0 and 6.9 a moderate quake and one between 7.0 and 7.9 a major quake.

Each whole number on the scale represents a tenfold increase in amplitude over the next lower number (so a 4.0 tremor is often said to be ten times stronger than one registering 3.0). But a tenfold increase in seismic wave amplitude actually translates into an energy release that is 31.5 times stronger than the next lower number.

The only problem with Richter's system is that in exceptionally strong quakes

(those with a magnitude of 8.3 or greater), the scale becomes "saturated" and less precise. In 1977, a geophysicist named Hiroo Kanamori introduced the Moment Magnitude Scale, which can more accurately measure exceptionally large temblors. Trying out his system on some historic quakes, Kanamori revised the magnitude of the Chilean Earthquake upward, from 8.9 to 9.5, and pegged Alaska's Good Friday Quake at 9.2 instead of 8.6.

In the past, very few earthquakes were measured using instruments, and reports of damage from various localities were frequently all that researchers had to go on. The Mercalli Intensity Scale, revised periodically over the years, describes the felt intensity and physical damage from an earthquake in 12 steps ranging from I ("Not felt except by a very few under favorable circumstances") to XII ("Damage total. Waves seen on ground surfaces. Lines of sight and level distorted. Objects thrown upward into the air."). Since it relies on human observations and concerns (right down to cracked foundations and broken crockery), the Mercalli scale appeals to the nonscientist interested in determining the impact of earthquakes on human lives.

San Francisco's Trial by Fire

The earth's surface rolled like the ocean, and then it seemed the entire city had burst into flames.

L IKE THE JOHNSTOWN FLOOD and the Great Chicago Fire, the San Francisco Earthquake lives on as one of the most compelling disasters in U.S. history. The tale is a true American tragedy, full of

We choose not 'tween good and bad but 'tween bad and worse.

pride and ego, greed and corruption, nobility and ignorance—all of the human passions played out against the fearsome backdrop of a city in flames. San Francisco was changed forever by the events that began on April 18, 1906, a date San Franciscans will always remember as the defining moment in their city's history—the end of one era and the beginning of another.

At 5:12 A.M. on that Wednesday, most of the city was either sleeping or just beginning to stir. But in the produce stalls at the foot of Market

Undeterred by the chaos *that resulted from the great San Francisco Earthquake and Fire, journalist Henry Anderson Lafler set up his equipment outdoors and began transmitting the story of the disaster to the outside world.*

Street, business was already in full swing. Police sergeant Jesse Cook was walking a beat nearby when he heard a deep rumbling sound and saw the first signs of the earthquake.

"I could actually see it coming up Washington Street," he later recalled. "The whole street was undulating. It was as if the waves of the ocean were coming toward me, and billowing as they came."

Striking along the San Andreas Fault, which lies only eight miles from the center of San Francisco, the tremor (according to later estimates) measured 8.3 on the Richter scale. As it approached the city from its epicenter offshore, the quake left horrifying destruction in its wake— a taste of things to come. At Point Arena, 90 miles north of the city, the quake hit land, cracking the lighthouse. A locomotive and four railroad cars parked at Point Reyes Station were hurled into the air, and the train's fireman, Andy McNab, was thrown several yards away. Nine men working in the Loma Prieta sawmill were buried in a huge landslide triggered by the quake. The violent shaking destroyed 14 buildings at Stanford University in Palo Alto, killing two students. Outside of San Jose, 100 patients and staff of the Agnews State Insane Asylum died when the hospital collapsed around them. Rescue workers arrived to find many of the surviving patients in a violent state; with no buildings left standing in which to confine them, the patients were bound with cords, hand and foot, around

Confusion reigned in the city's streets as people attempted to flee— some with their most cherished possessions, most with only the clothes on their backs.

some small trees left standing on the property.

South of San Francisco, the massive iron pipes running from the Peninsula Reservoir ruptured, cutting off the city's main water supply. Within a few minutes of the earthquake, dozens of small fires had been reported in the downtown area. In the fiery days to come, city officials would remember the words of fire chief Dennis Sullivan, who had lobbied unsuccessfully for more water storage and better training for his men.

The chief himself became one of the early victims of the disaster. During the quake, the California Hotel collapsed on top of the central firehouse. Attempting to rescue his wife, Sullivan fell three stories through a hole in the floor and was carried out, unconscious and fatally wounded. And so it was that, in the early hours of the tragedy, the almost impossible task of fighting fires without water fell to John Dougherty, a fire department veteran who succeeded Sullivan as chief.

After the hard shock and the nauseating, two-foot-high earth waves that followed, the streets were filled with dazed survivors, many only half-dressed. The scene they witnessed was astonishing. Trolley tracks and streetcars were twisted into grotesque forms, and live wires wriggled on the ground like serpents spitting blue sparks. Cracks appeared everywhere in the streets, spurting water and gas from broken mains. Telephone and telegraph lines were down, and the city was cut off from the outside world.

From the relative safety *of Russian Hill, the sight of the inferno filled some onlookers with wonder, others with dread.*

By 7 A.M., nearly 20 major fires had broken out all over the city. Fire chief Dougherty declared that there was no way to save anything in the district south of Market, the city's widest street. Dougherty hoped that setting up a fire line there would help them contain the spreading conflagration.

Meanwhile, from his home above the city, the acting commander of the Presidio, San Francisco's army base, was making emergency plans of his own. Brigadier General Frederick Funston had little use for Mayor Eugene Schmitz and the civil authorities. Clearly, he thought, the Army would be needed to uphold order in the wake of this crisis. Acting on his own initiative, Funston effectively declared martial law in San Francisco, calling out armed soldiers from the Presidio, Fort Mason, and other installations. It was a decision that would be roundly criticized for years to come.

Around 9:30 A.M., another major fire started in the area known as Hayes Valley, between Van Ness Avenue and Market Street. A woman who had survived the earthquake decided to cook breakfast, but her faulty stove ignited what came to be known as the Ham and Eggs Fire, opening up another front in the war waged by overextended firemen.

By noon, a square mile of the city's center was in flames. The wood-frame houses south of Market Street, much of the financial district, and the area around Union Square were all involved. The hun-

Above: Brigadier General *Funston and his staff at the Presidio.* **Below:** *Structural damage from the earthquake was so great that many San Franciscans had to cook and eat al fresco in makeshift street kitchens.*

Silver Linings

AMADEO GIANNINI, the president of San Francisco's Bank of Italy, came into the city from his home in San Mateo on April 18, 1906, the day of the great earthquake. When he finally reached his building, he was appalled to find that two of his employees had drawn all of the bank's hard currency, some $80,000 in gold, from the vault in which it was kept and had opened for business as usual at 9 A.M., sitting around the office with the sacks of money. They were surprised at not seeing any customers.

Giannini immediately hired two horse-drawn wagons and started loading the wagons with almost everything in the building that wasn't nailed down. He hid the sacks of money under some oranges in the front of one wagon. Then he made the long, nerve-racking journey home, hiding the money in the ashes of his living-room fireplace.

A few days later, the Bank of Italy resumed operations. Because of the damage to other banks and their records, it was one of the few financial institutions in the city with access to large sums of ready cash—a fact that Giannini tried to keep quiet. He quickly started making loans, however, to people who were working to get back on their feet after the earthquake and fire. Giannini's savvy in beating his competitors to the punch paid off handsomely, and he later went on to found another famous institution—the Bank of America.

Except for the far-sighted A.P. Giannini and his Bank of Italy, the earthquake and fire brought San Francisco's banking industry to a screeching halt.

A bad day has a good night.

When the smoke cleared, *five square miles of San Francisco lay in smoldering ruins.*

Living on Borrowed Time

THE TRACK OF the 1906 San Francisco Earthquake has been virtually erased in the years since the tragedy took place. How? Scientists at the U.S. Geological Survey note with horror that rows of houses now straddle that line.

dreds of thousands of gallons of water in the city's cisterns had long since run out, and firefighters concentrated on what they could save, such as the Ferry Building at the foot of Market Street. By pumping water from the bay, the firemen managed to spare the building, and with it an important exit for the refugees fleeing the quake and the fires. In the days to come, thousands of city residents would walk silently down Market Street, between two walls of fire, to the ferry docks. From there they took passage across the bay to Oakland—and safety. Some regular ferries charged 25¢ or 50¢ per person for the short crossing; other boat owners, more profit-minded, ran their prices up to $10.

On the south side of the city, firemen also saved the Southern Pacific Railroad yards. In the days following the quake, the railroad ran free trains continuously out of San Francisco, eventually evacuating around 300,000 people (an average of 70 per minute) from a city whose population in 1906 was only around 425,000.

By 8 P.M. on Wednesday night, the fire covered a three-mile front, and people living 50 miles away in Sonoma and Santa Clara looked up at a sky that was so bright they could read a newspaper by its light. In San Francisco's Union Square, thousands of people spent an uneasy night sleeping on the grass and waiting for evacuation to permanent camps being assembled at Golden Gate Park and the Presidio.

As night fell, a horrifying new drama was played out in the city. General Funston had ordered his men to kill any looters or other lawbreakers on sight. Mayor Schmitz, who had at first been slow to respond to the crisis but was by now attempting to manage it, issued a proclamation confirming Funston's order and setting up a dusk-to-dawn curfew. By this time, federal soldiers, local police, state troops, and deputized bands of volunteers patrolled the city's streets. Reports began to come in of people being summarily shot or bayoneted for refusing an order to stop. Some of the victims, it was feared, were homeowners trying to salvage their own belongings.

The strategy for fighting the fires that raged through the night took a bizarre turn when General Funston ordered artillery and explosives brought in. Around 9 P.M., he informed Mayor Schmitz and the newly formed "Committee of Fifty" (a group of local businessmen and other bigwigs) of his plans to dynamite a fire line through a significant part of the city. By destroying buildings in the path of the fire, Funston planned to create a firebreak that would contain the blaze—something that the waterless fire department could not hope to accomplish.

Already that evening, an inexperienced crew of soldiers had tried to blow up a drugstore at the corner of Clay and Kearney streets—using black powder to do the job. The resulting explosion carried flaming bedding and debris from an upstairs apartment into the populous Chinatown neighborhood, spreading the fire instead of containing it.

Thursday, April 19, brought mixed blessings to the beleaguered city. The fires still raged out of control, but by early afternoon the wind had shifted slightly, blowing the flames back and giving exhausted firefighters new hope. Off the coast of California, the flagship *Chicago* of the Navy's Pacific Squadron had received a message that San Francisco was in ruins, and Admiral Caspar Goodrich immediately ordered his ships into port. Marines and sailors began directing demolition crews along the fire line. The Navy water tender *Soto Kano* supplied fresh water to the city's fire engines, and sailors laid water pipes up Telegraph Hill from the harbor. By late afternoon, fire chief Dougherty learned that workers had repaired some of the water mains into the city and that the fire had turned.

The reprieve proved to be short-lived. Around 3 A.M. on Friday, it began to appear as if the fire line that had been set up along Van Ness Avenue would not hold back the flames. Firemen, who had been working almost nonstop since the earthquake, began to collapse one by one from heat and exhaustion; so did their horses, some of which died in their harnesses. Just when all seemed lost, the firefighters caught sight of their chief, riding the length of Van Ness, shouting, cajoling, and swearing at them. Men somehow found their second wind.

Silver Linings

DURING THE evacuation of San Francisco after the 1906 earthquake, a young fisherman named Giuseppe Alioto met a girl named Domenica, who was crossing the bay on a fishing boat. The two began to talk, one thing led to another (as these things do), and the two were eventually married. Sixty-two years later, their son, Joseph Lawrence Alioto, was sworn into office— as mayor of San Francisco.

Joseph Alioto, an unexpected blessing from the big quake.

TEST YOUR EARTHQUAKE KNOWLEDGE

1. **What is the minimum number of seismographs needed to locate the epicenter of an earthquake and measure its magnitude?**

       a. one   c. three

       b. two   d. six

2. **You are on a ship at sea when a significant earthquake occurs nearby. Theoretically, would you be able to feel it? What if you were onboard an airplane?**

3. **True or false: A tsunami is the same thing as a tidal wave.**

4. **Alaska experiences scores of earthquakes every year, more than any other state, including California. About what percentage of the seismic energy released around the world each year occurs in our 49th state?**

       a. 4 percent

       b. 7 percent

       c. 13 percent

ANSWERS: 1. c. Scientists need readings from at least three different seismographic stations to locate the epicenter of an earthquake, based on how long the primary shock wave (or P wave) takes to reach each location. One seismograph is needed to calculate for each of three unknowns: latitude, longitude, and time of origin. 2. You should be able to detect an earthquake onboard a ship because you would feel the primary, or P, waves, though not the secondary, or S, waves, which are transmitted only through the ground. As for the plane, you probably wouldn't notice the earthquake. Even though some of the high-frequency P waves would be refracted into the air as sound, they would be pretty small and insignificant to a jet setter. 3. False. The definition of a tsunami is a seismic ocean wave, and it may be caused by an earthquake on an ocean fault line, a mammoth landslide, a volcanic eruption or collapse, or a combination of these factors. It has nothing to do with the gravitational forces of the moon and sun, which govern the tides and thus can cause tidal waves. 4. b.

Even in the face of such heroism, the fire had taken on a far more frightening character. After burning almost unchecked for two days, the inferno had actually begun to create its own wind. Pockets of superheated air raced through the ruins of the city, fanning the flames higher like a gigantic bellows. Everything close to the fire was burning or melting. After the fire, the bodies of earthquake victims that were found were little more than stumps. In the district south of Market Street, the heat was so intense that corpses melted in with the debris. The smell of death was sickening.

Around 11 A.M., the wind shifted again on the fire line at Van Ness Avenue. At nearby St. Mary's Cathedral, Father Charles Ramm noticed a small fire starting on the church's spire. Still wearing his black cassock, he started to climb the tower to put out the flames. Firemen tried to come to his aid, but their ladders wouldn't reach him. Climbing higher, the priest battled a feeling of vertigo as well as the stifling heat, which made breathing nearly impossible.

At the top of the spire, Father Ramm held on with one hand as he beat out the fire with a bag held in his other hand. For a moment the crowd that had gathered below was silent. Then they started cheering wildly.

At 4 A.M. on Saturday, fire chief Dougherty arrived at the Pacific Mail Dock Pier to supervise efforts there. For three days straight, he and his troops had been fighting a losing battle, and the exhausted men he found at the pier had begun to retreat from the fire. Suddenly Dougherty rushed forward, grabbed a hose himself, and headed for the pier. Once more the men rallied around their chief, and the fire was extinguished.

With that small victory, the tide began to turn at last. At 5:30 A.M., the fire at Van Ness Avenue was contained; and by 7:15 Saturday morning, 74 hours after it had started, the greatest inferno in San Francisco's history was over. At least 315 people had died in the earthquake and fire, and more than 350 others were listed as missing and presumed dead. Five square miles of the city (nearly 28,000 buildings) were destroyed. But the city, or what was left of it, had been saved. And then, ironically, a light rain began to fall.

The Loma Prieta Earthquake of 1989 reminded San Franciscans of the havoc that a strong quake can wreak in their beautiful city by the bay. Yet that tremor, though serious, can't compare to the stories still told of 1906—when San Francisco survived an earthquake only to suffer through days of terror from fire and the sword. ∎

Making Waves

THE VIOLENT SHAKING and damage we experience in an earthquake results from three distinct kinds of wave action, two of which are called *body waves* because they act on the earth's underground body of rock.

Primary waves, or *P waves,* are the fastest-moving shocks from an earthquake, and the ones that most people and seismographs feel first. P waves radiate out from the quake's focus, compressing and stretching the solid rock as they race through it. They travel through the rock in a way that is similar to sound waves passing through air, so it's no surprise that these are the waves that, when they reach the surface, cause the rumbling, thundering, or booming sound associated with major earth tremors.

Secondary waves, or *S waves,* are the other type of body waves that act on the underground rock. S waves are slower than P waves and are usually felt a few seconds after the first shock of the earthquake hits. As the S waves pass through rock, they shear it or twist it violently at right angles to the direction of the waves. This produces the familiar surface motion of earthquakes, which most observers describe as both an up-and-down and a sideways action. This combined vertical and horizontal motion is what causes the most damage to structures.

The third type of waves associated with earthquakes, *surface waves,* are slower than either P or S waves and occur only near the ground's surface. *Love waves* shake the ground horizontally and are particularly damaging to building foundations. *Rayleigh waves* cause both vertical and horizontal movement, but unlike S waves, the motion is in the direction of the wave, creating a sickening elliptical roll such as you'd experience on a boat in a heavy sea.

One of the most frightening things about P and S waves is that, once they reach the surface, much of their energy reflects back into the earth's crust. This can spell double trouble for people and objects at ground level, who get clobbered by what is known as *surface amplification.* In other words, waves heading up combine with waves heading down to make the shaking even worse.

Earth wave action on the Union Street cable line, San Francisco, 1906.

"God Save Us!"

For those who survived that first violent tremor in Charleston, it seemed the night would never end.

FOR THE PEOPLE OF Charleston, South Carolina, Tuesday, August 31, 1886, was a pleasant summer's day. As late afternoon passed into evening, the heat of the day lingered, radiating from the walls of the gracious old brick buildings that lined the streets of this prosperous southern city of 53,000.

The Ashley and Cooper rivers, which frame the peninsula on which Charleston sits, seemed to stretch out in the late-summer heat, their surfaces dead calm, reflecting the stars that shone brightly above in the clear, dark sky. The sound of dance music rose in the still air from the pavilion on James Island, where young people were attending a social event. But as the evening wore on, many other residents of the city were calling it a night and preparing for bed.

At 9:51 P.M., a slight shudder passed almost imperceptibly through the city, followed by an unusual rolling sound that increased in strength and ferocity until at last it became a deafening roar. Suddenly every object, person, and building—the very earth itself—was in motion as the tremor grew in its jarring intensity. For 35 or 40 seconds—what seemed like a lifetime to

Residents of Charleston, *South Carolina, camped in town squares after the earthquake of 1886.*

those who lived through it—the violent shock continued unabated. Then, just eight minutes later, a second strong tremor shook the city, driving thousands of frightened people into the streets. After the roar ceased, the earth became strangely quiet, but the night soon rang with cries of pain and panic.

The Great Charleston Quake had two epicenters: one near Woodstock, about 16 miles northwest of the city, and the other about 13 miles west in sparsely settled country. Near the village of Summerville, the quake had given notice of its coming several days earlier on August 27 and 28, when residents heard unexplained booms that sounded like artillery fire or explosions. On the night of the quake, residents of Summerville and nearby towns were tossed about and thrown to the ground by the violent shocks, while chimneys snapped off houses and were flung far away. Cracks opened in the ground, and towering jets of water, sand, and mud spurted out of basins in the earth. One such crater, near Ten Mile Hill on the South Carolina Railway, measured 21 feet in diameter.

Most houses in these rural areas were built of logs and suffered only moderate damage in the quake, but in Charleston itself, the damage to the old

A crater on Ten Mile Hill, *near the South Carolina Railway. One crater created by the earthquake measured 21 feet in diameter.*

brick homes of planters and other wealthy residents was severe. The earth's surface rolled in ground swells that some witnesses reported as being two feet high, pitching many buildings up and off their foundations. The shocks seemed to come from everywhere at once. Indeed, after the quake, headstones in cemeteries were found thrown down in every direction. And in some of the houses that withstood the shocks, framed pictures were found still hanging, their faces turned toward the wall.

In the *Charleston News and Courier,* a certain Captain Dawson described how one brick house fared during the quake: "The house seemed literally to turn on its axis. The first shock was followed by a second and a third, less severe than the first. The air was filled with the cries and shrieks of women and children. From every side of that normally quiet neighborhood came the cry, 'God save us.' "

After the first of the shocks, many of Charleston's terrified residents rushed to the city's public squares and parks—Marion Square, Hampstead Mall, Washington Square, and Battery Park—to escape collapsing and shaky buildings and to join in hymns and prayers for deliverance.

One Catholic priest reported that after the first shocks, many of his parishioners rushed for the refuge of the church, perhaps convinced that the unprecedented tremors were divinely inspired. "As soon as I felt the shock," he wrote, "I ran for the yard. In the streets were thousands of Catholics who wanted to enter the church. I closed and locked the iron gates, keeping the crowd from entering the church, which I feared might fall at any moment."

Unbeknownst to the victims in Charleston, the great earthquake that had paralyzed their city also had been felt by millions of people all over the eastern United States and beyond—from Canada to Cuba, from Iowa to Bermuda, almost 1,000 miles away. The vibrations shook the steeple of New York City's Bedford Avenue Church, 600 miles from Charleston, causing the bells to sound. In Raleigh, North Carolina, 215 miles away, the shocks were strong enough to ring doorbells.

After the initial shock, the night returned to normal for people far from the center of the quake. But for the citizens of Charleston, the nervous waiting had just begun. The lurid glow of fires punctuated the darkness. Broken water mains hampered firemen's efforts, as did the towering piles of debris that rendered many streets impassable. The smell of sulfurous gas released by the quake made the hellish scene complete.

At 2 and 4 A.M., two strong aftershocks broke the uneasy calm of the city and toppled many buildings that had survived the earlier quake. Throughout the night, small groups of rescuers searched among the ruins for the living and the dead; the injured numbered in the thousands. Four ships moored in the estuary were turned into floating hospitals and morgues, as local doctors worked through the night.

Wednesday's dawn brought a measure of comfort to those who had survived the anxious night, but it also revealed the full extent of the city's devastation. Most of the buildings along Market Street had been destroyed by the tremors, and Hanes Street also was partially demolished. Much of Charleston had been built on reclaimed land or fill, but even some structures that stood on well-compacted earth proved no match for the violent shaking. Ironically, some of the older houses in the city, made of rough handmade brick, fared better than newer brick structures. In some cases, recent additions to houses collapsed, while the original houses withstood the shocks.

Once news of the earthquake reached the outside world, assistance began pouring in. Clara Barton, president of the American Red Cross, paid a visit and inspected hospital facilities. Even Britain's Queen Victoria cabled her sympathies to President Grover Cleveland as news of the tragedy spread around the globe.

A total of 17 major shocks destroyed more than 100 buildings in Charleston, an estimated 90 percent of the city's brick structures. Total damage from the quake nationally amounted to between $5 and $6 million. Yet, amazingly, only 40 people died as a result of the quake, with 27 of those lives lost in Charleston itself—a city jarred out of its quiet complacency by the frightful power of the earth. ■

A man does not always grow wise as he grows old, but he always grows old as he grows wise.

Terror on Good Friday

After March 27, 1964, Alaska was never the same again.
Some of it wasn't even in the same place.

I N THE LATE AFTERNOON of March 27, 1964, the 400-foot freighter SS *Chena* docked at the port of Valdez on Alaska's Prince William Sound and began to unload its cargo. The arrival of a ship was always a welcome occasion for the 1,000 residents of this small town, the northernmost ice-free port in America. At one time, Valdez had been a prosperous city

of 12,000 people, but the railroads had been run through other towns, and in 1964 the Alaska Pipeline was only a twinkle in some engineer's eye. Valdez was dying, and excitement was where you could find it—such as on the city docks, watching a freighter come in. The dock where the *Chena* rode at anchor was busy on this Good Friday afternoon, as longshoremen went onboard the ship to unload cargo from the hold, and a small crowd of children and adults looked on from the pier.

At 5:36 P.M., 13-year-old Tom Gilson was riding in the back seat of his brother's car, heading for the waterfront. When the ground

started to shake, Tom and his friends thought that someone had climbed onto the back of the car and was jumping up and down on the trunk. After they managed to get out of the vehicle, they watched utility poles collapsing near them and heard the earth rumbling as an enormous shock shook the town for half a minute or more.

Onboard the *Chena,* Captain M.D. Stewart raced to the bridge as soon as he felt the earthquake. Looking on helplessly, he saw people running as the dock started to disintegrate beneath them. Just then, a towering wave lifted the *Chena* and heeled her over until she listed 50 to 70 degrees to port, striking bottom heavily in the place where the dock had stood just moments before. The warehouses, cannery, and packing plant were swallowed up in the jaws of the great tsunami (seismic ocean wave) that rolled through Valdez.

Each succeeding wave battered the freighter, driving it ashore through the debris of the waterfront, which by now had been

FOR THE RECORD

Even before the Good Friday Quake, Alaska had its share of healthy tremors. Between 1899 and 1961, a total of seven earthquakes measuring 8.0 or greater struck the state.

Large sections of *Fourth Avenue, as well as other streets in Anchorage, subsided in the earthquake and landslides that struck Alaska on Good Friday, 1964.*

FOR THE RECORD

ON SEPTEMBER 10, 1899, AN earthquake measuring 8.6 on the Richter scale struck Yakutat Bay in Alaska. Near the epicenter of the quake, the maximum uplift (vertical displacement) observed along the fault was 47 feet 6 inches—the greatest ever recorded in the state. The resulting tsunami that struck the coastline after the quake was 35 feet high.

completely submerged. Captain Stewart and his crew tried desperately to start the *Chena*'s engines while it was still afloat in the roiling water. As the ship scraped along the soft mud bottom, the backrush of the wave carried the freighter clear of the dock and pointed its bow seaward. Shaken but largely undamaged, the ship made for deeper water. In his report to the *Chena*'s owners, Captain Stewart wrote, "On our back roll off the beach it seemed certain that we were capsizing, but the following wave righted us. It is a miracle that the vessel survived."

Jim Bedingfield, the owner of the Valdez Hotel, abandoned his pickup truck when the earthquake struck. He started off on foot to gather his family but almost immediately fell into a deep fissure as the ground opened under his feet. The force of the water spurting from the crack pushed him back up to the surface, surprised but not seriously hurt.

The powerful earthquake that devastated many of Alaska's coastal towns and villages had its epicenter about 50 miles west of Valdez, deep beneath the waters of Prince William Sound. No seismographic stations were located in the state in 1964, but scientists estimate that the quake hit 8.6 on the Richter scale—making it one of the most powerful temblors on record, second only to the disastrous quake that struck Chile in 1960.

In Anchorage, 80 miles west of the epicenter, the initial shock lasted for a full four minutes, much longer than most other quakes. With a pop-

Governor William A. Egan
*returns to his home town
of Valdez to survey
the damage.*

ulation of about 100,000 in 1964, Alaska's largest city stood poised on the brink of a development boom that would replace the remaining vestiges of frontier life with modern high-rise office and apartment buildings. The Four Seasons, a six-story apartment complex, had just been completed but was still empty at the time of the quake. In the long, hard shake of March 27, the brand-new building collapsed, telescoping in on itself.

Much of the damage caused by the quake resulted from the shifting of the loose, silty clay soil that underlies much of the city. Four major landslides swept through downtown Anchorage and through the exclusive neighborhood of Turnagain Heights, cracking streets and damaging buildings. In the downtown area, about 30 blocks of homes and businesses along Fourth Avenue and L Street were destroyed. At Turnagain Heights, 75 houses slid toward the tidal flats of Knik Arm. And up on Government Hill, the south wing of an elementary school plunged 30 feet, while its east wing split lengthwise and crashed to the ground.

In the aftermath of *the quake, Vivian Garrath draws water from an Army supply tank.*

One block south of the Fourth Avenue slide stood the new five-story J.C. Penney department store. The store was scheduled to remain open until 6 P.M., but business was slow on this Good Friday, as many people who worked downtown had left early and were headed home. Larry Gage was working behind the jewelry counter at Penney's when the quake struck at 5:36. He remembers instinctively reaching behind himself to grab the ankles of a mannequin in a bridal dress, to keep it from crashing into his glass display case. As the building jerked violently, the store's fluorescent lights went dark and the emergency lights came on, casting light and shadow on the confusion. Shelves collapsed and displays cracked, and

THE TOTAL ENERGY released in the 1964 Alaskan earthquake has been estimated as the equivalent of one hundred 100-megaton underground nuclear explosions placed in line.

Except for the home *of one defiant resident who vowed to stay and rebuild, this housing development in Anchorage was almost completely destroyed.*

Gage joined the group of customers and employees fleeing down the stalled escalators toward the Fifth Avenue exit.

Reaching the outer glass doors, Gage saw a crowd of frightened people debating what they should do—whether they should leave the groaning building or stay put. Outside on the street, the ground motion was lifting cars five feet off the pavement, and pedestrians couldn't keep their balance. Gage and another man linked arms to prevent anyone from leaving the store. Only moments later, the decorative concrete panels that lined the front of the building came crashing to the street, burying cars and killing two persons outside.

By 5:41, the first shock of the earthquake had ended, and as evening approached with all power knocked out in the city, Anchorage city officials began to mobilize for the crisis. But in the small towns and native villages that dot the coastline of south central Alaska, the tragedy had just begun.

The violent movement of the fault line beneath Prince William Sound triggered numerous underwater landslides, sending seismic ocean waves—like the destructive tsunami that struck Valdez—bearing down on Alaska's bays and inlets. The first wave struck the village of Chenega even before the shaking had stopped. Of the 76 residents, the tsunami drowned 23; only 5 bodies were ever recovered. Most of the homes in town, as well as the local church, were destroyed, and the entire island moved 55 feet to the south. At Old Harbor, Kaguyak, and Afognak, the story was much the

San Francisco school kids practice for the next Big One.

What to Do When an Earthquake Hits

1. Remain calm. Unless the tremor is a particularly strong one or strikes relatively close by, most people (especially in areas where quakes are rare) don't even realize what it is and attribute it to some other cause, such as a sonic boom or a passing truck.

2. If you find yourself indoors, stay there. If you are outside, stay outside. Many earthquake-related injuries are caused by people rushing in or out of buildings during the shocks.

3. If you're indoors when the shaking starts, crawl under the sturdiest piece of furniture in the room—a heavy chair or table, for instance. This will protect you from falling debris such as ceilings and light fixtures. Stay clear of windows and outside doors.

4. If you're outdoors, stay in the open, away from buildings and overhead power lines. If you're in a city, move to the middle of the street to avoid falling glass and masonry.

5. If you're in a car, park it in the open, away from buildings, power lines, bridges, or overpasses and stay put until the shaking stops.

6. After the shaking subsides, if you are indoors, get out of the building as soon as possible. Use stairs instead of elevators. Most tremors are followed by aftershocks that can further damage or collapse a weakened building.

7. Check for leaking gas or water lines and shut them off if necessary. Use a flashlight rather than a candle or other open flame.

8. If you're near a beach or waterfront, evacuate to higher ground in case of a tsunami, which can strike some time after the initial shock. Take a radio to listen for emergency instructions.

Through the ages natural forces have been shaping and reshaping our earth. Earthquakes, volcanic eruptions, fire, hurricanes, and floods—man suffers the immediate havoc of these. But by these, in the infinite patience and pattern of time, the living balance of the earth is created. And it is by this man lives.

same. Native residents, used to earthquakes and high waves, moved quickly to higher ground and watched as their homes were washed away. After they had been evacuated, some people never returned. Most did, however, and rebuilt their villages in new locations.

In Valdez, a total of 32 people were killed as the waves battered the town. Two of the dead were longshoremen who had been crushed by shifting cargo in the hold of the *Chena*. The low-lying delta on which Valdez was built had subsided in the quake, and with all the damage to the port and downtown area, the residents decided to rebuild their city about four miles away from the old site, near a place called Mineral Creek.

The Good Friday Quake caused ripples all around the world. The shock itself was felt over 1 million square miles, all across Alaska and in parts of western Canada. The powerful tsunami generated by the earthquake killed at least 15 people when it came ashore later that night on the coast of Oregon and at Crescent City in northern California. Shock-induced waves formed in the Gulf of Mexico, causing high water in Texas and Louisiana, and water levels in wells as far away as South Africa were affected.

Given the awesome power of the quake, which was estimated as having released twice the energy of the San Francisco Earthquake of 1906, the relatively low death count—115 people in all—seems almost miraculous. Most of the victims died in the tsunami and the local ocean waves that scoured the coastal deltas and harbors. If a quake had to happen, its timing—on the afternoon of Good Friday, when schools and most businesses were closed—could not have been better. Many people were in their cars, a relatively safe place to ride out an earthquake. Also, the tremor struck while it was still light, at a time of year when the long nights of Alaska's winter were giving way to spring. The temperatures, in the 20s and 30s, remained mild by Alaskan standards, which made life a little easier for the thousands who lost their homes.

Today Anchorage has nearly twice as many residents as it had in 1964. As opposed to the people of Valdez, who rebuilt on higher ground, the residents of Anchorage seem to have forgotten the lessons of the past. High-rise hotels and other buildings stand on the bluffs of the growing city, perilously close to where the slides of 1964 wreaked their havoc. The attitude of the developers may be justified; perhaps, as they argue, the Good Friday Quake was the kind of thing that happens only once in a hundred years. Earthquakes, after all, are a fact of life in Alaska. But even the cockiest natives would not dispute those geologists who say that it isn't a question of *whether* another major quake will strike, only when. ∎

No Time for Surfing

EARTHQUAKES ON OR NEAR A coastline are frequently followed by tsunamis (seismic ocean waves), which pose a deadly threat of their own. The Pacific Tsunami Warning System in Honolulu warns that you should never go down to the beach to watch for a tsunami. When you can see the wave, the authorities explain, you are too close to escape it.

A Japanese depiction of a tsunami as a "typhoon dragon."

VOLCANOES

MOST AMERICANS THINK of volcanoes as distant curiosities, something spectacular, to be sure, but unlikely to have much bearing on their daily lives. Yet of the 500 or so volcanoes considered active in the world, roughly 50 are in the United States. In Hawaii, Alaska, and along the Pacific coast, volcanic peaks are commonplace. And the 1980 eruption of Mount St. Helens in Washington State proved that volcanoes have the incredible power to awe every one of us.

Although scientists have studied (and argued) the effect of volcanoes on the world's climate for more than a century, the need to understand this relationship has never been greater than it is today. Even amidst fears of global warming, most experts believe that great volcanic eruptions can block the sun and actually cool our planet for years at a time, triggering a massive shift in world weather patterns. As catastrophic as eruptions are to the people living near a volcano, they have a profound influence on the rest of us as well. ■

Lava advances toward Hoopuloa Landing in 1926 during the eruption of Hawaii's Mauna Loa volcano. Despite prayers and offerings to Pele, the fire goddess, the village was completely destroyed.

Mount St. Helens: The Greatest Show on Earth

On a May morning in 1980, professional observers suddenly found themselves part of the main event.

O**N SUNDAY MORNING**, May 18, 1980, Dr. David Johnston was working at the Coldwater 2 Observation Post, six miles north of the summit of Mount St. Helens in southwest Washington State. Having monitored the mountain ever since it had started rumbling nearly two months earlier, Johnston, a field volcanologist with the U.S. Geological Survey, had been the first scientist to climb down into the volcano to retrieve ash samples. He also had been the first to notice a blue flame flickering inside the expanding crater—a sure sign that Mount St. Helens was coming to life after more than a century of quiescence.

On this sunny spring morning, Johnston had a spectacular view of Mount St. Helens from his post, located on a small mountain nearby. A bulge had recently developed on the mountain's north side, and Johnston and his colleagues believed that magma (molten rock) was welling up into the shallow recesses beneath the summit, heating the ground water and continuing the process that meant a major eruption was near. It was only a question of time.

At 8:32 A.M., a 5.0-magnitude earthquake shook the scenic area around the mountain. This was immediately followed by another tremor, triggering a massive landslide that moved the whole unstable north face forward. Suddenly released from the overlying rock that had contained them, superheated water and magma lay exposed to the open air. They exploded violently, blasting out 600°F steam clouds from the ruptured peak.

The eruption occurred around 8:39. At about that time, there was a radio transmission from Coldwater 2. David Johnston's excited voice came on the line: "Vancouver! Vancouver! This is it!" Then silence.

The violence of the eruption was beyond anyone's wildest imagination. A fast-moving cloud of hot ash and gas, described by some

A month before the big *eruption, federal workers measure the snow pack near Mount St. Helens.*

The main event on May 18, 1980, sent a plume of volcanic ash and debris nearly nine miles high.

The violent eruption *obliterated the whole north side of the mountain, creating a huge, horseshoe-shaped crater.*

witnesses as a fiery hurricane, fanned out laterally as the whole north side of the mountain was obliterated. Coldwater 2 lay directly in the path of the blast; searchers later scanned the area for Johnston but could find no sign of either him or his observation trailer. The area where the camp had once stood lay under four feet of ash and rock. At Coldwater 1, eight miles northwest of the summit, photographer Reid Blackburn also was listed as missing; all that was left at the post was his burning car.

Rolling over ridges and valleys, the dark, hot blast cloud scorched the earth to bedrock and scattered lofty Douglas firs like match sticks. In less than ten minutes, more than 150 square miles of standing timber had been destroyed, blown down in windrows pointing away from the fuming peak. And the mountain had barely begun its work.

When the gases trapped within the underground magma hit the air, they exploded like bubbles from a huge bottle of soda that had been shaken up and then pried open. Ash and gas formed a vertical cloud rising nine miles high. Inside the black plume, streaks of lightning flashed, igniting fires that by Sunday evening would engulf 3,000 acres in flames. People in Vancouver, Washington, more than 50 miles to the southwest, witnessed the eruption, and the shock waves from the first cataclysmic blast were felt 200 miles away.

That Sunday morning, Pam Siddens and Terry Clayton were asleep at their campsite on the shore of Riffe Lake, 20 miles north

FOR THE RECORD

THE ERUPTION OF ALASKA'S Mount Katmai on June 6, 1912, created an ash cloud that traveled as far as the Yukon Valley, 1,000 miles to the north. The accumulation of floating pumice in the Shelikof Strait between Kodiak Island and the mainland was said to be thick enough to support a man's weight. Coast Guardsmen reported that in the heart of the ash cloud, it was impossible to see a lantern that was held at arm's length.

of Mount St. Helens, when they were shaken awake by the force of the blast and the lightning that was crashing around them. Attempting to flee in their car, they drove toward the main highway over bridges covered with water and mud until they spotted a Coast Guard helicopter overhead. Abandoning the car, the pair flagged down the chopper and were flown to safety, over a landscape that all at once looked appalling and unfamiliar.

Below them, it seemed that everything had been either buried or carried away by steaming mud flows, which had knocked out concrete-and-steel bridges and destroyed houses, cars, and logging equipment. The mud, a slurry of red-hot ash and rock combined with melting snow and ice, surged along at 50 miles per hour, heading for Spirit Lake and the Toutle River. Hitting the cold water, the hot mud swelled the north fork

Harry R. Truman became *a national celebrity when he refused to evacuate his lodge on Spirit Lake, vowing to "spit in the mountain's eye."*

Does a Free Fall Count for Bonus Miles?

ON DECEMBER 14, 1989, Alaska's Mount Redoubt volcano began erupting for the first time in 23 years. Situated about 110 miles from Anchorage on the western shore of Cook Inlet, the 10,000-foot peak threw a cloud of fine ash 40,000 feet into the air, sprinkling the town of Talkeetna and delaying holiday air travel in and around Anchorage.

The next day, the 245 people aboard KLM Royal Dutch Airlines Flight 867 learned just how dangerous that ash could be. The pilot of the Boeing 747 jumbo jet, en route from Amsterdam to Tokyo, hadn't received the Federal Aviation Administration's advisory on the volcano and didn't know anything about the fine ash until it appeared on his windshield. Suddenly, at 11:50 A.M., the flight crew reported smoke in the cockpit and the loss of power in all four engines. The plane was going down.

For the passengers and crew of the stricken plane, the next few minutes must have seemed like an eternity. The powerless jet went into a 13,000-foot free fall as the pilots frantically tried to restart the engines. At 11:58, two of the choked engines coughed back into life, and the other two quickly followed. At 12:25, the plane made a successful emergency landing at Anchorage. This particular drama was over, but air traffic was halted for days to come.

of the river to three times its normal width and raised the temperature of the water to around 100°F. Millions of salmon died, and witnesses saw fish leaping onto the banks in a desperate attempt to escape being poached alive.

Helicopters buzzed the area looking for survivors. Some would-be rescuers watched helplessly from the air as people were overtaken while trying to escape the fire and flood of the eruption. Fred and Margery Rollins of Hawthorne, California, were sitting inside their car about 15 miles from the mountain when the glowing steam cloud reached them. A helicopter pilot reported that they were fried alive by the intense heat even before the hot mud buried them.

At his resort on Spirit Lake, 84-year-old Harry R. Truman had stubbornly refused to evacuate, despite warnings from local officials and pleas from his family and friends. Truman had lived in the shadow of Mount St. Helens for more than 50 years, and since the mountain had started rumbling in March, he had become a national celebrity, granting interviews to reporters who loved his gruff demeanor and his vow to stay put and "spit in the mountain's eye." In the weeks before the eruption, he had received fan mail from all over the country saying "Give 'em hell, Harry," and he had even received a proposal of marriage.

Truman's sister recalled that he had often talked about a secret mine shaft where he would go for shelter if Mount St. Helens ever exploded. But the speed and fury of the eruption left no time for escape. When a search party finally reached the spot where his lodge had stood, they found only mud, 30 feet deep, entombing him in the place that he had loved too much to leave.

By Sunday evening, a huge, horseshoe-shaped crater had begun to form on the mountain's north face, from which thick, billowing clouds of ash continued to rise. At Camp Baker, about 15 miles west of the volcano, almost a foot of ash had fallen by the end of the day. At Walla Walla, 160 miles east, streetlights winked on in the unnatural twilight. About half an inch of ash fell on the streets of Missoula, Montana, 500 miles away, and visibility was reduced to near zero. Schools and businesses closed, and people were advised to stay indoors to avoid breathing the choking soot.

Thousands of motorists who had tried to escape the ash found themselves stranded, either by the treacherous road conditions or because their cars' air filters had given up the ghost. In Ritzville, Washington, seven inches of ash blanketed the ground, and 2,000 travelers sought shelter in local churches and schools, doubling the size of the small town overnight. Road crews mounted snowplows and took to the highways, but the slippery coating of ash proved to be much more of a problem than even the worst winter storm. Hundreds of miles of roads were closed, and air and rail service was suspended. As far away as Wyoming, the acidic ash blistered the paint on cars.

As the fine ash from *Mount St. Helens drifted east, it dusted streets as far away as Minnesota, leading to concerns about health and making driving treacherous in some locations.*

By Tuesday, the ash had stopped falling in the six-state area around the volcano, but the cloud continued to head east, dusting windshields in North Dakota and Minnesota. Before it completed its journey, the cloud would pass over every state east of the Rockies except Texas, Louisiana, and Florida.

Mount St. Helens continued to erupt, though more benignly, through the early fall, steadily building a new lava dome inside its crater. Finally, after an eruption late in 1986, the mountain entered a period of temporary repose.

Standing 9,677 feet high before its catastrophic rebirth, Mount St. Helens lost some 1,300 feet during the eruption. But the mountain that claimed 57 lives on that memorable spring day is far from dead. Although it spent much of its fury in 1980, the odds are that Mount St. Helens—a young volcano—will have another violent convulsion before the middle of the next century.

Actually, of the 15 or so volcanoes in the Cascade Range that are considered active, almost any is likely to flip its lid with virtually no notice. In fact, some of Mount St. Helens's sister volcanoes could cause even greater destruction should they erupt violently. Nearby Mount Rainier has more snow and ice on its flanks than all of the other Cascade peaks combined. If all of that water should melt in a large eruption (like the nine that have occurred there since the last Ice Age), the ensuing avalanche could reach as far as Puget Sound, almost 50 miles away—making the mud slides at Mount St. Helens look puny by comparison.

Neither Rain, nor Snow, nor That Little Gritty Stuff . . .

IN THE TOWN OF PASCO, Washington, about 100 miles east of Mount St. Helens, several local residents decided to mail out some of their surplus volcanic ash to friends and family as a souvenir. The only trouble was that some of the envelopes broke open as they were being postmarked and sorted. The sharp little pieces of ash spilled out, wrecking the machinery—and causing postal workers to erupt.

Sales of Mount St. Helens memorabilia skyrocketed after the eruption.

The Place That Gave Volcanoes a Bad Name

THE ISLAND OF VULCANO, one of the Aeolian Islands lying off the coast of Sicily, was one of the first volcanoes ever known (at least in the Western world). Its name eventually became associated not only with a certain type of eruption (vulcanian) but with all places where eruptions occur.

Vulcano was named for Vulcan, the Roman god of fire. In the fifth century B.C., the Greek historian Herodotus called the mountain Hiera, for the vent of the great god's forge. This, it was said, was where Vulcan fashioned immortal armor for the hero Achilles, and the vapor cloud that rose over the mountain was a sign that he was hard at work.

Still blowing its top from time to time, Vulcano has been comparatively quiet since May of 1890, when its last great eruption ended.

While man may suffer immediately from earth's violence, he can destroy far more swiftly and permanently than nature. Just possibly he is learning to understand this.

Was the spectacular eruption of Mount St. Helens a preview of coming attractions? Look at the record, say the two geologists who predicted back in 1978 that Mount St. Helens would erupt sometime this century. Dwight Crandell and Donal Mullineaux of the U.S. Geological Survey designed the method now used around the world to figure the likelihood of a volcano erupting. Simply put, if it's happened before, it will happen again. ■

"Eighteen Hundred and Froze to Death"

In 1815, a volcano erupted in Indonesia. In 1816, it snowed in New England in July. Any connection? You bet.

Wise men make weather proverbs and all fools repeat them.

AS LONG AS THERE IS a New England, there will be stories told of 1816, the famous Year Without a Summer, which brought snow and killing frosts to the northeastern United States and Canada in June, July, and August and which even reached across the Atlantic to cause widespread famine in Europe. The effects of the cold weather were immediate and obvious to the hardscrabble farmers of rural New England, yet no one at the time suspected that this unnatural season had sprung from

The cataclysmic eruption *of Mount Tambora in the Dutch East Indies affected weather worldwide.*

Nothing is certain except the unexpected.

an event deep within the bowels of the earth—an event that had taken place a full year earlier and half a world away.

In early April of 1815, the volcano Mount Tambora, on the island of Sumbawa east of Bali, began a catastrophic eruption that many experts believe to have been the most explosive in the past 10,000 years. By the end of its major convulsions on April 12, the peak had lost 4,200 feet of its 13,000-foot height and had spewed at least 25 cubic miles of ash into the upper atmosphere, causing a profound darkness that lasted for three days in areas as far as 200 miles away. A one-foot-thick layer of volcanic debris covered the surface of the sea, and four years after the eruption, mariners still reported sighting large floating islands of pumice.

Working from the reports of a survey ship sent out immediately after Mount Tambora's eruption, Sir Charles Lyell described the local aftermath of the eruption in his landmark book *Principles of Geology* (1830):

> Out of a population of twelve thousand, only twenty-six individuals survived on the island. Violent whirlwinds carried up horses, cattle, and whatever else came within their influence, into the air, tore up the largest trees by the roots, and covered the whole sea with floating timber.

Going from Bad to Verse

BACK IN THE NINE-teenth century, folks just seemed to versify a lot more than they do these days. Give them a good, juicy disaster and off they went, in search of pen and ink.

In the case of the famous Year Without a Summer, an anonymous poet captured a sense of the times:

The trees were all leafless, the mountains were brown,
The face of the country was scathed with a frown;
And bleak were the hills, and the foliage sere
As had never been seen at that time of year.

In a sense, the volcano's 10,000 or so immediate victims were the lucky ones. Over the next year, the heavy ash fall and other effects from Mount Tambora's eruption would claim 82,000 more lives on Sumbawa and its neighboring islands, mostly from starvation. And as the huge column of dust and sulfurous gases from the eruption rose high into the stratosphere, swift winds began to spread the volcano's veil of dust around the globe. Over the next few years, this hazy shroud would cause the sun to appear dull and reddish in the sky and prevent a portion of its warming rays from reaching the earth. For millions of people in North America and Europe, the results of this global cooling proved as disastrous as they were bizarre.

At first, the spring of 1816 seemed no different from any other. Although frosts in mid-May had delayed planting, by the end of the month temperatures had moderated, and farmers all over New England began putting in their corn, beans, and pumpkins. But things were about to change, and not even the crustiest old-timer could fail to be impressed by what happened next.

When farmer Hiram Harwood of Bennington, Vermont, went to bed on June 5, it was rainy with a gusty northeast wind. Despite the inclement weather that evening, it had been a warm, sunny day with temperatures approaching 90°F, and Harwood had been out planting with his father. In his diary, he described what he saw when he awoke the next morning: "The heads of the mountains on every side crowned with snow—the most gloomy and extraordinary weather."

Thursday, June 6, was Inauguration Day in Concord, New Hampshire, and it was cold enough in the unheated State House that the chattering of teeth from the audience punctuated Governor William Plumer's address. Outside the hall, a fierce, gusting wind swept snow flurries across the sky.

The cold snap continued, with frigid temperatures and blustery winds lasting until June 11. People built roaring fires in their hearths, as killing frosts reached even into coastal Connecticut, turning leaves and gardens black.

Then, as quickly as it had come, the cold spell ended. The weather turned pleasant once more, and farmers hastily replanted their crops, still hoping for a good season.

A SURE-FIRE (?) WAY TO PREDICT THE WEATHER

Tune In to Your Local Volcano

IF YOU LIVE within sight of an active volcano, plan to sell your barometer at the next yard sale. The inhabitants of Stromboli, a volcanic island in the Tyrrhenian Sea near Sicily, have been forecasting the weather a day in advance for longer than anyone can remember.

By looking at the vapor column rising from Stromboli's crater, mariners and fishermen can gauge the current barometric pressure. And the density of the cloud reflects the moisture content of the air, indicating either rain or fair skies in the offing.

If you get good enough at forecasting, people may even make you a god. Some scholars believe that Aeolus, god of the winds, was originally a Grecian prince who ruled the islands north of Sicily. By observing the clouds over Stromboli, Aeolus became known as a crackerjack forecaster—and perhaps the world's first weatherman.

Their hopes were dashed in early July, when temperatures plummeted again. Caleb Emery of Lyman, New Hampshire, reported that in his town, a well eight feet below the surface of the ground was completely frozen on the Fourth of July—and that it remained iced over until July 25. Independence Day was so chilly that men pitching horseshoes in the

Silver Linings

THE "COLD SUMMER" OF 1816 made for a dreary Swiss vacation on the shores of Lake Geneva, where the British poet Percy Bysshe Shelley and his soon-to-be second wife, Mary, were visiting Lord Byron at the Villa Diodati. To pass the time during what Mary later described as "a wet, ungenial summer," the friends decided to write ghost stories for their rainy-day amusement.

For Mary Shelley, the exercise turned out to be much more than a parlor game. Her "ghost story" became her most famous literary work. It was published in 1818 under the title *Frankenstein*.

Boris Karloff, offering silent thanks for Tambora.

bright sunshine had to wear heavy coats and mittens to keep warm. On July 9, another heavy frost cut down the corn crop in all but the most sheltered locations. And in Canada, many small lakes were still frozen over in the middle of July.

Compounding the problems of the cold weather, drought conditions prevailed throughout much of the summer in New England. Yet despite heavy losses of corn and a scarcity of good hay, some crops, such as oats, were actually thriving. Sidney Perley, in his *Historic Storms of New England,* relates the story of Jacob Carr of Weare, New Hampshire, who boasted that he harvested no fewer than 500 bushels of potatoes an acre that year and never allowed a specimen to be picked up that was smaller than a teakettle. (Like many stories about the Cold Summer, it's possible that this one was exaggerated just a bit.)

Hot and dry conditions lingered on through the first half of August, but then the fickle weather began to change again. On August 20, temperatures began to dive. On the night of August 21, hard frosts killed crops in northern New England and were felt as far south as Boston. Another snowstorm whitened the peaks of the Green Mountains of Vermont. By August 29, the frost had reached Berkshire County in western Massachusetts, and with it went all hopes for salvaging much of the already poor corn crop.

In 1816, as today, corn was far and away the largest and most important crop in America, and the poor harvest meant that livestock feed would be scarce during the coming year. The price of corn on the Philadelphia market shot up from $1.50 a bushel in April of 1816 to a whopping $3.11 a bushel in May of 1817. Those who had managed to salvage any part of their crop, whether through dumb luck or good husbandry, realized huge profits by selling corn to their neighbors. Abraham Sargent, Jr., sold seed corn for $4 a bushel. At the same time, meat prices plunged as livestock were slaughtered for lack of feed. One desperate man reportedly sold a $1,000 Merino ram to the butcher for $1.

The price of hay also skyrocketed. A ton of hay that might have fetched $30 early in 1816 cost $180 the following year. "Going down to Egypt" was how cropless farmers described the humbling experience of buying hay—many for the first time in their lives—from their more fortunate neighbors.

Not all farmers were quite so profit driven. On Christian Hill in the town of Ashland, New Hampshire, a locally famous tombstone commemorates Reuben Whitten (1771–1847). The clear inscription reads:

TEST YOUR VOLCANO KNOWLEDGE

1. True or false: All active volcanoes are located on or near the edges of the earth's moving crustal plates.

2. Mount St. Helens was the second volcano in the lower 48 states to erupt in this century. Which of the following peaks was the first?
   a. Mount Shasta
   b. Mount Hood
   c. Lassen Peak
   d. Mount Rainier

3. What is the difference between *magma* and *lava*?

ANSWERS: 1. False. About 5 percent of volcanoes are located somewhere inside the margins of the earth's geologic plates and are thought to be created and fed by stationary "hot spots" deep within the mantle. The Hawaiian Island chain, in the middle of the Pacific plate, is an excellent example. **2. c.** All four volcanoes have erupted in the past 200 years, but only Lassen Peak, in northern California, has flipped its lid this century—from 1914 to 1917. **3.** *Magma* refers to molten rock and the gas it contains as it exists underground. *Lava* is magma that has reached the earth's surface and exists in either liquid or solid form.

"Son of a Revolutionary soldier. A pioneer of this town. Cold Season of 1816 raised 40 bushils of wheat on this land whitch kept his family and neighbours from starveation."

According to Northeastern University professor John D. Post, the poor harvest of 1816 didn't cause widespread famine in the Northeast and Canada, but it did lead to serious food shortages in isolated parts of northern New England, the Canadian Maritimes, and elsewhere. In Vermont, some families reportedly subsisted on hedgehogs, boiled nettles, and clover heads. Farther south, New England's coastal fisheries took up some of the slack, and the change in many people's diets is reflected in another nickname for 1816— "The Mackerel Year."

For many Yankees who had contemplated moving to newly opened lands in the Midwest, the Year Without a Summer provided the last excuse they needed. Thousands of New England farmers either sold out or abandoned their homes and left for good. The number of migrants during 1816–17 was almost double that for the rest of the decade. Some places became virtual ghost towns. At one time, Granby, Vermont, had been a prosperous town with more than a hundred families. After the "Cold Summer," only three remained.

Westward ho!
The Cold Summer of 1816 prompted many Yankees to set out for greener pastures.

As bad as the summer of 1816 was in New England, it was infinitely worse in much of Europe, where cold weather and heavy rains contributed to a disastrous harvest. Crops rotted in the cold, wet ground, and as 1817 began, famine became widespread and severe. Food riots broke out in France and Switzerland. Grain hoarding and government embargoes sprang up everywhere. In Ireland, a cold rain fell on 142 out of 153 days during the summer of 1816, and 65,000 people died of hunger and from an ensuing typhus epidemic. Spreading quickly to other parts of Europe, the epidemic ultimately killed some 200,000 people.

The climatic chicanery that Mount Tambora's eruption inflicted on the world had profound and long-lasting effects on most of the Northern

Hemisphere. Today's scientists often debate the relative influence that major volcanoes have on climate and world weather patterns, but even the largest eruption of this century (that of Mount Pinatubo in the Philippines in 1991) can't hold a candle to the awesome power of Mount Tambora, which exploded with the power of 25,000 one-megaton bombs and turned the very seasons upside-down. ■

Told You So!

LEGEND HAS IT that the best forecast *The Old Farmer's Almanac* ever made was for the summer of 1816.

At the time, the Almanac was still being edited by its founder, Robert B. Thomas. The story goes that, in 1815, Thomas came down with a bad case of the flu and had to take to his bed, just at the time copy for the 1816 Almanac was due at the printer. Short on time and patience, someone (either a whimsical printer's devil sent to fetch the copy or the delirious Thomas himself) filled in the weather prediction for mid-July to read, "Rain, hail, and snow."

When Thomas discovered the "error," he recalled all (or at least most of) the copies of the 1816 edition and ordered the whole thing reprinted—this time with safer forecasts, such as "sultry with thundershowers." But somehow word got out, and Thomas spent the next few months trying to live the story down.

In July and August of 1816, much to Thomas's (and everyone else's) amazement, rain, hail, and snow *did* fall in New England. Thomas, of course, calmly boasted that he had predicted it all along, but to this day no one (to our knowledge) has ever seen one of the fabled "snow" editions of 1816.

Apocryphal? Perhaps. But think what one of those editions would be worth today.

Robert B. Thomas and the (corrected) 1816 Almanac.

The House of Everlasting Fire

To thousands of native Hawaiians, Kilauea is the home of Pele, the fire goddess. To scientists, it's the laboratory of a lifetime.

According to legend, *the fire goddess Pele appears to Hawaiians as either an old woman or a beautiful young girl. How well she's treated by the people she meets determines how explosive her reaction will be.*

ONE OF THE MOST SPECTACULAR natural sights in America has to be the Kilauea (pronounced kill-a-WAY-ah) Crater on the big island of Hawaii. Sitting 10,000 feet below the summit of Mauna Loa, Kilauea at first appears to be only a subsidiary crater on the southeast flank of its larger neighbor. But scientists consider it a volcano in its own right, and since 1912 they have operated the Hawaiian Volcano Observatory near the lip of the summit caldera (volcanic crater), making the mountain perhaps the most studied peak in the world.

Kilauea's low elevation above sea level (4,090 feet) can be misleading. Rising from a base some 15,000 feet beneath the waves, the volcanic seamounts that have risen one by one from the ocean floor to form the Hawaiian Islands are really some of the loftiest mountains on earth. The Hawaiian volcanoes are unlike most others. Scientists believe that the magma that formed Hawaii, and that continues to feed the active volcanoes there, comes from an unusual stationary "hot spot" located 25 to 40 miles beneath the earth's surface, circulating an almost endless supply of hot material from its deep reserves of molten rock. As the great Pacific plate moves toward Asia at the rate of about four inches a year, it drifts over this hot spot, snuffing out the fires of old volcanoes and bringing new ones (such as Kilauea) to life.

Another aspect of Hawaii's volcanoes that separates them from their fellows around the globe is the relatively gentle nature of their eruptions. Thousands of lava flows have gradually built up, layer upon layer, to form broad, flat, shield-type volcanoes such as Mauna Loa. Unlike the sudden, violent eruptions characteristic of places such as Mount St. Helens, Hawaiian volcanoes have a style all their own. Eruptions usually begin with a spectacular show, as fountains of lava spray out of fissures in the earth, sometimes to a height of 500

The Kilauea crater—"Pele's living room."

Dramatic and beautiful curtains of lava called "fire fountains" usually signal the beginning of an eruptive cycle. The sheets of flame shoot upward, sometimes to a height of 500 feet or more.

feet or more, forming a brilliant curtain of fire. Huge volumes of lava are usually released in the first few days of an eruption, and the lava fountains continue their pyrotechnic display until most of the volcanic gases have been released. At this point, they subside, and the magma continues to ooze out of a vent farther downhill along a rift.

Compared to a volcano like Mount St. Helens, Kilauea is a geologic pussycat, usually giving fair warning so that people have plenty of time to get out of its way. This volcanic style has a lot to do with the character of Kilauea's magma. Many volcanoes, such as Mount St. Helens, have stiff or sticky magma that traps expanding gases inside until they explode violently in a sudden burst of energy, flinging out ash and rock in what scientists call a *pyroclastic blast* (pyroclastic means "broken fire"). Hawaiian lava, by contrast, is thin and fluid, allowing gases to bubble to the surface and escape.

That's not to say that Kilauea is always so mild mannered. Some explosive eruptions have occurred over the years due to ground water seeping into a vent as the magma drains out. When the two mix, the water flashes into steam and explodes, resulting in what volcanologists call a *phreatic eruption*. In 1790, the summit of the mountain was buried under 30 feet of pyroclastic debris, and 80 Hawaiian warriors who were traversing the flank of the mountain were suffocated by the hot gas. Some say their footprints are still visible in the

FOR THE RECORD

IN THE FIRST SIX YEARS OF ITS latest eruption (1983 to 1989), Kilauea Crater disgorged an estimated 850 million cubic meters of lava—enough to pave a highway that would circle the earth four times.

ash deposits. In May of 1924, another phreatic eruption formed a tremendous dust cloud four miles high, with one eight-ton boulder blown three-quarters of a mile from the lava pit.

The most fascinating and unusual feature of Kilauea is the bubbling lava lake that periodically fills within its caldera. Hawaiians call this molten lake Halemaumau, "the house of everlasting fire," and according to their religious tradition, it is the home of Pele, the goddess of fire. The lake can expand, shrink, or even disappear altogether following a flank eruption on the mountain, but even if it stays around for years, it can maintain a temperature of around 1,800°F at its surface. Roughly 1,300 feet deep, the lake's

Many Hawaiians consider *Kilauea part of Pele's body, and leave offerings to the goddess at the edge of the caldera's lava pit. Here, demonstrators protest a geothermal power project designed to harness the volcano's energy.*

level rises and falls within its circular "fire pit," sometimes overflowing the depression as the magma rises from below and the mountain swells.

On the morning of January 1, 1983, just after midnight, Kilauea began sending out the familiar signs of another impending eruption: earthquake swarms, a low-frequency volcanic tremor, and the subsidence of the summit (indicating that magma was moving from underneath the caldera toward a volcanic rift on the mountainside). Two days later, on January 3, lava fountains began their display in the remote Napay Crater, in the East Rift Zone.

Over the next few years, geologists watched as Kilauea slipped into a pattern of eruption—lava fountains that lasted for several hours or days alternating with rest periods, during which the magma welled up beneath the caldera on the summit. The instruments used to measure the rising and falling of the mountain itself are called *tilt meters,* which work in much the same way as an extremely sensitive carpenter's level. By measuring when the volcano is "out of plumb"—inflating or deflating between eruptive episodes—scientists can predict fairly accurately what Kilauea is about to do next.

But predicting what a volcano might do next is a far cry from being able to control it, or to mitigate the damage it might cause. Most people think of volcanoes merely as a destructive force, but in Hawaii the issue is more ambiguous. After all, the islands wouldn't exist were it not for volcanic eruptions. Since the first stirrings of its current activity in 1983, Kilauea has sent tongues of fire lapping over 30 square miles of land—burning more than 160 homes, burying a highway, and spreading a blanket of basaltic lava over everything in their path. But the mountain also has added some 400,000 square meters to the island of Hawaii as the lava flows down to meet the sea.

An engineer checks a tilt meter, which monitors the subtle swelling and subsidence of a volcano— and indicates when an eruption may be near at hand. This one is located near Mt. St. Helens.

To the thousands of native Hawaiians who still practice the old ways, the mountain represents Pele, the fire goddess incarnate, and her home at Kilauea is considered hallowed ground. At Hawaii Volcanoes National Park, dozens of worshipers every day bring gifts to Halemaumau—known as "Pele's living room"—to propitiate the goddess. Flowers, incense, meat, and rocks wrapped in ti leaves are left beside the lava pit. Believers say that Pele sometimes appears to humans in the guise of an old woman or a beautiful girl. The hospitality she receives from the people she meets determines whether she is appeased or angered, and hence dictates the severity of the eruption.

A number of visitors to the park have experienced the wrath of Pele when they've tried to remove rocks or black sand from her domain. Almost every day, park rangers receive a few packages containing souvenirs from the volcano that have brought the pilferers nothing but bad luck. Not ones to tempt fate themselves, the rangers return the stolen items to the volcano.

888   LLAO CLIFF (1997 FT.) AND WIZARD ISLAND, CRATER LAKE, OREGON

HARWOOD PHOTO

5A-H1445

The secretive worship surrounding Pele might have remained only a curiosity to the outside world had it not been for a controversy that erupted during the time that Kilauea was brewing in the mid-1980s. A plan to build geothermal power plants in the volcano's East Rift Zone drew sharp criticism from Pele's worshipers, who contend that every part of the mountain is a part of Pele's body and that harnessing power for energy is sacrilege, interfering with the goddess and their First Amendment right to worship her. The Supreme Court of Hawaii heard the case in 1987 and decided for the state and against the worshipers. The following year, the U.S. Supreme Court refused to hear the case, and that, it seemed, was that.

But environmental advocates have raised new concerns about the threat to the Wao Kele o Puna ("the green forest of Puna"), a 27,000-acre parcel that represents much of the last tropical rain forest in the United States. Although the state and the energy company developing the site maintain that only a small fraction of the forest would need to be developed to generate the 500 megawatts of power planned by the year 2007, opponents argue that the noise of the wells and the stench of hydrogen sulfide gas could upset the fragile ecosystem.

For all the attempts to harness her power and defend her honor, Pele may yet have the last word in the debate. Some Pele worshipers note that the mountain began erupting on the same day the geothermal permits were filed. But no matter how Hawaiians look at their volcano—as a natural deity or a natural power source—Kilauea will remain the great builder and destroyer, determining the fate of humans and not the other way around. ■

FOR THE RECORD

THE DEEPEST LAKE IN THE United States (some 2,000 feet) is Oregon's Crater Lake, all that remains of a massive prehistoric volcano that has been dubbed Mount Mazama. When Mount Mazama erupted violently 7,000 years ago, the whole top of the mountain collapsed to form the huge caldera, which measures six miles in diameter.

Welcome to the inferno.
Lava flowing from Hawaii's Mauna Loa volcano lights up the night sky on December 27, 1935.

The Day We Bombed Hawaii

The lava was flowing, and the city was directly in its path. Then they called in the Air Corps.

NOTHING SEEMS AS INEXORABLE as molten lava flowing out of a volcano. It runs, you run, and everything left in its path—houses, trees, even whole towns—becomes a burnt offering to the fire gods.

But back in 1931, Dr. Thomas Jaggar, director of the Hawaiian Volcano Observatory, came up with a novel idea for steering a lava flow away from inhabited areas: Bomb the heck out of it. By 1934, Jaggar had plotted the recent history of eruptions for the Mauna Loa volcano and predicted another major lava flow sometime in the next two years. Then he had sat back and waited to test his hypothesis.

Right on schedule, molten lava started flowing from the north flank of the mountain on November 21, 1935, just where Jaggar expected it would. On December 22, the lava, which had been pooling harmlessly in the saddle that lies between Mauna Loa and Mauna Kea, suddenly turned toward the coastal city of Hilo, about 20 miles away. Jaggar decided to call for an air strike.

The type of lava called *pahoehoe* (pa-HOY-HOY) by Hawaiians develops a skinlike surface as its porous outer layer cools in the open air. This crust covers the still-liquid lava inside, building a roof and walls that insulate the flow. Jaggar reasoned that if a bomb were to break through the walls and roof of the flow, side flows would spread out in different directions, and the lava would be diverted or stopped in its tracks. The basic idea wasn't new, but the use of air power was.

On December 27, the U.S. Air Corps Bombing Squadron from Honolulu dropped twenty 600-pound bombs at two points in the lava channel. Already the lava had traveled five miles, one-quarter of the way to Hilo. At noon on the 27th, the flow had been moving at 800 feet per hour; by noon the next day, the lava had slowed to 44 feet per hour; and by 6 P.M., the lava flow had stopped completely. Hilo had been saved.

Some skeptics said that the lava probably would have stopped without the bombing, but Jaggar repeated his experiment in 1942 with essentially the same results— once again using weapons of war to save human lives. ■

As director of the Hawaiian *Volcano Observatory, volcanologist Dr. Thomas A. Jaggar called in an air strike in an attempt to save Hilo.*

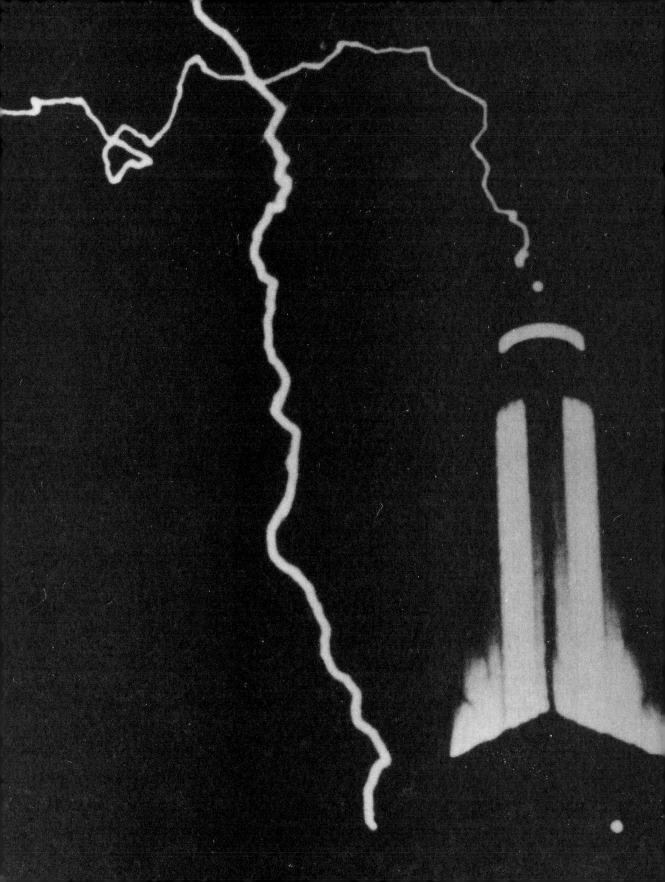

LIGHTNING

ALMOST NOTHING IN NATURE can match the awesome power and beauty of a thunderstorm. Nothing beats watching a real rip-snorter from the safety of the house, and few things are as frightening as being caught outdoors when the wind whips the trees, the bolts flash down, the thunder crackles and rolls, and the dog hides under the porch.

No wonder, then, that nearly every culture on earth has considered lightning something special. In many early religions, the sky god reigned supreme, and thunderbolts were his emblem of absolute power over heaven and earth. We even have a day of the week—Thursday, or "Thor's day"—named after the Norse thunder god.

Every second, about 100 lightning bolts strike the earth; that amounts to somewhere between eight and nine million strikes per day. Fortunately, the earth is an awfully big place, and you're about as likely to get hit by lightning as you are to win a big lottery jackpot. That may put your mind at ease, as long you don't think too much about it. After all, somebody *does* win the lottery. . . . ∎

Lightning strikes one of its favorite targets—New York's Empire State Building—in November of 1930.

Drama on Mount Whitney

Caught in a violent thunderstorm, the hikers raced for the only shelter they could find—a refuge that for one of them proved fatal.

AT AN ELEVATION OF 14,496 FEET, the peak of California's Mount Whitney is the highest in the Lower 48 states. The spectacular view from the summit stretches westward over Sequoia National Park and the Great Western Divide. Hikers from all over the world come to the Sierra Nevada range to climb this mountain—to escape the pressures of modern life, to reconnect with the wilderness, or just for the challenge and exercise of reaching the top.

On Friday evening, July 13, 1990, four friends left Huntington Beach, a southern suburb of Los Angeles, on a journey to the High Sierras. For Matthew Nordbrock, 26, and his roommate Jim Swift, 24, the weekend trip was fairly typical; they and their two other friends, Kent Kroener and Steven Hellman, both 23, often went cycling or on other excursions together. Another roommate, Joseph Cotti, was working that weekend and had to stay behind.

Almost everybody liked Matthew Nordbrock, who worked as a credit analyst for a company in Lynwood. Athletic and gregarious, he had a good sense of humor that helped him make friends easily. But as they drove out of Huntington Beach that Friday evening, none of Nordbrock's companions could have dreamed that, less than 24 hours later, they would be struggling to save his life as well as fighting for their own.

Around 10 or 11 on Saturday morning, the four hikers broke camp and began their ascent of Mount Whitney. Other groups of hikers had already started up the mountain, including James MacLeod, 24, and his brother Glen, 37, of Long Beach, who had slept in their car Friday night with a friend, Calif Tervo, 44, of San Diego. At around 8 A.M., the three men passed Whitney Portal, the mountain's eastern trailhead, and began the winding, 10.6-mile climb to the summit. The day was clear and hot, fine weather for hiking. By mid-afternoon, the trio had climbed nearly three-quarters of the way up the mountain when they noticed clouds beginning to form over the distant peaks. A little before 5:30 P.M., as they approached the summit, a thunderstorm struck in all its fury.

"We heard thunder at a distance, but we didn't think much of it at the time," James MacLeod recalled later in an interview with the *Los Angeles Times.* "When it started raining, our first thought was to get dry."

Thunder in the morning signifies wynde; about noon, rayne; in the evening, a great tempest.

As rain and hail began to fall, the three looked around for any shelter they could find. Close to the summit, they saw an old stone building with a corrugated metal roof and immediately headed for it. They couldn't believe their luck. Ten other hikers in the vicinity, including Matthew Nordbrock and his friends, had the same idea.

The stone cabin they fled toward was known as the old Smithsonian hut, built in 1909 to house equipment for a group of scientists who were working on the summit. Like people who run under tall trees to stay dry during a downpour, the 13 hikers acted instinctively when they sought out the shelter. Outside, the thunder and lightning were pounding the summit, and it seemed that any haven was better than none.

Hikers from around *the world flock to California's Mount Whitney—at 14,496 feet, the highest peak in the Lower 48 states.*

A helicopter crew evacuates *survivors from Mount Whitney on Sunday, July 15, 1990—the day after a fierce thunderstorm hit the summit, killing one hiker.*

Even as Matthew Nordbrock ran for cover, he joked with his friends that he had nothing to fear. "I've been hit by lightning before, so I won't get struck," he said, according to Jim Swift.

More than ten years earlier, Nordbrock and his younger brother had been sitting in a rowboat on a lake in Arizona's White Mountains when a thunderstorm came upon them suddenly. A bolt of lightning flashed close by, temporarily stunning them, but only one of the boys, who was wearing wire-rimmed glasses, had been seriously hurt. On the summit of Mount Whitney, Nordbrock took heart from the fact that he had survived that previous experience. What he didn't stop to consider was that *he* was now the one who was wearing glasses with metal frames.

Inside the stone hut, the 13 hikers huddled together as the storm rumbled outside. E.J. Wueherer, 32, from Tehachapi, California, was one of those in the cabin. He remembered later that the group began to talk about whether the metal-roofed structure was really the safest place to be during the thunderstorm.

"It actually seemed to be abating," Wueherer said after the storm. "I was figuring, 'Oh, it's over.' " Just then, the bolt struck.

The lightning scored a direct hit on the stone house, coursing through its frame and making the floor crackle with electricity. Everyone suddenly felt pain and numbness in their legs. A moment later, as they realized they had been hit, they looked around the hut and saw two bodies lying on the floor.

James MacLeod remembers sitting with his back to the wall of the cabin as he talked to the other hikers. The next thing he remembers are the faces of his companions staring down at him and asking him questions. He'd been knocked out by the force of the blow, and they told him that he had been unconscious for more than 20 minutes.

Doctors later told MacLeod that the lightning had entered his right shoulder, leaving a circular wound four inches in diameter, and had exited his body in at least a dozen places, where it also left the unmistakable marks of its passage. "It's unbelievable what it did to me," MacLeod later told a reporter from the *Los Angeles Times*. "Every article of clothing I have has holes in it, except my shoes. Every muscle in my body must have contracted. I'm sore all over."

MacLeod's life may have been saved by the quick actions of his companions, who, after the shock of the lightning strike, started to administer cardiopulmonary resuscitation (CPR) to him and to Matthew Nordbrock, the other hiker who lay unconscious on the floor. MacLeod recovered quickly, but for the next five hours, the group worked feverishly over Nordbrock in a desperate attempt to keep him alive.

In a living human body, there are no preferred pathways for lightning. The bolt courses through tissue at speeds of 90,000 miles per second, so fast that victims often don't suffer much permanent internal damage from what doctors call fourth-degree burns. The main threat usually comes from the powerful electric current, which can paralyze the respiratory center of the brain and cause every muscle in the body to contract—including the heart, which stops its coordinated, continuous beating. By administering CPR to a lightning victim, a person performing first aid can sometimes

TEST YOUR LIGHTNING KNOWLEDGE

1. In which direction does forked lightning travel?
   a. up
   b. down
   c. in both directions

2. What kind of clouds are the most common source of thunderstorms?
   a. altocumulus
   b. stratocumulus
   c. cumulonimbus
   d. cirrus

3. In arid and semiarid climates, clouds tend to be higher above the earth, and forked lightning is less common than in other areas. In such regions, about what percentage of lightning bolts makes it to the ground?
   a. less than 5 percent
   b. less than 20 percent
   c. less than 40 percent
   d. less than 50 percent

ANSWERS: 1. c. A faintly visible forked channel called a stepped leader stretches down from the thundercloud until it induces a streamer of positive charge to rise from the earth to meet it. As soon as the two connect and form a pathway, the bright return stroke shoots up from the ground to the cloud in what we see as the brilliant flash of lightning. 2. c. A cumulonimbus is a towering cloud made up of individual cells. It rises thousands of feet in the air until it flattens out on top like an anvil. Temperature gradients of as much as 100°F have been recorded between the top and bottom of these clouds, which is one reason icy particles within them begin to separate and become charged, creating ideal conditions for lightning. 3. b. Although forked lightning in the desert is rarer than in other places, it is often quite spectacular. When the lightning strikes, it can melt sand into glassy ribbons called fulgurites, which are usually an inch or so in diameter and a few feet long.

When caught
by a tempest
wherever it be,
if it lightens and
thunders beware of
a tree.

get the victim's heart and lungs to begin functioning again on their own. Sometimes, with luck, the person struck by lightning will recover. But Matthew Nordbrock was not one of the lucky ones. Doctors later said that his metal-rimmed glasses may have been one of the reasons he died and the others lived.

As his companions tried to keep Nordbrock alive, other hikers in the hut decided to go for help. Calif Tervo and Morgan Milligan, 35, began hiking down the trail to Whitney Portal, but Tervo's legs still felt numb, and he couldn't keep up. Milligan raced on ahead, arriving at Whitney Portal around 6:30 P.M. A few minutes earlier, Tervo had encountered on the mountain a group of Girl Scouts, who used a radio they were carrying to call for help. A passing jetliner picked up their signal and radioed the message to Los Angeles air traffic controllers, who in turn relayed it to the Inyo County Sheriff's Department around 6:15.

Later that evening, a helicopter evacuated Nordbrock, Swift, and James MacLeod to the Southern Inyo Hospital in Lone Pine, where Nordbrock was pronounced dead. The remaining eight hikers, suffering from muscular aches and first- and second-degree burns, spent the night together in the stone house, crowding close together for warmth as the temperature dropped and a light snow dusted the summit. The next morning, more helicopters arrived and evacuated the hikers, ending their long ordeal.

Considering the violence of the storm and the number of people exposed to the lightning, rescuers said that it was fortunate that only one person had died. Although they were glad to be alive, however, Matthew Nordbrock's friends and the other hikers couldn't help second-guessing the personal decisions they had made at the summit that fateful afternoon.

"It all makes sense, in retrospect," E.J. Wueherer reflected in an interview with the *Los Angeles Times.* "We were asking for trouble. We were on the highest mountain, in a metal-roofed cabin, at the peak, in the middle of a rainstorm. What did we think was going to happen?

"I know now." ∎

A Superstition Ends

O N APRIL 15, 1718, a total of 24 churches of St. Pol de Leon in Brittany, France, started ringing bells to keep away lightning. All were struck. The six churches whose bells were not ringing were not struck. Thus ended a superstition.

The Father of the Lightning Rod

MOST AMERICANS REMEMBER Benjamin Franklin first and foremost as one of our nation's founders. In fact, Franklin was active in many endeavors, from philosophy to printing. One of the most enduring contributions this Renaissance man made to the world was the little piece of metal that protects your home from lightning.

In his *Poor Richard's Almanack* for 1753, Franklin published a little notice titled "How to Secure Houses, &c. from Lightning." The inventor went on to experiment with lightning rods on his own house and on those of fellow Philadelphians. In 1760, when the Philadelphia home of a merchant named William West was hit during a thunderstorm, the "Franklin rod" performed just as Franklin had predicted, and the house remained unscathed.

Many people in Europe immediately hailed Franklin's invention, but others were skeptical or downright antagonistic to the idea. For one thing, church leaders didn't like the idea of protecting steeples from lightning, which was thought to come from God. Despite all evidence to the contrary (including the great number of churches that had been damaged or destroyed over the years), many clergymen couldn't believe that God would actually strike a house of worship.

Military authorities in Italy considered churches to be so secure from lightning that they stored large quantities of explosives in their vaults. In 1767, a cache of 100 tons of gunpowder ignited when lightning struck the church of St. Nazaire in Brescia. In the huge explosion that followed, 3,000 people died and one-sixth of the city was destroyed. Suddenly, Franklin's modest invention didn't seem so foolish.

We tend to take the lightning rod pretty much for granted these days. So the next time you hear thunder overhead, think of Ben Franklin, whose simple yet brilliant invention is still keeping us safe today.

In 1752, Ben Franklin *performed his famous kite experiment, proving once and for all that lightning is a kind of electricity—and that kites are not only for kids.*

Yule logs provide good cheer at Christmastime and good luck year round.

1. Rekindle the Christmas spirit. In Germany and many other parts of Europe, the burning of a huge block of oak, called the yule log, is a time-honored Christmas tradition. Like many common rites, this one predates Christianity, and it may have had some connection with the ancient Aryan creed, which associated the oak tree with the all-powerful god of thunder.

In parts of Westphalia, in Germany, the custom called for withdrawing the yule log from the fire as soon as it became slightly charred. From then on, it was kept in the house throughout the following year and placed on the fire during thunderstorms. The people believed that lightning would never strike a house in which the yule log was smoldering.

2. Wear some bay leaves. Just as oaks (a symbol of the thunder god) were thought to get hit by lightning more often than other trees, the bay laurel *(Laurus nobilis)* was thought to be immune to the deadly stroke. Roman generals wore laurel wreaths when they entered the Eternal City in triumph, to protect them from the jealous anger of the god Jove. The emperor Tiberius wore laurel whenever a thunderstorm threatened (though Augustus preferred a sealskin coat). And the ancient prac-

The Roman emperor Tiberius—wearing his leafy lucky charm.

tice of awarding the laurel wreath to champions in athletic competitions (as is still done at the annual Boston Marathon) probably stems from the same belief.

3. Go to sleep. The ancient historian Plutarch believed that the body of a sleeping person was "loose" and lifeless, offering no resistance to lightning, which could pass right through without hurting the sleeper. Many others have believed that anyone who was asleep was protected from lightning's harm.

4. Carry a lucky charm.

French peasants used to carry thunderstones (or *pierres de tonnerre*) in their pockets to ward off lightning. When they heard thunder, they would recite this little verse: *Pierre, pierre, garde moi de la tonnerre* (Stone, stone, protect me from the thunder).

It was thought that these thunderstones (small oblong pieces of rock) were the spearheads of spent lightning bolts. After thunderstorms, people used to comb the fields for the objects, which actually may have been Stone Age artifacts. As recently as the 1870s, German soldiers carried thunderstones *(donnerkeile)* into battle, convinced that the stones would make them impenetrable to bullets.

5. Ring a bell.

In medieval Europe, church bells were cast with the Latin inscription *Fulgura Frango,* "I break up the lightning strokes." Bell ringers reported to church steeples during thunderstorms in an attempt to disperse the lightning, and this dubious practice continued in some places well into the eighteenth century.

No one records whether bell ringers received hazard pay for this job, but they certainly deserved it. One eighteenth-century book records no fewer than 386 church steeples receiving direct hits in one 33-year period, killing a total of 103 bell ringers. Finally, in 1786, the city of Paris made bell ringing during thunderstorms illegal, determining the issue to be a matter of public safety.

A "bell-glass preserve," to guard against lightning.

Mayday at 5,000 Feet

"Mayday, mayday, mayday. Clipper 214 out of control. Here we go."

In addition to getting *weather information from air traffic controllers, commercial airplanes now carry onboard radar that can track nearby thunderstorms.*

N THE LATE EVENING OF December 8, 1963, over Elkton, Maryland, Pan Am Flight 214 was in a holding pattern, awaiting clearance to land at Philadelphia International Airport, where a thunderstorm with gusty surface winds made landing treacherous.

At around 8:51 P.M., the flight crew of the Boeing 707 informed the Philadelphia tower that they were ready to start their approach as soon as the squall had passed. Then, at 8:59, Philadelphia controllers received another message: "Mayday, mayday, mayday. Clipper 214 out of control. Here we go." And nothing more. A few seconds later, the first officer of a National Airlines plane flying 1,000 feet above Flight 214 reported, "Clipper 214 is going down in flames."

The Pan Am plane crashed in open country east of Elkton, instantly killing all 81 persons on board and scattering debris over an area four miles long and one mile wide. Many people who witnessed the accident reported seeing a strong lightning flash, a glowing ball at the end of the flash, and then the airliner hurtling toward the ground in flames.

Following an investigation, the Civil Aeronautics Board decided that lightning had indeed caused the tragedy, damaging the left wing tip of the plane and somehow igniting fumes from the fuel vent and the left reserve fuel tank, which caused a fire and explosion. As a result of the tragedy, one of the fuels that the airliner was using, called JP-4, was banned from use on commercial flights, and extra design features were recommended to make planes safer from direct lightning strikes.

Lightning frequently strikes airplanes, usually running from nose to tail or from wing tip to wing tip and then discharging into the air. Normally the bolts cause only minor damage. As a precaution, however, commercial airliners now carry onboard radar that tracks thunderstorms nearby, as well as sophisticated systems to vent excess fumes from partially filled tanks during flight.

According to the National Transportation Safety Board (NTSB), the odds that lightning could cause another disaster like that aboard Flight 214 are extremely remote. The real danger from thunderstorms comes from wind shear, intense bursts of cold air that are found beneath the bellies of storm clouds. Wind shear can catch a descending plane in a strong tail wind, then switch directions and act as a head wind, forcing the plane down swiftly as it loses its lift. The phenomenon has been blamed for several airline disasters in recent years, including the following:

• **July 9, 1982.** Pan Am Flight 759 crashed after takeoff in Kenner, Louisiana, outside New Orleans, killing 145 people on board and eight people on the ground.

• **August 2, 1985.** A Delta Air Lines jumbo jet crashed on its final approach to Dallas–Fort Worth International Airport, killing 133 people, including one man on the ground who was decapitated when the plane struck his car.

In each case, witnesses reported lightning struck the plane before it crashed, but officials cited wind shear as the primary cause of the disaster. ■

If there be sheet lightning with a clear sky on spring, summer, or autumn evenings, expect heavy rain.

Lightning May Be Man's Best Friend

*Lighting may have been responsible for the first life on
earth. But what has it done for us lately?*

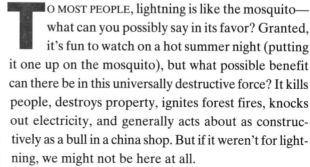

TO MOST PEOPLE, lightning is like the mosquito—
what can you possibly say in its favor? Granted,
it's fun to watch on a hot summer night (putting
it one up on the mosquito), but what possible benefit
can there be in this universally destructive force? It kills
people, destroys property, ignites forest fires, knocks
out electricity, and generally acts about as construc-
tively as a bull in a china shop. But if it weren't for lightning, we might not be here at all.

According to scientists, the earth is about 4.5 billion years old, but the oldest fossil remains date only from about 3.8 billion years ago. In the 700 million years that intervened, lightning may have played a crucial role as the spark that created life on earth.

In the early years of our planet, the earth's atmosphere bore little resemblance to what we now think of as air. Methane, carbon dioxide, and hydrogen, as well as ammonia and water vapor, were all present in abundance, but it was lightning that provided the energy to form complex organic chemicals in the air. These chemicals rained down on the oceans as amino acids and other molecules, which in turn became proteins, then one-celled organisms, and then, a few billion years later, became ingrates like us who complain that our golf game has been canceled due to lightning.

In 1953, Harold Urey and Stanley Miller performed an experiment at the University of Chicago that attempted to simulate lightning's effect on the earth's early atmospheric gases. Eventually, they discovered a dark-colored liquid in their closed environment: Amino acids had precipitated into their own little primordial soup, simulating the earth's oceans at an early age. Lightning, Urey and Miller concluded, could have acted as the catalyst for all life as we know it.

Okay, so we're alive, but what has lightning done for us lately? Here are a few examples of the important roles lightning plays.

• **Lightning as farmer.** Nitrogen now represents about 80 percent of the gases in our atmosphere, and lightning works with the nitrogen to produce a kind of fertilizer in the air. As a lightning stroke heats the air around it, the energy combines nitrogen and oxygen molecules into nitrous oxide, a water-soluble chemical that plants can use for growth. The rain that usually accompanies lightning delivers this natural fertilizer to the soil as dilute nitric acid (which is what causes that pungent, tinny odor you smell in the air during a thunderstorm). The amount of fertilizer produced is small but significant. In areas of heavy thunderstorm activity, it can be the equivalent of five pounds of fertilizer per acre per year.

Journeying in Tropical Florida

FOR THE RECORD

SOUTHERN FLORIDA HAS the greatest amount of thunderstorm activity in the continental United States, with an average of 80 to 90 thunderstorm-days per year. The region with the fewest thunderstorm-days is the Pacific Coast, averaging fewer than ten a year.

The difference is in the two climates. Southern Florida has generally hot and humid weather, whereas the West Coast stays fairly dry throughout the summer.

Not surprisingly, the places on earth that see the greatest number of thunderstorms include the world's tropical rain forests. The city of Bogor, in Indonesia, holds the world's record with 322 thunderstorm-days per year. (Planning a picnic there must be really frustrating.)

Flash

BEING STRUCK BY LIGHTNING IS not always a tragedy. In the world of comic book superheroes, it can be quite a boon. Barry Allen was a mild-mannered scientist who was working late one night when a bolt of lightning struck him through an open window. The chemicals he was working with exploded all around him, and the combination of chemicals and electricity transformed him into "Flash: The Fastest Man Alive." Like most superheroes, Flash spends his life fighting crime and rescuing maidens in distress—a definite step up from all those late nights in the lab.

• **Lightning as electrician.** Most of us incorrectly assume that the earth is stable and neutral, but in regions of fair weather, the voltage between the earth and its electrosphere (located about 30 miles above the surface) amounts to some 300,000 volts. To maintain this voltage, the earth holds a negative charge on its surface, with an equal positive charge being distributed throughout the atmosphere.

Where the weather is fair, atmospheric currents continually drain the earth's negative charge. As early as 1887, researchers determined that the earth would lose all of its charge in less than an hour if it were not continually renewed. When lightning strikes the ground, it helps keep things in balance. About 1,800 thunderstorms occur worldwide every hour, sending enough electricity to the ground in that time to equal the total charge of the earth. According to lightning expert Martin Uman of the University of Florida at Gainesville, thunderstorms around the world act "as a kind of battery to keep the fine weather system charged."

• **Lightning as forester.** Forest and brush fires started by lightning blacken millions of acres annually, but they also perform an essential function in maintaining and renewing a natural mosaic of plant species. Our attitudes toward fire and our ideas of wilderness have changed over the years, but in recent times, fire ecology has become an accepted practice in our national parks. When "natural fire" in the form of lightning strikes (as it did at Yellowstone National Park a few years ago), forest managers tend to let the fires burn with minimal interference. Burning the thick underbrush and opening up space in the wilderness, natural fires caused by lightning actually benefit many fire-dependent species, such as the jack pine and the giant sequoia.

So lighten up on lightning. It can be a minor inconvenience, sure, but a little common sense will usually keep you safely out of harm's way. Once you're out of the elements, make some popcorn and settle in to watch the show—which just may have been the original warm-up act for life on earth. ■

Silver Linings

MOST PEOPLE WHO have survived being hit by lightning consider themselves lucky just to be alive. But in 1980, a bolt from the heavens blessed one man in an extraordinary and miraculous way.

In February 1971, Edwin Robinson of Falmouth, Maine, jackknifed his truck while trying to avoid hitting a skidding car on an icy overpass. His head went through the back window of the truck, and he suffered severe damage to the occipital area of his brain. Over the next few months, Robinson began to lose his eyesight. Gradually, he became completely blind and so deaf that he had to wear a hearing aid. During the next nine years, he learned Braille and coped as well as he could with his disability.

On June 4, 1980, Robinson walked out into his yard with his aluminum cane and began clucking for his pet chicken, to get her in out of the rain. As he walked underneath a poplar tree, he felt "like somebody cracked a whip over my head." The bolt of lightning knocked him face-down on the ground, where he lay unconscious for 20 minutes. When he regained consciousness, he felt very tired and went back inside the house to lie down.

After he got up from his nap, he went into the kitchen for a sandwich. Suddenly, he remarked to his wife that he not only could see a plaque on the wall, but also could read what it said. His wife asked him if he could see the clock on the wall. He told her it was five o'clock.

Two days later, Robinson's sight had improved enough so that he could walk outside without a cane. His doctor pronounced the 62-year-old Robinson cured. He couldn't move his eyes, but his central vision and his hearing had both returned.

In a television interview, Robinson was asked how he felt after his ordeal. Pretty good, he admitted, except for a strange feeling in his scalp that felt like "whiskers on top of my head." Robinson's bald head had begun to grow a new crop of hair.

Edwin Robinson, the world's luckiest lightning victim.

Different Strokes for Different Folks

Sometimes looks can be *deceiving. What appears to be "black lightning" in this photograph may only be shadows of the bolts as seen against the clouds behind them.*

THE KIND OF LIGHTNING with which we're all familiar is the dramatic cloud-to-ground variety known as forked lightning. Some of us also have heard of ball lightning (see page 220). Closely related to these forms are a number of other electromagnetic phenomena, some quite rare and beautiful.

• **Heat lightning** or **sheet lightning** is actually regular lightning that lights up distant clouds. The reason you don't hear any thunder is that the clouds are so far away. The sound of thunder rarely carries more than 15 miles. Heat or sheet lightning usually doesn't bring rain immediately, but it indicates that unsettled weather is on the way.

- **Ribbon lightning** appears only infrequently, when strong winds blow a cloud-to-ground lightning channel for some distance between multiple strokes, so that each stroke in the flash is visibly separated.

- **Bead lightning,** another rarity, occurs when the lightning channel to the ground encounters some atmospheric obstacle and breaks up (or appears to, anyway) into glowing segments that look like beads or sausage links. The beads seem to persist longer than a normal lightning flash, usually for half a second or so.

- **Positive** or **top-of-cloud lightning** occurs when a single stroke shoots out from the top of the cloud and strikes the ground either ahead of or behind the main thundercloud. The reason thunderclouds have electrical potential is that a negative charge builds up in the lower part of the cloud and a positive charge builds up in its upper reaches. Almost always, ground flashes come from the bottom of the cloud, but occasionally they come from the top. Positive lightning strokes can be much larger and stronger than typical strokes, and for some reason, positive lightning is far more common in winter than in summer.

- **Clear-sky lightning** seems to strike as a "bolt from the blue," when there aren't any thunderclouds overhead. Usually this happens when a strong bolt shoots out from a storm several miles away. Under certain rare conditions, clear air can generate enough electricity to produce lightning, especially when triggered by an airborne object such as an airplane or a rocket.

- **St. Elmo's fire** is familiar to mariners, pilots, and mountain climbers. This spooky but harmless glow appears around high objects, such as the topmast of a ship or the wing tips of a plane. It forms when misty air ionizes around the tip of an object. As electrons from the surrounding air are pulled toward the area of positive charge, the air glows green.

St. Elmo (a corruption of the name Erasmus) was a fourth-century martyr. Just how he became a patron saint of sailors is unclear, but legend has it that Ferdinand Magellan's crew, mutinous and tired of stormy weather on their voyage around the world in 1519, saw St. Elmo's fire on their masts and spars and took it as a sign from heaven of calm seas ahead. ∎

Lightning in the south is a sign of drouth.

St. Elmo's fire reassured *Magellan's edgy crew, allowing the explorer to continue his circumnavigation of the globe.*

Great Balls of Fire

THE STARTLING APPEARance and behavior of ball lightning have terrified witnesses and perplexed scientists for centuries. In fact, many researchers steadfastly refuse to admit that such a thing as ball lightning exists, chalking it up as either an optical illusion or the product of overactive imaginations.

On rare occasions, people have reported sighting glowing spheres that drop out of the sky during or just after a violent thunderstorm. When they get near the ground, the balls seem to move horizontally, parallel to the ground,

Physicist Pyotr Kapitsa.

and sometimes meander hither and yon as if they had minds of their own. The size of these luminous orbs can be as small as a marble or as large as a basketball, and the color varies from red or orange all the way to blue and white. Reports of ball lightning inside buildings commonly refer to it as having entered through an open door or window or down the chimney, but it also has been seen coming straight through solid walls. There have been several accounts of ball lighting appearing inside metal airplanes.

The glowing ball usually moves around for a few seconds before it disappears with a loud bang. Some witnesses claim to have touched the ball and felt no heat, but one famous account describes the fireball as having entered a window and dropped into a cask of water, which it heated to boiling. Sometimes there are signs of damage, such as a charred piece of wood, but in other cases, the lightning vanishes without a trace.

A Russian physicist, Pyotr Kapitsa, was one who thought

Peasants having a ball.

that these reports were more than just folklore, and he spent considerable time trying to explain the nature of ball lightning and why it might exist. Kapitsa suggested that the balls were composed of plasma, ionized atoms similar to the air found in a lighting channel. Somehow, he believed, these atoms were stimulated by radio waves and began to emit light.

A few years later, scientists discovered a way to produce something like ball lightning in the laboratory using microwave radiation. The only trouble was that the balls disappeared as soon as the power was shut off. In nature, no one has yet been able to explain what causes ball lightning and how it can stick around—hanging fire—for such a long time.

Misogynists Prefer Mondays

N HIS *Prognostication everlasting of ryghte good effect,* an English author named Digges presented the then-common interpretation of thunder's various and complicated prophecies, all dependent on which day of the week it was heard. (Hint: Unless you're a confirmed misanthrope, pray for Thursday.) Digges wrote:

"Some wryte (their ground I see not) that Sondaye's thundre should brynge the death of learned men, judges, and others: Mondaye's thundre, the death of women: Tuesdaye's thundre, the death of harlottes, and other blodshede: Thursdaye's thundre, plentie of shepe and corne: Fridaye's thundre, the slaughter of a great man, and other horrible murders: Saturdaye's thundre, a generall pestilent plague and great deathe."

Before braving the elements, make sure that it's your lucky day.

One More Reason King Kong Should Never Have Left the Ground

WHO CAN FORGET THE IMAGE of King Kong climbing the Empire State Building, actress Fay Wray clutched in his giant hands, in the 1933 movie that was named for him? Climbing the skyscraper was a bad move on the part of the huge ape, but his fate could have been even more dramatic if someone had checked the weather statistics. It turns out the Empire State Building is struck by lightning nearly once every other week on average. Maybe it's a good thing the filmmakers didn't know that.

King Kong, in one of his stormier moods.

If There's No Time to Count, You're Too Darn Close

HOW CAN YOU estimate the distance of an approaching storm? One way is to count the seconds between a flash of lightning and the thunder that accompanies it. A flash of lightning travels many miles instantly. Sound is much slower, taking five seconds to travel a mile. If the thunder lags ten seconds after the flash, the storm is 2 miles away. Fifteen seconds equals 3 miles. If no thunder follows the flash, the storm is probably more than 20 miles away.

It's lightning, by Jove.

Fatal Attractions

THE NATIONAL WEATHER Service has reported that in 1990 only 74 Americans died as a result of lightning, while 247 were injured. Extrapolating from those figures, your odds of getting fatally zapped are about 1 in 3 million. Just for comparison's sake, you have a 1 in 5,800 chance of dying in a traffic accident, a 1 in 39,000 chance of dying from a fall at home, and a 1 in 342,000 chance of perishing in an airplane crash.

Don't get too cocky, though; 1990 was a below-average year for lightning fatalities. The latest 20-year figures for lightning deaths put the average at 83 per year, although the number of people struck by lightning has been dropping since the turn of the century. The reason? More people have moved off the farm and away from rural areas into towns and cities, where they are less likely to be hit.

Much less likely, in fact. Of the 74 persons killed by lightning in 1990, 71 of them died outdoors. Only 1 victim was listed as being "in or near a house" when the fatal blow struck. Although the total number of lightning deaths has decreased steadily, the percentage of people hit while engaging in outdoor recreational activities has skyrocketed. Roughly 15 percent of all lightning victims are struck while standing under tall trees. Some people just never learn.

Be Careful What You Wish For (It Just Might Come True)

JAMES OTIS WAS A Massachusetts lawyer and legislator, a passionate advocate of colonial rights and a hero of the American Revolution. Otis often told his friends and family that when his time came, he wanted to die as a result of a bolt of lightning. His reasons for this preference remain obscure; he was probably just a flashy guy who wanted to make a memorable exit.

Whatever his motive, on May 23, 1783, Otis got his fondest wish. While he was leaning against a doorway at his home in Andover, Massachusetts, lightning struck the chimney, shot through the frame of the house, and killed him.

Lively James Otis.

RAIN, HAIL & ICE STORMS

IN ANCIENT SOCIETIES, the rainmaker was the most important official in the village, commanding even more respect than the king or chief (although sometimes he was one and the same person). Maintaining a steady supply of such a vital commodity as water required a full-time miracle worker, and people developed a wide array of rituals to summon clouds by means of either magic or religion. The Nootka Indians of British Columbia, for example, painted their faces black and then washed them, to represent rain dripping from black clouds.

Even in our own time, we still have an imperfect understanding of clouds and exactly what it takes to make them release their moisture. Cloud seeding from airplanes is the most recent (and definitely the most scientific) chapter in the long history of rainmaking, and it suggests that someday we may indeed be able to modify our weather—bringing rain to the desert, suppressing damaging hail and lightning, dissipating hurricanes before they hit land, and so on. Yet even with the latest technology, we have not advanced—from a practical standpoint—very much beyond face painting.

This presents a problem because, unfortunately, gentle rains aren't the only items produced by the liquid factories of storm clouds that race across our skies. Most raindrops begin their lives as ice crystals high up in the clouds, melting as they fall to the ground. But in the complex and turbulent world of weather, all kinds of frozen precipitation can combine to keep things interesting—from freezing rain that turns a superhighway into a skating rink to hailstones that crash to earth, flattening crops and shattering windows. Like Dr. Jekyll and Mr. Hyde, the clouds can come as either our friends or our destroyers. ■

Few things in nature can match the splendor—and sheer destructive power—of an ice storm.

When Hatfield Called, the Heavens Answered

From the Yukon to Honduras, many parched communities considered rainmaker Charles M. Hatfield "the real McCoy."

I N THE 1890s, CALIFORNIA was America's land of promise, and few communities were growing faster than San Diego. The city fathers, worried that the periodic droughts common to southern California would limit San Diego's expansion, decided in 1897 to build the Morena Dam 60 miles east of the city, in the mountains near the Mexican border. The dam's location was excellent, at the head of a small stream-fed lake between two canyon walls.

Despite the dam, the situation worsened in the next decade and a half, as concern about drought turned to alarm after several successive dry seasons, and in 1912 the San Diego Wide Awake Improvement Club first broached the topic of hiring a rainmaker. The city council scoffed at the idea, but the Wide Awakers insisted that their man, Charles Mallory Hatfield—the most famous rainmaker of his time—had proven his precipitation prowess. Near the town of Vista, where the Hatfields had settled, Charles and his younger brother Paul had built a 20-foot platform atop their windmill and started evaporating chemicals into the air one bright, sunny morning, causing (they claimed) the only rainstorm that day in all of California. And in 1904, when the Los Angeles Chamber of Commerce had offered Hatfield $50 to bring rain to that city, the former sewing-machine salesman had erected another tower in the hills near Pasadena and again sent his con-

coctions swirling into the air, promising rain in not less than three hours or more than five days. On the fourth day, it began to rain heavily, dropping well over an inch on downtown L.A. and even more in the foothills—much to the chagrin of George E. Franklin, the chief of the U.S. Weather Bureau in Los Angeles and one of Hatfield's harshest critics.

As Hatfield took to the lecture circuit with the discourse "How to Attract Moisture-Laden Atmosphere," his admirers took to calling him "Professor." His mother attributed his gift to some divine power, but his detractors maintained that there was nothing miraculous about his rainmaking abilities. On the contrary, they claimed, Hatfield carefully schooled

Left: Charles M. Hatfield *mixing his secret rain-making chemicals in 1919.* Above: *The Hatfield brothers' tower at Coalinga, California, in 1924.*

In 1916, Hatfield produced *so much rain that flooding brought down this San Diego bridge.*

himself in the weather records and rain cycles for every area he worked (mostly in California) and timed his "experiments" just before showers were logically scheduled to arrive.

By the time Charles Hatfield arrived on the scene, the "science" of rainmaking (or pluviculture, as it was later dubbed by educator David Starr Jordan) had become a hotly debated topic in the United States. Ever since the last years of the nineteenth century, when settlers farming the Great Plains had encountered serious drought conditions for the first time, most ordinary people (though few scientists) had been willing to listen to almost anyone who promised to produce rain. Some believed that artillery fire during battles caused rain to fall, while others claimed that prairie fires could create clouds and showers. Congress, pressured by western senators who hoped to bring more rain to their arid states, spent more than $20,000 testing the concussion, or "boom-boom," theory in Texas in 1891, exploding the theory along with the blasting powder. And a whole school of rainmakers using chemicals and electricity to produce rain—the so-called smell makers—plied their trade throughout the Midwest and the Great Plains, each one jealously guarding his own secret formula.

Despite Hatfield's many well-publicized "successes" (including an episode in the Yukon, where Canadian officials were at first hesitant to hire him, lest he tinker with Providence and flood the whole continent), San Diego balked. Finally, though, on December 8, 1915, Hatfield made the desiccated city an offer it couldn't refuse: to produce 40 inches of rain at Morena Dam at no expense. The city council agreed, and the next day Hatfield arrived, holding a carefully worded contract that read as follows:

I will fill the Morena Reservoir to overflowing between now and next December 20, 1916, for the sum of $10,000, in default of which I ask no compensation, or I will deliver at Morena Reservoir thirty inches of rain at no charge, you to pay me $500 per inch from the thirtieth inch to the fiftieth inch—all above fifty inches to be free—on or before the first of June, 1916. Or I will discharge forty inches during the next twelve months, free of charge, provided you pay me $1,000 per inch for all between forty and fifty inches, all above inches free.

The council chose to pay Hatfield the flat fee of $10,000 to fill the reservoir but decided not to sign the contract.

The Hatfield brothers constructed a 20-foot-high tower near Morena Dam, built a fire, and started to cook their chemicals, sending noxious fumes into the air on the inauspicious date of Friday the 13th of January 1916. (One earlier observer, commenting on what Hatfield had described as

Attention Shoppers: Snowstorm Approaching in the Frozen-Food Aisle

THE CHEMICAL COMPOUND most commonly used today to seed clouds and produce rain or snow is silver iodide, a substance also important in photography and medicine.

Bernard Vonnegut, a physicist who worked with Irving Langmuir and Vincent Schaefer at General Electric on cloud-seeding research in the 1940s (see page 231), decided to experiment with using silver iodide because its crystalline structure is the closest thing there is to ice crystals formed from water— with only about a 1 percent difference.

Pure silver iodide is far too expensive to throw to the winds, so Vonnegut developed a smoke generator that split the chemical into tiny crystals. When he tested the generator in his lab, the smoke reportedly drifted six miles and started a small snowstorm in the frozen-food section of a grocery store.

Unlike dry ice, silver iodide smoke doesn't have to be dispensed from an airplane. Today many rainmaking and snowmaking efforts burn the chemical in generators placed on the ground or atop towers, letting it waft upward into the clouds. Ironically, this is much the same technique that Charles Hatfield and the other "smell makers" used to coax precious water from the skies back in the early 1900s.

Rainmakers, Inc.

THE RAINMAKING CAPITAL of the United States, at least during the heyday of the industry in the 1890s, was Goodland, Kansas, a small farm town located in the western part of the state. Frank Melbourne, the famous "Australian rain doctor," had tried in vain to squeeze a few drops from the uncooperative clouds over Goodland in October 1891. Even though his attempts had failed, the hoopla that had accompanied his arrival inspired several local entrepreneurs and investors to form cloud-busting corporations of their own.

The first and largest of these was the Inter State Rain Company, which offered its stock to the public at a whopping $1,000 a share. The Goodland Artificial Rain Company and the Swisher Rain Company quickly followed suit and began selling their services to desperate, drought-stricken farmers. Most of the rainmaking was done in the local area, although Inter State worked as far west as California's San Joaquin Valley.

Not every customer was completely satisfied. When a Goodland Company rainmaker failed to produce even a heavy dew after five days of hard work in Minden, Nebraska, irate residents tied him to a telegraph pole, and the local fire brigade turned their hoses on him—a case of poetic frontier justice.

Hollywood's The Rainmaker, *with Burt Lancaster in the lead.*

the "mild odor" of the chemical brew, had compared it to the stench of a Limburger cheese factory: "These gases smell so bad that it rains in self-defense.") Early the next morning, a heavy overcast enveloped the area, and by noon a downpour began to fill the rivers. The newly opened Agua Caliente Racetrack was forced to cancel its races.

Three days later, the rain was still coming down in buckets. Roads were underwater, and bridges and railroad tracks had begun to wash away. At Hatfield's platform, crews worked day and night to keep the rainmaking concoction boiling during the deluge. On January 20, the rain continued to fall. A few miles north of San Diego, the passengers on a stranded train had to be rescued by means of an ocean launch. Houses and several bodies floated out of the canyons. The rain tapered off briefly, then resumed on January 26—with a vengeance.

By now the water at Morena Dam was rising at the rate of two feet an hour. Desperate engineers opened two 24-inch spillway valves to divert backed-up water around the dam. On January 29, when the hard rain finally stopped, the water crept to within 5 inches of the top, but the dam—and, doubtless, hundreds of lives—had been spared. Total rainfall for the month of January 1916 amounted to an incredible 38 inches, a local record that has yet to be broken.

Charles Hatfield and his brother stayed at the dam for three more days, dismantling their tower and raking the ground beneath it to remove any trace of the chemicals they were using. A message got through to them that an angry crowd—possibly a lynch mob—was coming up the mountain to find them, but the brothers somehow managed to avoid the posse and return to San Diego.

On February 4, Hatfield told reporters that he was not responsible for the flood damage. "It was up to the city to take precautions to protect the citizenry if they wanted that much water," he said. The city council refused to pay Hatfield, claiming that if they did, they also would have to assume liability for all the destruction and the 15 lives lost in the flood. Hatfield tendered a compromise bill for $4,000, which he said was for legitimate expenses, but he never was paid and never pressed the issue much. Some 30 years later he told a newspaper reporter, "I've never felt right about that San Diego city council."

Letters poured in from all over the world—Australia, Africa, Arabia—requesting Hatfield's help in making rain. Hatfield generally preferred to operate closer to home, although he and his brother did travel to Honduras in

The First (Accidental) Cloud Seeding in History

THE AFTERNOON OF JULY 13, 1946, was a hot and humid one in Schenectady, New York. Vincent J. Schaefer, a scientist working at the General Electric Research Laboratory, returned from lunch to find that the temperature in his laboratory "cold box," which he was using for his cloud research, was too high. Schaefer had been searching for the right substance to make ice crystals form in a chamber of supercooled (below 32°F) cloud droplets, so far with no success. He had tried volcanic ash, sand, quartz, diatomaceous earth, sulfur, carbon, talc, even common table salt—but nothing seemed to work. When he decided to cool the chamber quickly by inserting a chunk of dry ice (frozen carbon dioxide gas at –108°F), however, something strange and wonderful began to happen. First, a blue cloud of tiny ice crystals formed, and then, with a little more fiddling, Schaefer found that he could actually create a miniature snowstorm inside the chamber.

Schaefer and his cloud chamber.

Four months later, on November 13, Schaefer decided to put his theory into practice. In a small plane at 14,000 feet, he spread dry ice into a cloud over Mount Greylock in western Massachusetts. From above, Schaefer watched the cloud "explode," while a colleague on the ground saw snow fall nearly 2,000 feet before it evaporated.

It was Schaefer's discovery that, at long last, attached some scientific respectability to the mystical art of rainmaking.

TEST YOUR PRECIPITATION KNOWLEDGE

1. **On an average day, approximately what percentage of the earth's surface is covered by clouds?**
   - a. 35 percent
   - b. 40 percent
   - c. 50 percent
   - d. 60 percent

2. **What is the least likely time of day for hail to fall anywhere in the United States?**
   - a. 1 A.M.   c. 2 P.M.
   - b. 6 A.M.   d. 7 P.M.

3. **Strong updrafts within thunderstorms are necessary to support the kind of large hailstones that sometimes fall. What kind of wind velocity would have to be present in an updraft to support a hailstone three inches in diameter?**
   - a. 40 miles per hour
   - b. 60 miles per hour
   - c. 75 miles per hour
   - d. 100 miles per hour

4. **Many people claim to be able to "smell" rain coming. Is this ability real or imagined?**

ANSWERS: 1. d. 2. b. Hail is associated with large thunderstorms that typically develop in the afternoon due to surface heating. **3. d. 4.** Real, although what they smell probably isn't the rain itself but the odor of volatile organic chemicals released by certain plants. When the air's relative humidity is high, these smells may become more noticeable.

1929 to try to save a banana plantation for a New Orleans fruit company. Later, during the Great Depression, Hatfield offered to bring rain to the nation's Dust Bowl for only the cost of his expenses. Admirers urged President Franklin D. Roosevelt to employ his services, but pressure from the U.S. Weather Bureau, which had always been skeptical of rainmaking schemes, stopped the project.

How exactly did Hatfield make rain? His brother Paul, when asked many years later to explain the secret, said, "Only Charles knew. He just stumbled on a formula that someone will discover again someday. After all, they are beginning to seed clouds to make rain." At one time, Hatfield talked freely, in general terms, about his method: he mixed 23 different chemicals in casks, allowing them to age for a few days, then placed them in evaporating pans atop his towers. He got the idea, he claimed, from noticing that steam in teakettles would move toward certain chemicals.

Among Charles Hatfield's papers in the Denver Public Library are two well-thumbed books, *Elements of Meteorology with Questions for Examinations, Designed for Schools and Academies,* published in 1848 and reprinted in 1860 by John Brocklesby, and *Elementary Meteorology* by William Morris Davis, published in 1894. Also included are rainfall data for selected California locations, stretching as far back as there were records, as well as a barometer and a rain gauge.

As late as the 1970s, Paul Hatfield continued to maintain that he and his brother had conducted 503 rainmaking experiments without a single failure. There had been failures, of course, although the newspapers had seldom reported them. And sometimes it had begun to rain while the Hatfields were still in the process of setting up their towers, making it difficult even for them to take the credit.

Charles Hatfield died in 1958 at the age of 83, but he is still remembered today as the most skillful (or luckiest) of America's many self-proclaimed rainmakers. Every so often, the press rehashes his colorful and controversial career. And in 1973, a group called the Native Sons of the Golden West erected near Lake Morena a six-foot-high granite marker dedicated to "Hatfield the Rainmaker"—the man who gave the citizens of San Diego everything they bargained for. And more.

— RAYMOND SCHUESSLER ∎

It's Never Raining Rain, You Know

THE WEATHER HISTORY of the United States is replete with all kinds of examples of weird precipitation. A few of the more unusual and well-documented cases include the following:

- **June 6, 1869.** At Chester, Pennsylvania, a light rain shower was accompanied by **falling snail shells,** which one witness described as having descended with a slow, whirling motion. Specimens of the snails, identified as *Gemma gemma,* were later exhibited at Philadelphia's Academy of Natural Sciences.

- **December 15, 1876. Live snakes** fell on the south side of Memphis, Tennessee. The snakes were a dark brown, almost black, color and 12 to 18 inches long. The weather observer at Memphis noted that a light morning rain had turned torrential around 10:20 A.M. and continued for 15 minutes. Immediately after the heavy rain, the snakes were found crawling all over an area of two blocks along Vance Street. The snakes lay on the sidewalks and streets, in yards and gutters, but, strangely, no one had actually seen them falling from the sky, and none of the snakes were found on rooftops or anywhere above the ground. For this reason, some people considered the event a hoax, but the snakes themselves were real enough, and no one ever produced any other plausible explanation to resolve the mystery.

- **October 1881. The Great Cobweb Storm** was observed from Milwaukee to Sheboygan, Wisconsin, along the western shore of Lake Michigan. This event was caused not by rainfall, but by the migratory habits of certain species of spiders, which cast their silk on a breeze and tag along for a ride as the wind bears them away.

Observers reported that the webs appeared to come from across the lake (the opposite shore being nearly 100 miles away) and to fall from a great height. At Green Bay, too, residents couldn't fail to notice the strong, white strands, which varied greatly in size, from mere specks to 60 feet in length, and which filled the sky thickly as high up as the eye could see.

Joe and Jill Von Newham of Norborne, Missouri, hold some truly spectacular hailstones.

The Icy Stones of Summer

When the clouds turn dark blue-green, westerners know all hail is about to break loose.

AROUND DINNERTIME ON AUGUST 3, 1985, a heavy rain began to fall on Cheyenne, Wyoming. No one thought that this was anything out of the ordinary—just a typical summer thunderstorm that was passing through town, dropping a quick deluge and clearing the air. But by 9:45 P.M., some three hours after it had started, the storm had dumped more than six inches of rain on the city, about one-half of the total precipitation that Cheyenne normally receives in a year.

The flooding from the sudden downpour would have caused enough damage all by itself, but with the rain came severe hail—the summer scourge of the eastern Rockies. The hail slashed at trees, cars, and buildings, shattered windows and windshields, and drifted into five-foot-deep piles that had to be cleared away by city crews. After the storm, 12 people lay dead and 70 more were treated for injuries. The storm was one of the worst in the city's history, but just another example of the havoc caused by hail each year, especially in the western United States.

Cheyenne is located in the southeast corner of Wyoming, in the region that meteorologists call Hail Alley. In this area—comprising northern Colorado, southeastern Wyoming, and western Nebraska—residents can expect hail, on average, about nine or ten days each year. That may not sound like much (especially considering that the worst hail zone in the world, the Kericho and Nandi hills in Kenya, averages about 132 hail days a year), but the hailstones that fall in the eastern Rockies and on the Great Plains are the largest and most destructive in the nation and among the worst in the world.

A hailstone begins its life within a thunderstorm as a tiny ice pellet or dust particle, something like the nucleus of an atom. As the particle circulates within the updrafts and downdrafts of a storm, it collides with supercooled droplets of water (unfrozen but with temperatures below 32°F), which freeze and adhere to the surface of the particle. Above the freezing level in the cloud, moisture freezes very quickly on the growing hailstone, trapping air bubbles within it and forming a milky, opaque layer of ice. Below the freezing level, the ice forms more slowly, and a clear layer is added to the stone. The growing hailstone repeatedly travels up and down within the storm center as if on an elevator to nowhere, until the stone either is thrown clear of the updraft "chimney" or gathers so much mass that the air currents can no longer hold it suspended aloft, at which point it drops to the ground.

To qualify as hail, a particle must be at least two-tenths inch in diameter. The majority of hail is the kind referred to as "pea-sized," but larger

Every year hailstones *cause major damage to farm crops and property —and as the owners of these automobiles in Dallas, Texas, could attest, 1926 was no exception.*

stones are also classified loosely and compared to golf balls, marbles, hens' eggs, baseballs, softballs, grapefruits, and other common spherical objects. (It's hard to maintain a scientific detachment when you're being pelted with these things.) Actually, the larger a hailstone is, the less likely it is that it will look like a perfect sphere by the time it hits the ground. The greatest mass of ice coats the outer layer of a large hailstone as it plummets through the lower levels of the cloud, and repeated melting and icing can form knobs or knuckles, lending a misshapen appearance to the falling projectile.

We don't hear much about hail disasters here in the United States, although the damage this odd precipitation causes to crops and property each year is significant. Hail destroys an estimated 2 percent of the nation's agricultural crops, with losses topping $800 million annually—about half of those losses occurring in the Great Plains. Many farmers, especially in the hail-prone western states, take out crop insurance against hail; others simply gamble that the next hailstorm will hit their neighbor's field, not their own.

In fact, hailstorms are often as localized as they are destructive. The area in which hail falls during any one storm is called a *hailstreak,* a roughly rectangular patch that is about five miles long and half a mile wide on average. Like a tornado, though, a hailstorm can skip around and leave a discontinuous track over hundreds of miles—showering stones down on one community, but leaving another town in its path unscathed.

The amount of damage a hailstorm causes is a function of its intensity. This depends not only on the size of the hailstones that fall but also on the velocity and violence of the storm's gusting winds, which add force to the falling ice. Fortunately, few people are actually killed in hailstorms in the United States, although many injuries occur when people are caught outside, and numerous livestock and other animals die as a result of hail each year. Other more populous areas of the world are less fortunate. In May 1986, a hailstorm in China's Sichuan province killed more than 100 people and injured 9,000 others. And on April 30, 1888, a storm dropping hailstones "as large

Ring Around the Hailstone

BECAUSE A HAILSTONE can get tossed around in a cloud's updraft several times before it falls to earth, acquiring another layer of ice each time, it ends up resembling an onion with one distinctive layer for each trip to the top of the cloud. The next time you are unfortunate enough to get caught in a hailstorm, try gathering a few of the larger stones (but cover your head first). Then cut them in half and quickly count the number of rings to find out how many times the stone was pushed upward before it became too heavy for the cloud to support it. Remember: The stronger the winds within a hail cloud, the larger the hail will be.

A hailstone's rings tell its history.

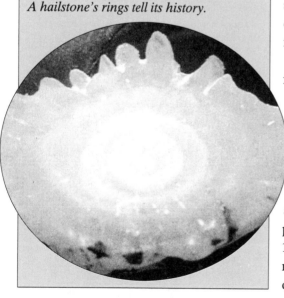

as cricket balls" claimed 246 victims near Moradabad in northern India.

Hailstorms occur most frequently during the late spring and summer months, with a peak in May and June. The severe thunderstorms that form tornadoes (especially the strong, isolated storms known as supercells) also can carry hail, which often accompanies torrential rain as a harbinger of the approaching twister. The strongest hailstorms usually form in the warm air just in advance of an approaching cold front, and the dark blue-green color of their clouds is a dead giveaway (for those who know what to look for) that hail is on the way. This unusual greenish appearance, much like that of clouds preceding tornadoes, is caused by the reflection of light off the large hail and water droplets inside the clouds.

Other weather events may be more widespread or catastrophic, but few can match the hailstorm's bizarre special effects. A backyard covered with tiny balls of ice in the height of summer is a picture few people ever forget. To most Americans, hail is a rare and freakish inconvenience that may knock a few holes in the tomato plants or at worst break a window or two. But to the people of Cheyenne, Wyoming, and their neighbors on the plains, hail season is no laughing matter. When the greenish storm comes near, it pays to have the car in the garage, the kids inside the house, and a healthy amount of insurance on everything you own. ■

Trucks slosh through *hubcap-deep hail after a storm in Trinidad, Colorado, on June 14, 1937.*

FOR THE RECORD

THE COSTLIEST HAILSTORM in the nation's history occurred on June 11, 1990, when golf-ball- to baseball-size hail caused an estimated $625 million damage in sections of Colorado's Front Range stretching from Colorado Springs to Estes Park. The heavy rain that accompanied the storm washed the hail into sewers, backing up water three to six feet on some streets. Sixty people were injured in the storm.

When the peacock loudly bawls, soon we'll have both rain and squalls.

Have a Conversation with a Cat

ALTHOUGH THE FICTIONAL Dr. Doolittle could actually "talk to the animals," most of us aren't anywhere near that clever. Fortunately, observing the behavior of certain animals can be the next best thing to having a heart-to-heart with old Rover. In fact, it's one of the most time-honored and reliable ways to predict a change in the weather, especially an approaching storm.

Farmers, fishermen, and herders have been watching animals, both wild and domesticated, for thousands of years. (Before cable TV, what else was there to do for fun?) Early on they realized that these creatures, which are much more sensitive and attuned to nature than most humans, can sense a change in the wind hours or even days before it arrives. Generations of folk forecasters have identified certain types of animal behavior (like livestock herding together or heading for shelter, or birds flying low) as sure signs of a storm. Although we don't claim that the following precepts will always ring true, they are all part of our common legacy of weather lore and shouldn't be discounted, even if they don't work every single time. After all, when was the last time you heard a weatherman declare a 100 percent probability of anything?

Rex Harrison as *Dr. Doolittle, with a few of his favorite listeners.*

ANIMALS	SIGNS OF RAIN
Ants	Close off the mouths of their nests
Bats	Cry out and fly into their houses
Bees	Stay close to their hives
Bulls	Lead the cows on the way out to pasture
Cats	Sneeze, or wash behind their ears
Cows	Turn up their nostrils and sniff the air, lie on their right sides, lick their forefeet, or don't give milk
Deer	Come down from the hills (also said of elk)
Dogs	Roll on the ground, act drowsy and stupid, eat grass, or straighten their tails
Dolphins	Swim to windward
Donkeys	Hang their ears downward and forward and rub against walls, or bray more frequently
Ducks	Fly backward and forward, plunge into the water, or wash themselves incessantly
Fish	Rise to the surface and "bite" (go after bait) more actively
Frogs	Croak and jump around more than usual (unless they croak at night, which predicts a fair day ahead)
Goats	Bawl, leave high ground, or seek shelter
Horses	Stretch out their necks and sniff the air, or pull back their lips and grin
Mosquitoes	Bite more frequently (true of most biting insects)
Owls	Hoot and screech (during a rainy period, this means that fair weather will follow soon)
Peacocks	Cry out in the night
Pigs	Carry straw in their mouths
Robins	Stay close to houses
Roosters	Crow late and early (especially during the night) and clap their wings more than usual
Sea gulls	Make more noise than usual in the morning, fly inland (also said of geese), sit on the sand, or wash themselves (indicates rain within 24 hours)
Sheep	Young ones frolic and leap about; old ones eat greedily
Spiders	Abandon their webs, or build webs in the grass during Indian summer
Swallows	Fly low over the ground or water (also said of other birds, such as herons)

"What's that, Flipper?
You say fair and warmer for the weekend with a 30 percent chance of thundershowers?"

The Quiet Killer

*You wake up in the morning to a world encased in ice.
It's beautiful—and deadly.*

IT BEGINS SLOWLY, with a gentle rain and the promise of an early spring or a midwinter thaw. It ends with broken trees, downed power lines, and impassable roads. Wherever it strikes, an ice storm can be the quietest disaster in nature's whole bag of tricks—a dangerous, expensive curse, yet also a sight of uncommon, almost surreal beauty.

Most of the United States experiences freezing rain at one time or another, but the conditions for a first-rate ice storm are relatively rare. Meteorologists refer to the kind of freezing rain that coats trees, wires, and streets as *glaze,* to distinguish it from the ice pellets known as *sleet* (raindrops that have frozen solid before striking the ground). Glaze-type freezing rain forms when raindrops fall from a height at which the air temperature is above freezing (32°F) and then pass through a thin layer of below-freezing air close to the ground. The rain doesn't freeze in the air, though. Instead, the supercooled droplets freeze on contact with a surface—almost any surface—glazing the world under a slick sheet of ice.

A typical winter storm in the Northeast brings a mixture of precipitation, with rain, freezing rain, sleet, and snow all lying in distinct bands that radiate away from the storm's center. Topography also comes into play; the temperature in one place may remain above freezing, while only a few miles away, at a slightly higher elevation, a destructive ice storm can cause severe damage. Both hilly areas and valleys (into which colder air sinks) are particularly vulnerable to icing. A severe glaze storm on March 22, 1837, caused more than $100,000 worth of damage in the Litchfield Hills of northwestern Connecticut. And on December 16–17, 1973, central Connecticut bore the brunt of another crippling storm, which caused more damage to trees than the famous New England Hurricane of 1938. The resulting power outages were the worst in New England history, as wires snapped and hundreds of thousands of homes lost electricity for days.

Hazy weather foretells frost in winter, snow in spring, fair weather in summer, and rain in autumn.

The threat to trees comes from the sheer weight of the clear ice, which can coat twigs and branches with sheaths as much as several inches thick, until they sag under the load like overdecorated Christmas trees. In November 1921, Professor Charles F. Brooks reported to the American Meteorological Society on an ice storm near Worcester, Massachusetts, and calculated that the load of ice carried on the sides of an evergreen tree 50 feet high and 20 feet wide would amount to something like five tons.

The worst ice storm in U.S. history struck the South from January 28 to February 1, 1951, glazing over states from Texas to West Virginia and resulting in some $100 million in damage. Twenty-five people died, and 500 were seriously injured as a result of accidents caused by the ice. Road travel in the hardest-hit areas, such as Tennessee, was virtually impossible for up to ten days after the storm.

One of the worst ice storms in recent years hit Portland, Oregon, on January 9–10, 1979. Lying near the western edge of the Columbia Gorge,

At the turn of the century, *an ice storm toppled utility poles in Three Rivers, Michigan.*

Mark Twain (inset) and his home in Hartford, Connecticut, surrounded by his favorite weather.

the city is the perfect candidate for ice storms. Cold, subfreezing air at the ground combines with rainy conditions in the upper atmosphere to produce some of the best (or worst) potential for icing anywhere in the country. On January 10, a heavy glaze of clear ice (which locals call a "silver thaw") forced the closing of Interstate 80 through the gorge and cut off power at Portland International Airport for nine hours, as well as electricity to some 75,000 homes and businesses. Five people died in accidents resulting from the storm.

And yet, with all its negative aspects, including the threat to our modern umbilical cord of electric power, the ice storm remains one of nature's most lavish and breathtaking displays. Mark Twain, a resident of Hartford, Connecticut (and an aficionado of New England's bizarre weather), celebrated it most eloquently in a famous address he delivered in 1876:

> . . . the ice-storm: when a leafless tree is clothed with ice from the bottom to the top—ice that is as bright and clear as crystal; when every bough and twig is strung with ice-beads, frozen dewdrops, and the whole tree sparkles like the Shah of Persia's diamond plume. Then the wind waves the branches and the sun comes out and turns all those myriads of beads and drops to prisms that glow and burn and flash with all manner of colored fires, which change and change again with inconceivable rapidity from red to blue, from red to green, and green to gold—the tree becomes a spraying fountain, a very explosion of dazzling jewels; and it stands there the acme, the climax, the supremest possibility in art or nature, of bewildering, intoxicating, intolerable magnificence. ■

Who soweth in rain shall reapeth in tears.

The Snow Queen

THE BEST AND MOST GRAPHIC weather stories come from fairy tales. They have ice kings and ice castles, hearts turned to ice by evil spirits or by accident. But the most touching story of true love thwarted by the cold is the Hans Christian Andersen tale "The Snow Queen." In it, a woman made of ice whisks a young boy named Kay away from his home and his best friend, Gretta. The queen's cold kisses make him forget his past and his love for Gretta. He even forgets how cold he is in the queen's presence. She hides Kay in her palace of snow, and to save him, Gretta must travel to the North Pole, find him, and warm him with her tears. The happy ending arrives in typical fairy tale fashion. Kay and Gretta leave the icy palace walking hand in hand, and everywhere they go it is springtime, warm and bright.

In the fairy tale, living with the Snow Queen was a chilling experience.

A Real Fish Story

You had to have been there—in Marksville, Louisiana, on the day it rained fish.

IT WAS A LITTLE BEFORE 8 A.M. ON Thursday, October 23, 1947. A fellow named A.D. Bajkov and his wife were eating breakfast in a restaurant in the small town of Marksville, Louisiana, when someone burst in the door and announced that fish were falling from the sky. Most people might have chalked up this comment to the effects of drink or dementia, but Bajkov, a biologist working for the state's Department of Wildlife and Fisheries, decided to go outside and take a look.

What he saw seemed incredible, even though the evidence lay all over the ground around him. In an area about 1,000 feet long and 80 feet wide, thousands of fresh fish had fallen from the heavens and landed along Main and Monroe streets, at an average of about one per square yard. Residents who had witnessed the piscine precipitation reported that the fish had fallen in a series of short intervals, landing on roofs, on the street, and in backyards all over the area. The director of the Marksville Bank, J.M. Barham, discovered hundreds in his own and his neighbor's yards. And Barham's cashier, J.E. Gremillion, was actually struck by a fish around 7:45 as he made his way to work (surely the most bizarre accident in commuter history).

Keeping his scientific wits about him, Bajkov began collecting specimens to preserve for museums. The fish he found were fresh, not frozen, and perfectly fit for human consumption. Of the species he identified, all were freshwater fish native to the area. The most common species he observed was hickory shad, although several kinds of sunfish and minnows and even a few bass and goggle-eyes were found among the litter. The fish ranged in size from two to nine inches in length, with a nine-and-one-quarter-inch large-mouth bass the largest specimen collected.

No one knows exactly what caused Marksville's Great Fish Fall. Other, similar, incidents had been reported in England as recently as the summer of 1918, when a rain of eel-like fish with the local name of sile fell near Sunderland. And certainly all manner of frozen animals—snails, small turtles, and other critters—have at one time or another been known to fall in this country, typically during violent rainstorms or hailstorms.

The really unusual thing about the Marksville incident is that the fish touched down on a morning that was foggy and fairly calm, with winds of only around eight miles per hour on the ground. No strong thunderstorm or heavy rain accompanied the flying fish. Bajkov did remember that, just the day before, he and a colleague had noticed a number of small tornadoes (so-called dust devils) in the area, but these may have had nothing to do with the weird phenomenon. In fact, to this day, scientific experts and ordinary folks alike remain stumped as to what caused the Great Fish Fall—a bizarre event that transformed an otherwise ordinary day into the most memorable in Marksville's town history. ■

Gene Kelly making quite a splash.

Singin' in the Rain

IN LITERATURE, POETRY, AND DRAMA, rain is an almost universal symbol of sadness, melancholy, and plain old bad luck. With all of this going for it, it's no surprise that musicians of the past century have so often used rainfall to illustrate one of their favorite themes: smiling through adversity. Otherwise known as, well, you guessed it. Here is a short list of the most famous tunes for soggy hearts:

"It Ain't Gonna Rain No Mo'" by Wendell Hall (1923)
"Stormy Weather" by Koehler & Arlen (1933)
"Pennies from Heaven," from the movie of the same name, by Burke & Johnson (1936)
"Into Each Life Some Rain Must Fall" by Allan Roberts and Doris Fisher (1944)
"The Rain in Spain," from the musical *My Fair Lady*, by Lerner & Loewe (1944)
"April Showers" by B.G. de Sylva and Louis Silvers (1945)
"Raindrops" by Dee Clark (1961)
"Rhythm of the Rain" by John Gummoe (1963)

Picture Credits

Front matter. ii: The Library of Congress. ix: The National Archives.

Introduction. 2–3: The National Archives.

Watching the Weather. 4–5, 6: Culver Pictures. 7 (all): Yankee Archives. 8: Culver Pictures. 9: courtesy The Whitby Museum. 10 (both): Culver Pictures. 11: The National Archives. 12 (left): Carl Kirkpatrick. 12 (right): Dover Books. 13 (both), 14, 15: The National Archives. 16 (top): courtesy NBC-TV. 16 (bottom): Carl Kirkpatrick. 17: Culver Pictures. 18 (top): Carl Kirkpatrick. 18 (bottom): Dover Books. 19: The National Archives.

Hurricanes. 20–21: The National Archives. 22 (top): Culver Pictures. 22 (bottom): Carl Kirkpatrick. 23: The Library of Congress. 24 (top): The National Archives. 24 (bottom): Carl Kirkpatrick. 25 (top): Carl Kirkpatrick. 25 (bottom), 26: Culver Pictures. 27: The National Archives. 28, 29, 30: Culver Pictures. 31: courtesy the collection of Wright Langley, Key West, Florida. 32 (top left): Carl Kirkpatrick. 32 (bottom left): Culver Pictures. 32–33 (center): courtesy the collection of Wright Langley, Key West, Florida. 34, 35: Culver Pictures. 36: Ken Brown. 37 (top): Culver Pictures. 37 (bottom): Dover Books. 38: The National Archives. 39: Carl Kirkpatrick. 40: Culver Pictures. 41 (both): courtesy Betty Hinman. 42: Maryann Mattson. 43: courtesy The United States Air Force. 44 (both): Culver Pictures. 45: AP/Wide World Photos.

Tornadoes. 46–47: The Panhandle-Plains Historical Society, Canyon, Texas. 48 (bottom): Carl Kirkpatrick. 48–49 (top), 50: The National Archives. 51: Ken Brown. 52: Culver Pictures. 53: Jill Shaffer. 54 (top): Carl Kirkpatrick. 54 (bottom): Reprinted with special permission of King Features Syndicate. 55: AP/Wide World Photos. 56: U.S Department of Commerce, Weather Bureau. 57: The National Archives. 58: AP/Wide World Photos. 59: courtesy Burnham and Associates. 60-61: courtesy St. Louis Mercantile Library Association. 61 (right): Carl Kirkpatrick. 62: Tim Marshall. 63: Jill Shaffer. 64: The National Archives. 65 (both): Culver Pictures.

Blizzards & Wintry Weather. 66–67: The Connecticut Historical Society. 68: *Harper's Weekly.* 69: Culver Pictures. 71: The New York Historical Society. 72: Culver Pictures. 73: The New York Historical Society. 74 (left): Carl Kirkpatrick. 74 (right): AP/Wide World Photos. 75 (left): Culver Pictures. 75 (right): Carl Kirkpatrick. 76: Yankee Archives. 77: Anthony Cardinale, Thorner-Sidney Press, Buffalo, New York. 78: Culver Pictures. 79: AP/Wide World Photos. 80: courtesy The Buffalo Bill Historical Center. 81 (both): courtesy The National Cowboy Hall of Fame and Western Heritage Center. 82: Dover Books. 83: Ken Brown. 84, 85 (both): AP/Wide World Photos. 86 (top): Culver Pictures. 86 (bottom): *Anchorage Daily News*/Jim Lavrakas. 87: courtesy of the Academy of Motion Picture Arts and Sciences.

Drought, Dust & Conflagration. 88–89: The National Archives. 90, 91 (top): The Panhandle-Plains Historical Society, Canyon, Texas. 91 (bottom): Carl Kirkpatrick. 92: Dover Books. 93 (all): The Panhandle-Plains Historical Society, Canyon, Texas. 94: The National Archives. 95 (top): Culver Pictures. 95 (bottom): The Panhandle-Plains Historical Society, Canyon, Texas. 96: Culver Pictures. 98 (top): Carl Kirkpatrick. 98 (bottom): The Panhandle-Plains Historical Society, Canyon, Texas. 99: Madonna and Child on a Curved Throne, Andrew W. Mellon Collection, © 1993 National Gallery of Art, Washington. 100–01: courtesy The State Historical Society of Wisconsin. 101 (right): Carl Kirkpatrick. 102: courtesy The State Historical Society of Wisconsin. 103: Carl Kirkpatrick. 104: Richard Scarry/Simon and Schuster, New York. 105: courtesy The State Historical Society of Wisconsin. 106: Ken Brown. 107: Dover Books. 108: Culver Pictures. 109: The National Archives. 110 (both), 111, 112–13: courtesy The Chicago Historical Society. 113 (bottom): Culver Pictures. 114: courtesy The Chicago Historical Society. 115: Culver Pictures. 116, 117: AP/Wide World Photos. 118 (top): Carl Kirkpatrick. 118 (bottom): courtesy The University of Washington Library, special collections, neg. # HE 6685. 119: courtesy U.S. Borax and Chemical Corps.

Floods. 120–21, 122–23: The National Archives. 123 (right), 124 (all): Culver Pictures. 125: The Library of Congress. 126: AP/ Wide World Photos. 127: The Library of Congress. 128: Johnstown Area Heritage Association. 129: The National Archives/The American Red Cross. 130–31: courtesy *Rapid City Journal.* 132: AP/Wide World Photos. 133: courtesy *Rapid City Journal.* 134: courtesy Shirley and Leo Hessman. 135, 136 (top): Culver Pictures. 136 (bottom): Ken Brown. 137 (top): Carl Kirkpatrick. 137 (bottom): AP/Wide World Photos. 138–39 (both): Yankee Archives/The Blackington Collection. 140: Carl Kirkpatrick. 141: Culver Pictures. 142, 143 (bottom): courtesy The University of Lowell, Special Collections. 143 (top): Carl Kirkpatrick.

Earthquakes. 144–45: The National Archives. 146 (left): Carl Kirkpatrick. 146–47, 148: courtesy State Historical Society of Missouri. 149: Culver Pictures. 150 (top): courtesy State Historical Society of Missouri. 150 (bottom): Carl Kirkpatrick. 151, 152, 153: Culver Pictures. 154 (left): Carl Kirkpatrick. 154–55, 156: The National Archives. 157: Culver Pictures. 158 (both): The National Archives. 159 (top): Carl Kirkpatrick. 159 (bottom), 160: The National Archives. 161: AP/Wide World Photos. 162: Ken Brown. 163: Culver Pictures. 164–65, 166: The National Archives. 167: Carl Kirkpatrick. 168–69: AP/Wide World Photos. 170, 171, 172: The National Archives. 173: AP/Wide World Photos. 174: Carl Kirkpatrick. 175: Culver Pictures.

Volcanoes. 176–77: The National Archives. 178, 179, 180: AP/Wide World Photos. 181: Roger Werth. 182: AP/Wide World Photos. 183: Roger Werth. 184: AP/Wide World Photos. 185 (left): Dover Books. 185 (right), 186 (left): Carl Kirkpatrick. 186–87: Yankee Archives. 188 (top): Carl Kirkpatrick. 188 (bottom): Yankee Archives. 189, 190: Culver Pictures. 191: Ken Brown. 192: Culver Pictures. 193 (both): Yankee Archives. 194: Culver Pictures. 195: The National Archives. 196 (top): AP/Wide World Photos. 196–97 (bottom): G. Brad Lewis/Omjalla Images, Pahoa, Hawaii. 198: courtesy Applied Geomechanics, Inc. 199: Yankee Archives. 200: AP/Wide World Photos. 201: The Library of Congress.

Lightning. 202–03: The National Archives. 204: Carl Kirkpatrick. 205: Culver Pictures. 206: J. Albert Diaz/*Los Angeles Times.* 207: Ken Brown. 208 (top): Carl Kirkpatrick. 208 (bottom): Culver Pictures. 209: Yankee Archives. 210 (both), 211: Culver Pictures. 212–13: AP/Wide World Photos. 213 (right): Carl Kirkpatrick. 214 (both): Jim Peaco/The National Park Service, Yellowstone. 215: Yankee Archives. 216: "THE FLASH" ™ © 1990 DC Comics, used by permission. 217: AP/Wide World Photos. 218: The National Archives. 219 (top): Carl Kirkpatrick. 219 (bottom): Culver Pictures. 220 (bottom): AP/Wide World Photos. 220 (top), 221, 222 (both): Culver Pictures. 223 (left): Culver Pictures. 223 (right): The Boston Public Library.

Rain, Hail & Ice Storms. 224–25: The National Archives. 226, 227, 228: courtesy The San Diego Historical Society, Ticor Collection. 229: courtesy the Jericho, Vermont, Historical Society. 230: Culver Pictures. 231: AP/Wide World Photos. 232: Ken Brown. 233 (all): Yankee Archives. 234: National Center for Atmospheric Research. 235: The National Archives. 236: National Center for Atmospheric Research. 237: The National Archives. 238 (top): Carl Kirkpatrick. 238 (bottom), 239: Culver Pictures. 240: Carl Kirkpatrick. 241: Collection of Gotham Book Mart, New York. 242 (top, both): courtesy the Mark Twain Memorial. 242 (bottom): Carl Kirkpatrick. 243: Crown Publishing, New York. 244: Dover Books. 245: Culver Pictures.

Note: Diligence was exercised in locating owners of all images used. If an image was uncredited or mistakenly credited, please contact the publisher and effort will be made to include credit in future printings.